Fat Politics

Fat Politics

The Real Story
Behind America's
Obesity Epidemic

J. ERIC OLIVER

OXFORD
UNIVERSITY PRESS

2006

OXFORD

UNIVERSITY PRESS

Oxford University Press, Inc., publishes works that
further Oxford University's objective of excellence
in research, scholarship, and education.

Oxford New York
Auckland   Cape Town   Dar es Salaam   Hong Kong   Karachi
Kuala Lumpur   Madrid   Melbourne   Mexico City   Nairobi
New Delhi   Shanghai   Taipei   Toronto

With offices in
Argentina   Austria   Brazil   Chile   Czech Republic   France   Greece
Guatemala   Hungary   Italy   Japan   Poland   Portugal   Singapore
South Korea   Switzerland   Thailand   Turkey   Ukraine   Vietnam

Published by Oxford University Press, Inc.
198 Madison Avenue, New York, NY, 10016
www.oup.com

Oxford is a registered trademark of Oxford University Press

Library of Congress Cataloging-in-Publication Data
Oliver, J. Eric, 1966–
Fat politics : the real story behind America's obesity epidemic / J. Eric Oliver.
p. ; cm.
ISBN-13: 978-0-19-516936-2
ISBN-10: 0-19-516936-0
1. Obesity—United States.   I. Title.
[DNLM: 1. Obesity—United States. 2. Health—United States.
3. Health Policy—United States. 4. Prejudice—United States.
5. Social Perception—United States.   WD 210 O48f 2005]
RA645.O23O45 2005
614.5'9398—dc22
2005012983

9 8 7 6 5 4 3 2 1

Printed in the United States of America
on acid-free paper

For Thea

Contents

Acknowledgments

This was not the book I intended to write.

When I first became interested in obesity, I, like most Americans, assumed it was a major health problem. At the time, I was on a post-doctoral fellowship at Yale University sponsored by the Robert Wood Johnson Foundation. The fellowship is aimed at getting young political scientists, like myself, interested in doing "health-related" research. In trolling for a topic, I happened across an article that described the soaring growth of obesity and its catastrophic consequences. I became intrigued and soon had all sorts of questions about how the "obesity epidemic" might be handled as a political issue. Yet when I went to look for some answers to these questions, I found that very little had been written. Politically speaking, obesity was largely uncharted terrain.

Luckily for me, Yale also happens to be the home of Kelly Brownell, one of the nation's leading obesity researchers. Ever generous, Kelly helped get me started in my research and put me in touch with numerous other experts who were equally helpful, including James Hill, Steve Blair, Jon Peters, and William Dietz. In the summer of 2001, I was able to bring these researchers together with other social scientists for a mini-conference. Many of the participants, including John Cawley, David Cutler, Rogan Kersh, Taeku Lee, James Morone, and Abigail Saguy, provided many great ideas. After three days of discussions, I had a clear idea about a book I wanted to write: how was America going to overcome the political challenges posed by the obesity epidemic? Soon afterward, I drafted a proposal and got a contract from Oxford University Press to write this book.

Then I started to do the research. In early 2002, obesity was only beginning to emerge as a major news item and so my first task was to prove that it was, in fact, the major health and economic threat I presumed it to be. I started to read through the research papers and science journals. Although I had no advanced training in medicine or biology, I had done a lot of graduate work in statistics and even though much of the terminology was obtuse, I could still evaluate the basic estimates and the data on which many of the health claims were made.

And that's when my mind began to change—for the more papers I read and the more experts I interviewed, the more I realized that there was a real problem with my basic argument. Most of the claims about obesity were based on very shaky evidence. (I didn't know it at the time, but, independently, Paul Campos, author of *The Obesity Myth*, was coming to a similar conclusion.) I was astonished about how weak most of the statistical claims really were. Public opinion researchers, like myself, often get accused of drawing unwarranted conclusions, but what we did paled next to the breathtaking inferential leaps that were regularly made in many of the top medical journals. Based on the statistics, most of charges saying that obesity caused various diseases or that obesity caused thousands of deaths were simply not supported. Yet consistently, these pseudofindings were promulgated as fact.

I also discovered another dirty secret about obesity research; many of the scientists who were sounding the alarms about the "obesity epidemic" were also on the payrolls of various pharmaceutical and weight-loss companies. In the course of my interviews, I started hearing stories about contradictory research that was hushed-up, bogus numbers being reported by health agencies, and shifty "scientific" organizations that were no more than fronts for the pharmaceutical industry. The politics of obesity were more different and interesting than I first knew. What I thought was an epidemic began to look at lot more like a politically orchestrated campaign to capitalize on America's growing weight.

Around this time I also started to confront my own fat prejudices. Early on in my research, I heard about fat rights groups, including the National Association to Advance Fat Acceptance, who argued that obesity was not a health risk. Like many people, I had largely dismissed them as a fringe and marginal group; after all, who was this weird bunch of people who were actually proud of being fat? But once I realized they were right about a lot of the junk science on obesity, I started to seriously consider their other arguments, particularly about the pervasiveness of fat prejudice in the United States. I realized that my own preconceptions coming into this project were shaped more by my own antifat biases than by any facts. If I was going to clearly examine the nature of America's obesity epidemic, I would have to come to terms with what was making me so judgmental against fat people. Once again, I was fortunate, and I came into contact with many generous activists including Jennifer Portnick, Marilyn Wann, and, most important, Lynn McAfee, a long-time fat activist and perpetual thorn in the side of the obesity research community. Although not a formally trained scientist, Lynn knows more about obesity than most "experts" and has a clearer perspective on this issue than anyone; she is also one of the most courageous people I've ever met. Lynn taught me a lot about speaking truth to power.

I also enjoyed tremendous support from a number of nonprofit organizations including the Robert Wood Johnson Foundation; the Time-Share Experiments for the Social Sciences, a program funded by the National Science Foundation; and the Russell Sage Foundation. The International Food Information Council provided an invaluable service with their daily Listserve of obesity news items. The University of Chicago was also supportive, allowing time off to write and letting me teach a seminar on this subject. Those sources aside, I did not receive any financial assistance from any food, restaurant, or beverage industry nor any party concerned with obesity policy nor any pharmaceutical company.

In addition, I have enjoyed critiques, comments, and research help from a number of academic colleagues and researchers including John Brehm, Paul Campos, Cathy Cohen, Jeffrey Friedman, Heena Patel, Bruce Schneider, Gary Taubes, Lisa Wedeen, and Diane Whitmore. Kathryn Flegal at the National Center for Health Statistics was particularly helpful in steering me through the methodological controversies. Although some may disagree with my take on this issue, all were extremely generous and forthcoming with their time and ideas. I am also grateful to my research assistants Zachary Callen, Andrew Dilts, Shang Ha, Matsutaka Harada, and Stephan Whitaker, as well as the students in my obesity seminars at the University of Chicago. My agent, Elizabeth Sheinkmen, helped me get the book project started and set me up with Oxford University Press and its great staff. At Oxford, I was extremely fortunate in having Tim Bartlett as an editor. The stamp of his keen insight, patience, and attentiveness appears throughout this work.

Finally, and most importantly, I could not have written this book without the unflagging support of my wife, Thea Goodman. Not only did she provide many keen ideas and much critical feedback, she gracefully endured my stress, distraction, and obsession, as well as countless dinner conversations dominated by this topic. I promise my next book will be on something that doesn't make us feel self-conscious about what we are eating.

JUNE 2005, OYSTER BAY, NEW YORK

Introduction:
A Big, Fat Problem

Over the past two decades, a plague has been sighted in our midst. It is said to afflict one in four Americans and kill as many as 400,000 of us every year. It is purported to cause heart disease, cancer, diabetes, asthma, hypertension, and numerous other ailments. It is estimated to cost us 100 billion dollars annually in healthcare expenses and, according to some, threatens to overwhelm our medical infrastructure. Surgeon General Richard Carmona says it's a greater threat than terrorism and former heath and human services secretary Tommy Thompson has named it a public health "crisis." Congress and numerous state governments are allocating billions of dollars in search of a cure while the media and health organizations regularly sound the alarms.

The "disease" I'm referring to is obesity and in the United States it has become, by most accounts, a full-scale epidemic. This certainly seems to be borne out by the statistics: in 1980, only about a third of Americans were considered overweight and only 13 percent were classified as obese, rates not much greater than in 1960. But in the past twenty-five years these numbers have skyrocketed. Today, more than *60 percent* of Americans are considered overweight and *one in four* is obese—a two-fold increase in less than three decades. Even more alarming is the rise in juvenile obesity; today, 15 percent of American children are considered obese, more than twice as many as in 1980. As a result of their weight, today's teenagers will be, according to some projections, the first generation in modern American history to live a shorter life span than their parents.[1]

America, it seems, has a big, fat problem.

Or at least this is what I thought when I started writing this book. Like many people, I, too, believed that America's growing weight was a genuine health quandary. Indeed, my initial plan for this book was to look at why we were gaining so much weight and what we could do to stop it. But then I started to examine the evidence and a funny thing happened—the more I read, the more I realized how misguided my initial assumptions about obesity were.[2] While it was true that Americans were getting heavier, it was less obvious that this was putting them in mortal danger or even that it was causing ailments such as diabetes, heart disease, and cancer. Like many headline-grabbing issues, the truth behind America's "obesity epidemic" was far different than the story I once believed.

What I came to realize was that, contrary to the conventional wisdom, obesity is not a problem because more than 60 percent of Americans weigh "too much." Nor is it a problem because hundreds of thousands are dying from being too fat. Nor is it a problem because it costs us hundreds of billions in healthcare expenditures. Obesity is not a problem for any of these reasons *because none of them are true.* While Americans do face many health challenges, few of these arise from our increasing weight. Our growing weight is merely a symptom of some fundamental changes in our diet and exercise patterns that may (or may not) affect our health. There is, however, little evidence that obesity itself is a primary *cause* of our health woes. In other words, telling most Americans they need to worry about their weight is like telling someone dying of pneumonia that they need to worry about how much they are coughing; it conflates the real source of our health problems with a relatively benign symptom.

Now, understandably, you might view these claims with some skepticism. After all, there is no denying that America is a very fat country. One need only take a stroll through any airport or shopping mall to witness the ample size of our population. And our fatness does carry some genuine health consequences—being very heavy puts more stress on one's joints and makes it harder to exercise, which is very important for one's health. Then there is all the information we get in the media about obesity's dangers—hardly a week goes by without some new story about another health problem that purportedly comes from being too fat. From fashion magazines to television shows such as *The Biggest Loser*, we are surrounded by messages that fatness is not only unhealthy, but also unsightly and immoral. And who among us doesn't worry, at some time, about weighing too much? Considering all our anxiety about our appearance and weight, it is perfectly logical to assume that our growing obesity portends a national health catastrophe. But if you suspend all these preconceptions, at least for a moment, and look briefly at the scientific evidence, you'll see a much different picture.

Let us start with the much-cited claim that obesity is a major killer. In April 2004, researchers from the Centers for Disease Control and Prevention (CDC) released a report in the prestigious *Journal of the American Medical Association* estimating that obesity was killing 400,000 Americans a year.[3] Given that *JAMA*, as the journal is known, is the most prestigious medical journal in the country and that one of the article's authors was the head of the CDC, this estimate had all the trappings of official truth. Soon afterward, public health officials began to use these numbers in press releases, reports, and in congressional testimony as evidence that obesity was a major threat. Scientists repeatedly cited them as a justification for further research funding to address this important problem. Newspaper headlines across the country trumpeted how obesity would soon overtake smoking as the number one cause of preventable death in America.

A closer look at the numbers, however, shows that they don't add up. Partly, this was because the CDC researchers did not calculate the 400,000 deaths by checking to see if the weight of each person was a factor in his or her death. Rather, they *estimated* a figure by comparing the death rates of thin and heavy people using data that were nearly thirty years old. Although heavier people tend to die more frequently than people in mid-range weights, it is by no means clear that their weight is the cause of their higher death rates. It is far more likely that weight is simply a proxy for other, more important factors such as their diet, exercise, or family medical history. The researchers, however, simply *assumed* that obesity was the primary cause of death, even though there was no clear scientific rationale for this supposition.[4] Moreover, they also made a number of errors in their basic calculations. When these facts came out (only after a congressionally initiated inquiry), the CDC was forced to conduct an internal investigation and ended up amending the report.

In fact, a 2005 study, also published in *JAMA*, by a different set of CDC researchers, offers entirely different mortality estimates. Rather than being in peril, it appears that moderately "overweight" people live longer than those at a "normal" weight. And instead of finding that obesity causes

400,000 deaths, the new study estimates that fewer than 26,000 Americans die each year from weighing too much, a number that is even smaller than those who are estimated to die from being "underweight."[5] Weighing "too much" is less dangerous, it seems, than weighing "too little."

A similar problem exists with the links between obesity and most diseases. Doctors, government health agencies, and the news media frequently warn of the connections between being too fat and various ailments. *Time* magazine, for example, recently proclaimed that "being overweight significantly increases the risk of a long list of medical complaints including coronary artery disease, congestive heart failure, hypertension, diabetes, depression, deep-vein thrombosis, fatigue, insomnia, indigestion, and impotence."[6] After reading such a long indictment, it would be quite natural to assume that being fat puts your health in grave danger. However, this, too, is a misperception. Obesity has not been found to be a primary *cause* of any of these conditions. Yes, heart disease, diabetes, and other ailments are more common among the obese than the nonobese, but there is little evidence that adiposity (that is, excess fat tissue) is producing these pathologies. Indeed, some types of body fat are actually protective against many diseases, particularly for women and people over sixty-five. Nor is there clear evidence that, *by itself*, weight loss reduces the risk of death or most diseases. In other words, not only do we lack proof that being fat causes us to contract most major illnesses, but we do not have any evidence that losing weight makes us any healthier.

The same situation holds for the prognostications about how obesity is costing Americans so much money. The researchers who estimated that obesity costs us 100 billion dollars a year did so by calculating all the expenses associated with treating type 2 diabetes, coronary heart disease, hypertension, gallbladder disease, and cancer, but, like the estimators of deaths, they did not take into account other factors such as diet, exercise, or genetics that also might be causing these conditions.[7] Once again, they simply assumed that if you got heart disease or breast cancer it was because you were fat.

In short, nearly all the warnings about obesity are based on little more than loose statistical conjecture. While heart disease, cancer, stroke, asthma, and diabetes are undoubtedly serious and costly health concerns, there is no convincing evidence that such ailments arise from our growing weight. In many respects, body weight is no different than any other physical traits, such as height, age, sex, skin color, and even left-handedness that can be associated with higher rates of death and disease. Based on our current evidence, blaming obesity for heart disease, cancer, or many other ailments is like blaming smelly clothes, yellow teeth, or bad breath for lung cancer instead of cigarettes; it conflates an associated trait with its underlying cause.

Given these facts, I soon found myself trying to answer a much different set of questions. Rather than trying to figure out how to "solve" the obesity problem, I realized that the more interesting question was why so many smart and seemingly well-intentioned people were claiming that obesity was a problem in the first place. Why was our growing weight being labeled an "obesity epidemic"? What does it mean to judge our health and well-being by how much we weigh? And what is the real reason we are gaining weight? The answers to these questions came as a great surprise.

The Real Sources of the "Obesity Epidemic"

What I came to discover was that, contrary to the conventional wisdom, the primary source of America's obesity epidemic is not to be found at McDonald's, Burger King, or Krispy Kreme Donuts. Nor is it how little we exercise, our declining smoking rates, a "fat virus," or any of the other theories that are often used to explain our rising weights. Rather, America's obesity epidemic originates in far less conspicuous sources.

The most important of these is America's public health establishment. Over the past two decades, a handful of scientists, doctors, and health officials have actively campaigned to define our growing weight as an "obesity epidemic." They have created a very low and arbitrary definition of what is "overweight" and "obese" so that tens of millions of Americans, including archetypes of fitness such as President George Bush or basketball star Michael Jordan, are now considered to "weigh too much." They have also inflated the dangers and distorted the statistics about weight and health, exaggerated the impact of obesity on everything from motor accidents to air pollution. And, most important, they have established body weight as a barometer of wellness, so that being thin is equated with being healthy.

Now some of this campaign has been motivated by good intentions—for those who are sincerely concerned with Americans' health, the "obesity epidemic" seems like an effective way to highlight the chronic problems with Americans' poor diet and lack of exercise. And some sincerely believe that having too much fat leads to harm and disease, even if the scientific evidence is inconclusive.

But much of this campaign is driven by less altruistic concerns and more by the particular interests among the various constituent groups within America's public health establishment. Consider, for example, what an obesity epidemic means for the following groups. For scientists researching issues of weight, an obesity epidemic inflates their stature and allows them to get more research grants. For government health agencies, it is a powerful rationale for increasing their programs and budget allocations. For weight-loss companies and surgeons, it is a way to get their services covered by Medicare and health insurance providers. And, for pharmaceutical companies it can justify the release of new drugs, and help inflate their stock prices. The very same people who have proclaimed that obesity is a major health problem also stand the most to gain from it being classified as a disease. For America's public health establishment, an obesity epidemic is worth billions.

Of course, obesity researchers, doctors, and drug companies are not solely to blame. Another reason why our growing weight has come to be viewed as an "obesity epidemic" is because of our cultural biases against body fat and fat people. It is common for white, middle-class Americans, in particular, to think of weight as a barometer of a person's character—if people are fat, it is only because they are too lazy or irresponsible to "take care" of themselves. With such a strong moral connotation, body weight has become one of our most potent markers of social status whereby those with the resources or wherewithal to keep themselves thin rightly deserve their place at the top of the social ladder.

Given all the negative associations we heap on our fatness, it is no wonder our growing weight is seen as a cause for alarm across the political spectrum. For some on the right, the obesity epidemic merely reinforces their beliefs about the cause of the ever-widening gap between the rich and poor or between whites and minorities. After all, if African Americans, Latinos, or the poor are becoming fatter than America's predominantly white elite, it is only more proof that they lack the responsibility to take care of themselves. For others, our growing weight highlights the precarious social position of the middle class in an ever-stratifying America—if middle-class Americans, particularly middle-class children, are getting fat, it surely indicates the frailty of their own class status. And for those on the left, the growth of obesity is further proof that large, multinational corporations are running amok, fattening a hapless public with their billion-dollar advertising campaigns and super size value meals. The American people, particularly the poor and minorities who have the highest obesity rates, they argue, need to be protected from these corporate behemoths.

Running throughout all these perspectives is a paternalistic condescension toward fatness and fat people—not only do people with this view assume that fatness is inherently bad, but they also presuppose that fat people (that is, minorities and the poor) are too ignorant to know that they should be thin. Thus, when the filmmaker Morgan Spurlock sneers at the black kids who actually like McDonald's food in his film *Super Size Me* or the writer Greg Critser derides the Latinos at his local donut shop in his book *Fat Land*, it is not simply because they are worried about America's moral decline or unbridled corporate power. For many people, trumpeting the "problem of obesity" is an opportunity for them to express both their own moral superiority and their latent class snobbery and racism.[8]

Yet, it is just these kinds of biases about fatness and its origins that are dictating how obesity is being portrayed as a health issue. And this is creating all kinds of inappropriate and ineffective suggestions and responses for dealing with the "obesity epidemic." Consider, for example, the contradictory policies coming out of Washington and various state legislatures. Either they assume that body weight is solely a matter of individual responsibility, as with the Personal Responsibility in Food Consumption Act, a congressional bill that protects fast-food chains from lawsuits, or they assume that obesity needs to be tackled by reining in the power of McDonald's, Coca-Cola, and other food companies as with the proposed restrictions on food advertisements and taxes on snack foods. As a result, we now have a curious combination of laws that simultaneously forbid people from suing restaurants for making them fat but also prohibit schools from selling sodas and snack foods because they allegedly cause our kids to be too heavy.

Neither of these approaches, however, will do much either to improve our health or strengthen our moral fiber because they mistakenly equate fatness with both illness and depravity. By calling our growing weight an epidemic disease, America's public health establishment is sending a message that we can be healthy (and righteous) by being thin. Not only is such a message inaccurate (weight loss has not, by itself, been shown to improve most people's health or reduce the risk of most diseases), but it ignores the real threats to our health of which our weight is only symptomatic. If we want to know why diabetes and other diseases are on the rise in the United States, we need to focus less on the mere fact that our weight is increasing and more on the question of *why* our weight is increasing. In other words, we need to listen to what our growing weight is trying to tell us.

Biological Responses to the American Way of Life

From a biological perspective, fatness is simply a protective mechanism against an irregular food supply. Our fat cells are the places where our bodies store energy for times when food is unavailable or when we are too busy or active to eat. Because fatness is so crucial for our survival, our bodies have numerous means for ensuring that we retain as many calories as possible, such as giving us an appetite for calorie-rich food and regulating our metabolism to keep our weight within a certain range. While some people have a metabolism that keeps them thin, many Americans are inclined to have a weight range that tends toward corpulence. This is particularly the case for people whose ancestors came from places, such as Africa and parts of Asia, the Pacific Islands, and the Americas, where a regular food supply was not always present. These same metabolic protections are also why it is so difficult for most people to lose weight—most of us are biologically programmed to operate as if a famine is imminent.

Although our bodies may be expecting another famine, our way of life floods us with an abundance of foods, particularly sugars and fats, and allows us to expend little energy at work or in household chores. When our biological safeguards against privation come into contact with an environment of abundance and leisure, it is not surprising that many consequences ensue. Not only do we gain weight, but our cholesterol levels change, our insulin levels rise, and our blood pressure increases.

And it is these other metabolic changes that are behind many of the diseases that are typically associated with being too fat. The reason that diabetes and some types of cancer are on the rise is not because Americans weigh too much, it is because their metabolisms are out of whack. Fatness may result from the metabolic processes that are behind these ailments, but it is the underlying metabolic processes, and not the weight, that cause us so much trouble. So if we want to know the *real* health challenges behind our growing weight, we need to identify what is causing us to eat so many fats and sugars and to exercise so little.

Here, again, is where political ideology and cultural stereotypes often cloud our perceptions. Many folks, for example, like to blame our gluttony on the extra-large portion sizes in restaurants and supermarkets— and with a super size value meal weighing in at 1,500 calories it is easy to see why fast-food has been cast as such a villain. But, once again, this stereotype is inaccurate. Americans are not consuming more calories because of how much they are eating during their meals. (Americans consume only slightly more calories in their meals today than they did in the 1970s.) Rather, Americans are consuming more calories because of how much they are eating *in between* their meals. The real culprit behind our increasing wieght is snacking.

Similarly, many public health advocates and urban planners like to blame our inactivity on cars, sprawl, and television. Given the four hours the average American spends each day behind the wheel or in front of the TV, this suspicion, too, is understandable. If we want to get Americans exercising more, it seems, we need to figure out ways to get them to drive less, watch less television, and redesign their communities to make walking easier.

Once again, however, focusing on driving and television in order to make Americans thinner misses the real, and important, health issue. For the problem with both our unhealthy diet and inactivity goes beyond how much junk food we eat, TV we watch, or miles we drive; the problem is with the very principles that define us as a society. Snacking, driving, and television are more than simple conveniences; they are expressions of our very core values—choice, freedom, and liberty. Snacks, sodas, and other prepared foods have liberated the American meal away from the domestic confines of the home, allowing us to eat by ourselves, when and where we want. Automobiles reduce the physical demands of walking and give us near-limitless geographic mobility. Television allows leisure to be spent with little physical effort and provides a terrific array of entertainment choices. In short, each is about fulfilling our wants in as efficient and easy a manner as possible, the very benefits that our liberal, free-market system promises.

So, from this perspective, the origins of America's growing metabolic problems, as well as its increasing weight, ultimately derive from its very core principles. The American credo of "life, liberty, and the pursuit of happiness" is about giving us the freedom to individually pursue our own gratification to the extent that we see fit, the very thing that snacks, cars, and television provide. It is about making us the ultimate arbiters of what is good for ourselves. The market, in turn, responds by providing us what we want in the most efficient and inexpensive manner. Thus if we want to eat tasty foods, move about with great speed and ease, and amuse ourselves in leisurely ways, this is our right. But this is also why all the public health pronouncements about dieting and nutrition, such as "eat less and exercise more," are so ineffective. Although such simple advice may seem reasonable, it flies in the face of a consumer economy that is constantly expanding our choices and freedom. Asking an American to "eat less and exercise more" is like asking an Eskimo not to fish or a devout Muslim not to say daily prayers—it runs afoul of the dominant logic of our very culture. Our growing weight is simply a natural and inevitable biological response to living in a consumer-oriented democracy.

Why Focusing on Fat May Be Harmful to Your Health

Yet, with respect to our appearance and our health, this freedom is presenting us with a dilemma. On one hand, the amenities that make our lives so easy are ill suited to our physiology, particularly in large doses. The same consumer conveniences that are adding to our waistlines are also contributing to our chronically high levels of diabetes, cardiovascular disease, anxiety, stress, depression, and sleeplessness. While undoubtedly the rise of such maladies is also coming from a medical culture that is quick to diagnose any ailment as a disorder, the prevalence of such chronic diseases is also the by-product of a fast-paced culture of instant gratification and individual license. On the other hand, few Americans want to relinquish their freedom, particularly with respect to what they eat or how they move. Few of us want to ban our snack foods, raise our gasoline prices, get rid of our televisions, or forcibly be put on any diet plan. When it comes to our diet, lifestyle, and health, we basically want to eat our cake and have it, too.

The easiest way of resolving this cake-eating dilemma is by simply treating its undesirable side effects. So, if snacking and inactivity are making our cholesterol level too high, we jump at the chance to keep it in check with a pill such as Lipitor, rather than force ourselves to change our diet or start exercising more. And, to the extent that we are able to treat these unwanted symptoms, such a strategy is a great success. For example, much of the recent decline in deaths from heart disease and other ailments, as well as our improved quality of life, have come from simple and undemanding treatments. Sometimes, alleviating unwanted symptoms of an unhealthy lifestyle is the most efficient and effective response.

Often, however, treating a symptom rather than addressing its root causes only causes more problems than it solves, and this is what is happening with weight. Ask any of the millions of frustrated dieters in America and they will tell you what molecular biologists have long known—for many of us, our bodies are quite resistant to being slender. Nor do we have a safe or effective mechanism for helping us lose weight. Indeed, the same doctors, health officials, and medical researchers who have spent the past four decades telling Americans they are too fat have not been able to devise a sound treatment for becoming thin. As a result, many Americans are going to extreme measures to make themselves lose weight, such as self-starvation, smoking, taking dangerous appetite suppressants, or even having their stomachs surgically shrunk. Not only are such practices ineffective, they often do more harm than good. Whether it is from a failed diet, a botched gastric-bypass surgery, complications from an eating disorder, or heart damage from diet drugs, every year thousands of Americans are literally dying to be thin.

Thus, with respect to our weight, we have put ourselves into a bind. In calling our growing weight an "epidemic," we have created a disease out of a physical symptom that, in turn, we are unable to treat. In calling fat people gluttonous and lazy, we are ascribing moral characteristics to what is largely a biological phenomenon. We are now being told to lose weight without understanding that our fatness is actually an expression of forces that are largely beyond our individual control or our collective will to change. From the misguided equation of thinness and health, millions of Americans are being told to lose weight, which is only likely to make them more miserable and possibly do them great harm.

In truth, the only way we are going to "solve" the problem of obesity is to stop making fatness a scapegoat for all our ills. This means that public health officials and doctors need to stop making weight a barometer of health and issuing so many alarmist claims about the obesity epidemic. This also means that the rest of us need to stop judging others and ourselves by our size.

Such a change in perspective, however, may be our greatest challenge. Our body weight and fatness are uniquely powerful symbols for us—something we feel we should be able to control but that often we can't. As a result, obesity has become akin to a sacrificial animal, a receptacle for many of our problems. Whether it is our moral indignation, status anxiety, or just feelings of general powerlessness, we assume we can get a handle on our lives and social problems by losing weight. If we can only rid ourselves of this beast (that is, obesity), we believe we will not only be thin, but happy, healthy, and righteous. Yet, as with any blind rite, such thinking is a delusion and blaming obesity for our health and social problems is only going to cause us more injury over the long haul.

So how might we change our attitudes about obesity and fat? As with any change in perspective, the first place we must begin is in understanding why we think the way we do. In the case of obesity, we need to understand both why we are gaining weight and, more important, why we are calling this weight gain a disease. In other words, if we are to change our thinking about fat, we need to recognize the *real* sources of America's obesity epidemic.

This book seeks to help in this effort. It is divided roughly into two parts. The first part, examines how and why our growing weight has come to be characterized as an "obesity epidemic." Chapters 1 and 2 examine the role of the health professions, drug companies, government, and diet industry in promulgating the idea that our growing weight is a dangerous disease. After reviewing both the scientific evidence and the history of "obesity" as a health concept, it becomes clear that America's "health-industrial complex" is far more responsible for the obesity epidemic than any other source. But the health warnings about obesity have not fallen on deaf ears and if Americans are truly worried about obesity it is because of their receptivity to the various health pronouncements. Chapters 3 and 4 examine why we in the West hate fatness so much, particularly in white women, while the rest of the world tends to celebrate it. As we'll see, our attitudes about fatness have much more to do with our concerns about social status, race, and sex than they do with health.

The second half of the book examines why we are gaining weight and what this weight gain signifies. Chapter 5 looks at the science of fat and what the genetic sources of weight tell us about our expanding waistlines and our health. Chapters 6 and 7 review the charges and evidence concerning food, exercise, and our growing weight. As we'll see, the most commonly accused culprits (fast-food, high fructose corn syrup, television, and automobiles) are merely accessories to the "crime"; meanwhile, the real source of our growing weight (the free market) goes largely unnoticed. Chapter 8 reviews the politics behind the various obesity initiatives coming from our state and federal governments. Not only are most of these policies unlikely to help us lose weight, they also reveal the fundamental problems with making weight loss a target of government action. In chapter 9, the conclusion, I discuss what I think our growing weight really means and what we can do to address the *real* problems of obesity in the United States.

one

What Is Fat?

"Am I fat?" My wife, Thea, is six-months pregnant and fretting over her appearance. I try to reassure her and tell her that she is beautiful, but it seems to have no effect. "Look at me—I'm a whale." I tell her that she looks terrific and remind her that what she is feeling is perfectly normal. As I'm saying these things, she nods her head. "Yeah, I know. Thanks." Then, after a pause, she looks at me and says, "But tell me, really, do you think I'm fat?"

Most Americans are probably all too familiar with this question. It looms over our culture like an ominous shadow. It haunts adolescence and ruins marriages. It feeds a mammoth diet and fitness industry. It motivates millions to battle with their own bodies. It is a national preoccupation. And, it is at the center of America's obesity epidemic.

To understand why more than 60 percent of Americans are considered "overweight" and 25 percent "obese," we need first to understand how these terms are being defined. After all, the very existence of an obesity "epidemic" hinges on what exactly obesity is. If someone is obese only if he or she weighs 350 pounds, then few Americans would qualify and there would be no epidemic; conversely, if obesity can be had with only 200 pounds, then many people will get this label and the term "epidemic" may be justified.

But the importance of this terminology goes beyond the question of whether too many Americans are "overweight"; it is also in the power this word has in our everyday lives. In America, being labeled or perceived as overweight means your life will be harder on a number of fronts. You may pay more for many goods and services such as airline tickets and insurance. You will receive different medical care. In some cases, you may be denied a job.[1] More important, the designation of overweight or obese also goes to the very core of a person's identity. To be *over*weight is to be, by definition, abnormal or different. By calling people "overweight" or "obese," we are not simply delineating them by their body mass, but we are relegating them to the margins of society. Such labels also become internalized by the "overweight" or "obese" who think that something is wrong with them or that they must change their behavior in order to meet a particular physical ideal. Ultimately, the power of this terminology is not just in the way the overweight are treated by others, but in the way it makes them see themselves.

Yet, the curious thing is that even though we worry so much about being "overweight" and we hear so much about our "obesity" epidemic, these terms have no precise definition.[2] The *American Heritage English Language Dictionary* defines overweight as "weighing more than is *normal, necessary,* or *allowed*," while obese is "*extremely* fat, *grossly* overweight" (my italics). These definitions may seem straightforward but they raise a host of political questions: What standard determines "normal"? By what criteria is something deemed "necessary"? "Allowed" by whom? What point is "extreme" or "gross"?

In the case of body weight, these questions have no clear answers. If normalcy and necessity are what define obesity, then one can easily name any number of different standards on which to base a norm or a necessity. For example, what is considered overweight on a Hollywood starlet or a supermodel is probably thin for most ordinary women; conversely what is overweight on most men is skinny on a professional football player. This problem is confounded because so many different groups profit from setting the definition of these terms at one level or another; the diet industry, for instance, benefits from labeling everyone as overweight, while the fast-food industry prefers that no one thinks of themselves as obese. How these terms get defined ultimately depends on who gains from making people concerned about their body size and who has an interest in getting people to try to lose weight. Which leads us to the story of how our current standards of overweight and obese came to be defined.

The primary reason why more than 60 percent of Americans are "overweight" has nothing to do with fast-food, cars, or television; it is not because Americans are eating too much and exercising too little; nor is it because of any "fat" gene within us. The reason why a majority of Americans are overweight is because a nineteenth-century astronomer, a twentieth-century insurance actuary, and a handful of contemporary scientists concocted some ideas about what a normal weight should be. These definitions have little to do with scientific evidence about weight and health and a lot to do with simple mathematics, insurance premiums, and the pecuniary interests of the pharmaceutical industry. If Michael Jordan is "overweight" or Arnold Schwarzenegger is "obese," (which they are according to our current standards), it is not because of their poor fitness or their precarious health; it is because a handful of people are defining these terms in ridiculous ways.

Damning Statistics

America's obesity epidemic originates in a simple measure, the body-mass index, or BMI. Most of us have had our BMI checked at one time or another: it's the test where you type in your weight and height and you're told if you're overweight. It is the most common method for classifying people's weight—used by nearly all doctors, government officials, and health organizations. The surgeon general and the Centers for Disease Control and Prevention (CDC) have used BMI as the primary basis for claiming that obesity is a major health epidemic. The National Heart, Lung, and Blood Institute and many weight-loss companies feature BMI calculators on their websites and many of us get pop-up ads asking us to check our BMI to see if we're overweight. BMI has become a ubiquitous part of the American lexicon. At first glance, BMI seems to be a relatively neutral way of determining weight status. It is simply the proportion of a person's height to weight. BMI has a curious history, though, that reveals much about the origins of America's "obesity epidemic."

Interestingly, the concept of BMI was not developed with any connection to body fat. The first person to use it was not even concerned with losing weight or with health but, rather, he was interested in the laws of the heavens. In the 1830s, a Belgian astronomer named Adolphe Quetelet was trying to test whether mathematical laws of probability could be applied to human beings.[3] These statistical laws were used in astronomy to predict the likelihood of a phenomenon based on repeated observations. Quetelet believed that such laws also governed human affairs. To predict human behavior, all one needed to do was gather

BMI Calculator*

Calculate Your BMI[a]		Obesity Class	BMI (kg/m^2)
Enter Your Weight (in pounds) _____	Underweight	–	<18.5
Enter Your Height (feet) _____	Normal	–	18.5–24.9
(inches) _____	Overweight	–	25–29.9
[CALCULATE] Your BMI = _____	Obese	I	30–34.9
	Obese	II	35–39.9
	Morbid obesity	III	>40

*A BMI calculator, typical of many websites, automatically determines one's weight status after one simply types in one's weight and height. In this instance, the purpose of the BMI calculator offered by the American Society of Bariatric Surgery is to determine who might be eligible for weight-loss surgery (www.asbs.org/html/bmi.html).
[a]BMI = weight/height^2; weight in kilograms = pounds × 0.45359237; height in meters = inches × 0.0254.

information on a large enough sample of a population and calculate general trends.[4]

To test his ideas, Quetelet began collecting information from French and Scottish army conscripts. Along with other details, Quetelet measured their weights and heights and plotted them along a distribution. For each height, he found a range of weights in what statisticians would later call a normal distribution or, more famously, a bell curve. At the center of the distribution (or top of the bell curve) Quetelet found the most number of cases, which was the average weight of the group. In charting these distributions, he happened to observe that the weight of "normal" conscripts (that is, those closest to the middle of the distribution) was proportional to their height squared; this general formula would later be used to determine BMI.[5] But Quetelet did not stop there. Since the average conscript's weight was proportional to his height, Quetelet reasoned that this must be what the ideal weight *should* be; anyone who deviated from this average could be considered either under- or overweight. This pseudoscientific conception of an "ideal" weight thus provided the first scientific notion of what overweight could be.

Quetelet's idea had deep political implications. Among his many accomplishments, Quetelet first derived the concept of the "average man." Because most people congregated around average points in their physical characteristics, Quetelet believed that deviants, criminals, or troublemakers could be identified by their physical abnormalities. A similar technique was now available for body weight. Not only could

Quetelet's method determine what was the "normal" weight for a population (which was simply the average), but it could also mathematically define who was abnormal or "overweight" by calculating how far someone "deviated" from the norm. The farther someone was from the average weight, the more they violated other social norms and the more they could be monitored, institutionalized, or controlled.

Quetelet's scheme was a harbinger of a larger wave of scientific attempts to measure and differentiate groups in society. Throughout the nineteenth and early twentieth century, scientists became enamored with measuring skulls, brows, body proportions, and other aptitudes. Following Darwin and the development of biology, it was the golden era of classification. Although these efforts were often done in the name of science, they sought to do more than merely taxonomize the population.[6] Most efforts at measurement were meant to identify miscreants and justify racial and economic prerogatives among a white, aristocratic elite. For example, in the late 1800s public officials and scientists went to great lengths to catalogue the physical characteristics of criminals, arguing that their delinquency was tied to their physiognomy.[7] By claiming that elite groups had certain traits, scientists could rationalize racial inequities in wealth, employment, and education—something that we see with the controversial claims linking race and I.Q. test scores today.[8] From Quetelet's measurement of BMI, the groundwork was laid for a similar process of classification for body weight. A high (or low) body weight, simply by being different from the average, was not only systematically identified, it was also problematized. Even though there was no linkage between weight and health, delinquency, or any social ill, just by being far from the average, overweight and underweight people were marginalized.

Although Quetelet's methods provided a "scientific" basis for classifying (and standardizing) body weight, BMI did not become widely used until a century later because body weight was not a very good mechanism for social differentiation. Most people in the nineteenth century struggled to get enough to eat and few had the luxury of worrying about whether they were too fat. Since only the rich and well-off could afford to be corpulent, there were few groups who were looking to differentiate people for being too heavy. That is, except for one—the insurance industry. For years, life insurance companies had been desperately trying to find mechanisms that would predict early deaths.

In the early 1900s, when medical technology was still crude, they had few diagnostic tools for determining who might die early, and thus be a greater policy risk. Even though they suspected that body weight (like other physical traits) could be a predictor of mortality, they had no way of systematically using it calculate their insurance premiums. In other words, because they had no way of knowing how much more of a risk a 240-pound man was than a 220-pound man, they did not know how much more that person should be charged for life insurance.

Seeking to answer this question, Louis Dublin, a statistician at the Metropolitan Life Insurance Company, started charting the death rates of its policyholders in the 1940s using a height-to-weight index. In line with industry expectations, Dublin found that thinner people lived longer. But, more important, he also found that the closer a person's weight was to that of the average twenty-five-year-old, the longer he or she would live, or least live before cashing out on their life insurance. From these findings, Dublin came up with some ranges for each height of what was an "ideal" body weight (that is, the weight at which a person had the longest life span). Although Dublin's classification scheme was primarily intended for insurance actuary tables, the tables soon took on a whole new function, thanks in large part to his tireless promotion of weight as a determinant of early mortality.[9] Following Dublin's lead, doctors, epidemiologists, and the federal government soon adopted these tables to analyze the "health" of the population. By the 1950s, the Met Life table was *the* method for determining who was overweight.

It is important to remember, however, that up until this point, BMI was never intended to be a gauge of someone's health. When Adolphe Quetelet came up with BMI, he was simply trying to classify the population and not make any predictions about death or disease. Nor were Louis Dublin's Met Life actuary tables based on any biological rationale; Dublin did not specify why heavier people would die earlier, nor did his model account for genes, diet, exercise, or many other influences on mortality. Rather, Dublin used weight because it was easy to measure and had a lot of statistical power to *predict* the likelihood of early death. But as a result of his use of the statistics, people came to think that body fat *caused* early death, an idea that Dublin himself propagated. Ultimately, the most influential factor in determining what Americans considered to be overweight was not based

Ideal Weight Table for Men and Women*

	Women				Men		
Height in Shoes	Small Frame (lbs.)	Medium Frame (lbs.)	Large Frame (lbs.)	Height in Shoes	Small Frame (lbs.)	Medium Frame (lbs.)	Large Frame (lbs.)
6'	138–151	148–162	158–179	6'4"	162–176	171–187	181–207
5'11"	135–148	145–159	155–176	6'3"	158–172	167–182	176–202
5'10"	132–145	142–156	152–173	6'2"	155–168	164–178	172–197
5'9"	129–142	139–153	149–170	6'1"	152–164	160–174	168–192
5'8"	126–139	136–150	146–167	6'	149–160	157–170	164–188
5'7"	123–136	133–147	143–163	5'11"	146–157	154–166	161–184
5'6"	120–133	130–144	140–159	5'10"	144–154	151–163	158–180
5'5"	117–130	127–141	137–155	5'9"	142–151	148–160	155–176
5'4"	114–127	124–138	134–151	5'8"	140–148	145–157	152–172
5'3"	111–124	121–135	131–147	5'7"	138–145	142–154	149–168
5'2"	108–121	118–132	128–143	5'6"	136–142	139–151	146–164
5'1"	106–118	115–129	125–140	5'5"	134–140	137–148	144–160
5'	104–115	113–126	122–137	5'4"	132–138	135–145	142–156
4'11"	103–113	111–123	120–134	5'3"	130–136	130–143	140–153
4'10"	102–111	109–121	118–131	5'2"	128–134	131–141	138–150

*In 1943, the Metropolitan Life Insurance Company introduced its standard height-weight tables for men and women. The numbers represent the weights in pounds of people between ages of twenty-five to twenty-nine, those with the lowest mortality rates. (They take into account indoor clothing weighing three pounds, and shoes with one-inch heels.) Met Life described these as "desirable" weights, but, over time, they became known as "ideal" weights.

on criteria of health but criteria of profit and measurement within the insurance industry.

Despite this dubious history, BMI remains the basis for much of our official health policy today, both in the way we think of obesity and how we measure it. Government health agencies, such as the Centers for Disease Control and Prevention (CDC) and the National Institutes of Health (NIH), rely on BMI as the primary indicator of weight, health, and mortality risk in the American population. Today, almost all government agencies consider anyone with a BMI of 25 or more as "overweight." For an American man who is the average height of 5'9" that would be 170 pounds; for an American woman who is the average height of 5'4" that would be 145 pounds. A BMI of 30 or more is "obese" (that is, 204 pounds for a 5'9" American male and 175 pounds for a 5'4" American woman). According to government health officials and many obesity experts, these BMI scales are a simple and easy method for gauging your health. All you need to do is check your height and weight and "voila!" you can tell not only if you are "overweight" or "obese," but also how well you are. Except for one problem—it's not true.

The Problem with BMI

Despite its ubiquity among government agencies, medical practitioners, and health researchers, BMI is not only a poor measure of health, it is actually a lousy measure of obesity. To begin with, BMI is a measure of proportionate body weight and not a measure of body fat. This is why many professional athletes are technically "overweight" or "obese" even though they have little body fat. If we think of obesity as an excess of body fat (which most people do), then BMI is an inaccurate gauge.

And the problem does not stop there, for BMI is also a poor predictor of mortality. It is not a simple fact that the heavier a person is, the more likely he will die. The association between mortality and BMI is more of a U shape—those at both the low and high ends of the weight spectrum have higher mortality rates than those in the middle.[10] The rates of mortality at the high end of the BMI scale do not become prominent for men or women until a BMI is generally over 35 (which applies to less than 10 percent of the population). This correlation also varies by age—among older people, a BMI is negatively related to mortality (that is, the heavier you are, the less likely you are to die).[11]

Nor does BMI tell us much about why thinner or heavier people die. Although people at the either end of the BMI scale may have higher death rates, we simply do not know if early death comes from having too much or too little adipose tissue or whether BMI is simply reflecting other unmeasured influences.[12] BMI does not take into account fitness, heart rate, or fat distribution, all of which relate to disease and mortality.[13] By some accounts, fat distribution may actually be a better predictor of mortality than body weight—one study found the mortality associated with higher BMI levels can be completely accounted for by waist circumference.[14] Fat on someone's hips and thighs seems to have little or no relationship to the risk of death; it is only fat in the belly that seems to be problematic. Thus, if our concern with obesity is that it is supposedly killing thousands of Americans, then actually BMI tells us very little about who those people may be.

But these issues pale in comparison to the biggest problem with BMI; we have no clear criteria of what points on the BMI scale should be classified as "overweight" or "obese." Over the past two decades, the BMI thresholds for these terms have yo-yoed, sometimes being pegged at one level, sometimes at another. For example, between 1980 and 2000, the U.S. Dietary Guidelines (a joint report from the Departments of Agriculture and Health and Human Services) have defined overweight at various levels ranging from a BMI of 24.9 to 27.1.[15] In 1985, the National Institutes of Health (NIH) consensus conference recommended that overweight be set at a BMI of 27.8 for men and 27.3 for women—by this standard, a 6' man would be overweight at 205 pounds, a 5'7" woman would be overweight at 175 pounds.[16] Then, in the 1990s, the World Health Organization (WHO) came out with a recommendation that a BMI of 25 to 29 should be considered overweight and a BMI of 30 or more obese (more on this below).[17] To make the United States consistent with this standard, many federal health agencies and researchers soon began adopting the lower BMI standards, thus creating a confusing set of standards and guidelines.[18]

Partly to sort through these conflicting measures, in 1988 the NIH convened a panel of more than two dozen experts from the fields of health research, epidemiology, and nutrition to review the "evidence-based" research of the past twenty years. This NIH report concluded that the official designations of overweight should be set at a BMI of 25 and obesity at a BMI of 30, the same standards established by the WHO. Soon, this became the definitive guide for determining what was officially overweight and obese in the United States.[19]

At the time it came out, the NIH report caused a lot of controversy because, overnight, more than 37 million Americans suddenly became "overweight," even though they had not gained an ounce. What few people noticed, however, was that the scientific "evidence" to justify this change was nonexistent. According to the NIH report, the classification of overweight at a BMI of 25 was based on the putative linkages to mortality. According to the report, people who have a BMI of more than 25 had "significantly higher mortality" rates than those under 25, but in both the WHO and NIH reports, none of the research really substantiated this claim.[20] For example, the major source cited by the NIH board was a 1996 review of studies linking BMI and mortality by the nutritionist Richard Troiano and his associates. Yet, strangely enough,

Troiano's findings actually contradict most of the recommendations of the NIH panel. Not only did he discover that mortality was highest among the very thin as well as the very heavy, but also that the increased mortality was typically not evident until well beyond a BMI level of 30. And until one gets to a BMI of 40 or more, the differences in mortality are still within the bounds of statistical uncertainty. From these findings, Troiano concluded that "This analysis of mortality suggests a need to re-examine body weight recommendations. Weight levels currently considered moderately overweight (i.e., a BMI > 27) were *not* associated with increased all-cause mortality."[21] Ironically, although the NIH panel did recalibrate body weight recommendations, they did so in the opposite direction, *lowering* the BMI designation of what would be considered overweight and obese.

The fact of the matter is that, with our current data and measurement techniques, it is impossible to calculate the mortality risks of obesity accurately. The epidemiological studies that have estimated the links between BMI and mortality are not based on studies of the entire population or of all deaths, but on large pools of survey data from various projects tracking health. In these samples, epidemiologists simply measure the association between death rates or various diseases and body weights. If deaths or diseases are more common as weight goes up, a trend is identified. But calculating mortality in this way is a tricky business, largely because the illnesses that cause most deaths in America (that is, heart disease, cancer, and stroke) have so many sources. In other words, heavier people may have a higher mortality rate but this does not necessarily mean that it is their body fat that is killing them. Their weight may simply be capturing the effects of other unmeasured variables. The validity of this research depends largely on the variables that are included in the estimates and the margins of error from the coefficients. In order to determine that a certain trait has a really significant impact, the differences in the statistical estimates must be great enough not to simply be caused by random error. Moreover, it must be verified that the trait in question is the direct source of the problem and not simply a proxy for other causes. For example, mortality rates may be higher among the obese because heavier people are less likely to seek regular medical care, the consequence of the prejudice they often encounter among medical professionals.

The problem is that the major studies on the number of deaths due to obesity are fraught with all sorts of problematic assumptions. The two most commonly cited studies that linked higher BMI with mortality were written by the obesity researcher David Allison and his colleagues in 1999 and by a collection of CDC researchers in 2004. Both appeared in the *Journal of the American Medical Association (JAMA)*.[22] And both studies calculated that obesity (defined as a BMI of 30 or above) was causing several hundred thousand deaths a year. Yet, in neither of these studies did the researchers actually measure the linkage between obesity and death nor did they take into account other explanatory factors, such as genes, diet patterns, or exercise, that might also explain why heavier people had higher mortality rates.

In the 1999 study, Allison and his colleagues assumed "that all excess mortality in obese people is due to obesity." But, in reality, no one has proven that adiposity (excess amounts of fat) is an independent cause of heart disease, cancer, and stroke.[23] Moreover, their methods of calculating the obesity effects were incredibly crude: they divided the population between nonobese and obese and assumed that any deaths that occurred among the latter were due to their excess weight. Even if an obese person died in a car accident or from a snakebite, the cause of his or her death was attributed to body weight. These claims are as ludicrous as arguing that the difference in mortality rates between blacks and whites are the result of their skin color.

The 2004 *JAMA* study is more careful in its language but equally problematic in its conclusions. This study, written by researchers and the director of the CDC, calculated that the diet and inactivity associated with obesity causes 400,000 deaths a year in the United States. While they actually attribute these deaths to "poor diet and physical inactivity," they nevertheless assumed that these factors work primarily through obesity rather than having a negative impact on their own. In their view, the problem with inactivity and poor diet is that they make you fat and being fat is what kills you rather than simply saying that poor diet and inactivity are themselves problematic. Yet, as we'll see in later chapters, there is much more convincing evidence about the immediate health hazards of a poor diet and inactivity than there is about being too fat.

Indeed, if you look at the actual numbers on death, you'll find a much different story. Each year, roughly two million Americans die from all causes. About 70 percent of these two million deaths are among people who are over 65. Among the elderly, obesity is not a major cause of death because overweight and obese senior citizens (those with a BMI above 24) actually live longer than those at a normal or below normal body weight (a BMI below 24).[24] Yes, that is correct—older people who are heavier live longer than those who are thin. So if obesity is not killing the elderly, it means that obesity can only be responsible for some part of the roughly 600,000 deaths among the remaining population under the age of 65. And what are these people dying from? The biggest killers among the nonelderly are largely unrelated to obesity; the top cause of death among people who are under forty-five is unintentional injury, primarily from automobile accidents; the top killer among people between forty-five and sixty-five is cancer, the leading cause of which is smoking. Among the top ten causes of death for people under sixty-five, only heart disease, diabetes, and a small fraction of cancer deaths have any plausible connection to body weight.

And, even if we *assume* that all the deaths from heart disease, diabetes, and other organ ailments are attributed to obesity, we only get, at most, about 174,000 deaths a year among people under sixty-five.[25] Yet this number is also too high because we know that plenty of thin people are also dying from heart disease, diabetes, and organ failure. In reality, we have no clear idea whether any deaths at all can be attributed solely to a person's body weight. After these and other discrepancies in the 2004 CDC report were brought to the attention of Congressman Henry Waxman in the summer of 2004 he asked the General Accounting Office of the U.S. government to launch an investigation. The CDC ended up retracting their earlier estimates and after an "internal review" in which the miscalculations were blamed on a "computer error" they released new estimates for which the annual rate of death attributed to obesity was only about 365,000 per year.[26] Even these numbers were based on specious reasoning; a more recent and reliable estimate from Kathryn Flegal, a researcher at the National Center for Health Statistics, puts the number of deaths attributable to "weighing too much" at fewer than 26,000 a year. In addition, Flegal found that people who are "overweight" (with a BMI of 25 to 29.9) live longer, on average, than those at a "normal" weight (a BMI between 18.5 and 24.9).[27]

These inferential problems get even worse when the discussion turns to the question of diseases. The 1998 NIH report made an extensive list of diseases that were "associated" with higher BMIs including hypertension, type 2 diabetes, coronary heart disease, stroke, gallbladder disease, osteoarthritis, and some types of cancer. As the NIH report went through the list of these diseases, it cited hundreds of studies to back its claims, the result of a seemingly exhaustive search of the scientific literature. This evidence was supposed to prove that, even more than being a cause of death, a high BMI was a major health risk. Except, once again, there were two major problems.

First, there is no uniform point on the BMI scale at which all these diseases become more evident. The relationship between BMI and each disease varies considerably depending on the condition in question. For some conditions, such as diabetes, an increased likelihood can start as low as a BMI of 22; for other health conditions, such as many types of cancer, the increased risks do not begin until a BMI is much greater than 30. And again, in many instances, these health pathologies might not arise from adipose tissue but from associated causes. For example, the association between heart disease and obesity may come from greater insulin resistance among the obese, a factor that can be alleviated through exercise, even when weight isn't lost.[28] These health effects are also subject to significant differences depending on race, gender, and age. Even worse, some studies show that higher BMIs are actually associated with lower rates of cancer and heart disease.[29]

Indeed, the problem of misattribution appears throughout the NIH report. For example, throughout the report boxed statements give particular emphasis to messages such as "Weight loss produced by lifestyle modifications reduces blood pressure in overweight hypertensive patients."[30] This type of message is repeated with numerous other diseases. Yet in none of the studies cited was it conclusive that the weight loss itself was responsible for the remediation of the illness rather than the change in lifestyle. In fact, it is far more plausible that the increase in exercise and change in diet that affected the weight loss is the real cause for the health improvement.[31] This is like saying "whiter teeth produced by elimination of smoking reduces the incidence of lung cancer." Nevertheless, the NIH report continues to emphasize that weight loss was a causal factor.

Second, nearly all the studies linking obesity with disease are epidemiological studies; that is, they are simply surveys of the population and not clinical experiments. Not only are these data often problematic (for instance, body weight is self-reported), but the inferences that can be made from the data are unclear. Epidemiology is a tricky business—one tries to find relationships between phenomena by examining large surveys of the population and seeing where statistical associations exist. To determine causality, such as with smoking and lung cancer, epidemiologists look for the strength of association (what percent of smokers get lung cancer?), the timing of the association (does lung cancer follow years of smoking?), and whether there is a plausible scientific explanation between the two (is there something in cigarette smoke that would trigger lung cancer?).[32] If these links are all clear, then causal inferences can be made with some confidence.

But in most studies linking body weight and disease, these conditions for determining causality are not met. Numerous critics, such as the editors of the *New England Journal of Medicine*, Dr. Glenn Gaesser of the University of Virginia and Professor Paul Campos of the University of Colorado, have pointed out that most of the evidence linking obesity, mortality, and disease is fraught with questionable methodological assumptions. In fact, many studies do not take into account other factors that might account for diseases such as smoking, access to medical care, family history, exercise, or diet.[33]

Perhaps the biggest problem with this research is that we do not have a good theory on why obesity causes heart disease, cancer, or other ailments. Indeed, the evidence does not support many of our common stereotypes about the health risks of obesity and disease. For example, it is common for people to think that being fat clogs your arteries, but there is no conclusive proof that having more body fat results in more atherosclerosis independent of one's diet.[34] There are only two medical conditions that have been shown convincingly to be caused by excess body fat: osteoarthritis of weight bearing joints and uterine cancer that comes from higher estrogen levels in heavier women (although this can be treated medically without weight loss).[35] All the other diseases are only linked to obesity through *associations* in large populations. It is not clear why having a lot of fat tissue would make someone more likely to have heart disease, asthma, or many of the other diseases commonly attributed to obesity.

Herein lies the biggest problem of making health-related claims about obesity—there is far more we do not know about the consequences of excess fatty tissue than we do. The hypotheses about the causal links between excess fatty tissue and most health pathologies are largely untested. Although some obesity researchers now believe that many diseases may be caused by the hormones and signaling compounds produced by fat cells, they still have not proven how excess levels of these hormones may be harmful. The effect of these hormones in causing disease is still a matter of speculation.[36] Nor, more important, is there any conclusion about at what level of obesity such excess hormones become dangerous. As obesity researcher and NIH panel chair Xavier Pi-Sunyer says, "It's a very complicated system, and the more we learn about it, the more complicated it becomes."[37]

The Politics of Defining Obesity

So, if the scientific evidence about the relationship between BMI, mortality, and other health conditions is so unclear, why did the NIH, putatively the most objective public health institution in the United States, endorse these low thresholds of overweight and obese? According to one NIH panel member, the overweight designation came from the "best scientific judgment" of the committee members.[38] But the decision to lower the weight scale was not based on any revolutionary research in the scientific community about what an ideal weight should be—with such fuzzy evidence, science could not have possibly informed this decision. The U.S. government's proclamation of what BMI level was overweight or obese was based, in reality, on a subjective and arbitrary call on the part of just a few researchers. Ironically, the same NIH panel that strove for "evidence-based" and objective criteria ended up making a major proclamation that, in retrospect, appears to have been for reasons that had do nothing with health and a lot to do with the funding dynamics within the scientific professions and the pharmaceutical industry.

To understand this point, it is important to go back to the 1995 World Health Organization report that helped establish the idea that a person is overweight with a BMI of 25. This document probably had more impact on determining how obesity was defined than anything else. And who wrote this important document? Most of it was drafted and written under the auspices of the International Obesity Task Force (IOTF). On the surface the IOTF seems to be a credible association of scientists interested in obesity research and policy. According to its website, the IOTF's mission is to "inform the world about the urgency of the problem and to persuade goverments [sic] that the time to act is now." Their website also displays the logos of both the WHO and the International Association for the Study of Obesity, legitimate health organizations, making the IOTF seem like a purely scientific organization.[39]

In reality, however, the IOTF is anything but an unbiased congress of scientists. The IOTF is an organization primarily funded by Hoffman-La Roche (the maker of the weight-loss drug Xenical) and Abbott Laboratories (the maker of the weight-loss drug Meridia).[40] Like other organizations financed primarily by drug companies that don the "neutral" mantle of science (including the American Obesity Association), the primary mission of the IOTF is to lobby governments and advance particular scientific agendas that coincide with the pharmaceutical industry's goals. Indeed, the initial mission of the IOTF was to get the lower BMI standards imposed on the WHO report. Few realize that the effort to establish a worldwide standard for what is overweight and obese was sponsored primarily by a company that makes a weight-loss pill.[41]

The IOTF's chair, British nutritionist Philip James, typifies this conflict of interest. James, a well-regarded scientist, also has many financial links to the pharmaceutical industry. He has been amply paid for conducting clinical trials of Sibutramine (Meridia) and Orlistat (Xenical). He also engages in regular promotional activities for Hoffman-La Roche and Knoll Pharmaceuticals, offering regular praise of their products in press releases. In fact, in 2003, he presented the Roche Gulf Awards for Obesity Journalism to reporters who promoted studies (on which James consulted) showing, not surprisingly, that patients taking Xenical were 37 percent less likely to develop type 2 diabetes than those losing weight through lifestyle changes alone.[42] In short, James is not only a consultant for the drug industry, he also works as one of their pitchmen.

The influence of the pharmaceutical companies doesn't stop with such faux health organizations. The drug industry financially supports many researchers who are on the advisory panels to both the WHO and NIH. Pharmaceutical companies influence the tenor of scientific research and interpretation both by funding research and by contracting with various health researchers to serve as "consultants" for their various products. For example, the chair of the NIH committee (and a member of the WHO panel) is a doctor and medical researcher named

Xavier Pi-Sunyer (the same one quoted above). In addition to being a professor of medicine at Columbia University, Pi-Sunyer is also the director of the Obesity Research Center at St. Luke's-Roosevelt Hospital in New York City and the director of the VanItallie Center for Weight Loss. While Pi-Sunyer has these impressive scientific credentials, he also is on the advisory board or is a paid consultant to several diet and pharmaceutical companies, including Wyeth-Ayerst labs (makers of the fen-phen diet drug that ended up causing heart valve damage), Knoll, Eli Lilly Pharmaceuticals, Genentech, Hoffman-La Roche, Neurogen, and Weight Watchers International.[43] Pi-Sunyer has been the highly paid principal investigator on recent clinical trials of the drug Rimonabant made by Sanofi-Aventis. Indeed, Pi-Sunyer has been named in a lawsuit against the drug company Wyeth-Ayerst because he agreed to have his name attributed to scientific articles about the costs of obesity that were actually written by Excerpta Medica, a medical consulting firm, and paid for by Wyeth-Ayerst.[44] Not surprisingly, Pi-Sunyer is also a member of the IOTF.

Pi-Sunyer is not alone in his connections to the pharmaceutical industry—many of the researchers on the NIH board (once again the group that basically defined what overweight and obese mean in the United States), as well as most of the top obesity experts in the United States, including David Allison, George Blackburn, Tom Wadden, James Hill, and Judith Stern, are financially tied to diet and pharmaceutical companies. A particularly egregious example among this group is George Bray, one of the first obesity experts and the editor of *Obesity Research*, the leading academic journal on obesity studies. In addition to his long list of research publications, Bray also has a side job as a developer and marketer of a "weight-loss" thigh cream that has had little long-term success. It is difficult to find *any* major figure in the field of obesity research or past president of the North American Association for the Study of Obesity who does not have some type of financial tie to a pharmaceutical or weight-loss company.

While the pharmaceutical industry did not necessarily dictate the decisions of the obesity experts, the conflicts of interest among the leading researchers in the obesity field are both undeniable and problematic. The IOTF's campaign to lower the standard of what is overweight directly coincides with the economic interests of the diet and pharmaceutical industries, especially in the case with weight-loss drugs such as Meridia and Xenical.[45] By lowering the BMI standard and making more people think they are overweight, the pharmaceutical industry can create a much larger market for diet drugs and diet plans.

Of course, the pharmaceutical industry is not alone in wanting to lower the standard for being overweight and to increase the number of people that fall into that category. Significant financial incentives also exist for university health researchers and health agencies within the U.S. government. In fact, the coincidence of interest between the pharmaceutical industry and public health researchers has created something in the field of obesity that could best be described as a "health-industrial complex." The health-industrial complex is built upon a symbiotic relationship between health researchers, government bureaucrats, and drug companies. Drug companies sponsor research that defines current health issues and fund researchers who sit on the NIH board and within medical schools; government bureaucracies such as the NIH and CDC rely on the expertise of researchers to back their claims for increased congressional funding; and drug companies use health warnings issued by the CDC to promote their products. As the health writer Thomas Moore notes, "The same medical school physicians who serve on NIH consensus and other panels also work as consultants to these drug companies and are paid handsome fees to speak at the medical conferences that these companies finance. It is a tightly interlocking system."[46]

A key part of the health-industrial complex arises from the funding imperatives within medical research institutes. Within most of the research institutions and universities where health research is conducted, a significant portion of the salaries of scientists and their staffs is based on grants from foundations and support from private industry or the federal government. The application process for these grants is very political—who gets funded and at what level depends on a number of factors including the importance of the research problem in question and how well it fits within the established health paradigms. Similarly, the funding levels of the CDC, the NIH, and other government agencies depend upon perceptions of the U.S. Congress about the validity of their efforts. Lobbying groups such as Research!America tirelessly promote the possibility of looming health catastrophes in order to secure greater federal funding of health research. Getting funds to do health research and promotion, whether one is in the private or public sphere, depends largely upon how serious a health problem one is researching. Pathologies affecting large or vocal populations, such as cancer or AIDS, get more money; conditions affecting smaller or less-represented groups get less.[47]

For obesity researchers, this means there are significant incentives to lower the threshold of what is considered overweight. By adopting the overweight standard of BMI at 25, they can add nearly 40 million people to the population at risk. For medical researchers focusing on weight loss, this quickly inflates the importance of their own efforts; for government agencies such as the CDC and NIH this gives them a new reason for expanding their own missions and increasing their budget requests; for both groups it provides a rationale for expanding their power.[48] Thus, it was not mere coincidence that soon after the NIH report the congressional budget appropriations for obesity-related programs in the CDC and NIH were increased. Nor does it seem like mere coincidence that one of the lead authors of the *JAMA* article that attributed 400,000 deaths a year to obesity was the director of the CDC (Julie Gerberding) and that she used the information in this article in her congressional testimony requesting a larger CDC budget.[49]

These efforts to lower the BMI threshold of what is considered overweight have further obfuscated the complicated relationships between body weight and health. Once the "experts" come out with evaluations of what is overweight or obese, even the most exaggerated or misinterpreted claims take on a life of their own and become accepted as unquestioned truth. After researchers first identified the growing weight of the American population in 1994, a host of news items and scientific articles sounded the alarm about the increase in body weight of the American public.[50] Obesity began to be paired with terms such as "epidemic," first, in a careful or measured way, but inevitably without criticism or introspection.[51] By the end of the decade, scholarly articles, government reports, and the news media were proclaiming obesity an epidemic with little acknowledgment of the medical complexity and problematic assumptions of this claim.

Although the media often sensationalize and oversimplify complicated issues in order to attract public interest, in the case of obesity this has been taken to great lengths. Consider these two examples. On March 10, 2004, the *New York Times* ran a headline "Death Rate from Obesity Gains Fast on Smoking." This major story presented the conclusions of the 2004 *JAMA* article that "obesity-related" deaths in the United States would soon top 400,000 and overtake smoking as the number one cause of preventable death in the United States without a single hint of criticism.[52] It reiterated the various costs associated with obesity but never questioned how these numbers were reached. Similarly, on January 8, 2003, the Associated Press ran a story with the headline "Obesity at Age 20 Can Cut Life Span by 13 to 20 Years." Only later did the story reveal that the obesity in question was at a BMI of 45 (that would be more than 340 pounds for a six-foot man), which affects less than 1 percent of the population.

With this growing consensus about the threat of the obesity "epidemic," it became increasingly difficult for ideas or findings that contradicted, or least questioned, the claims about obesity to gain any attention or audience. This occurred not only in the press but also among the very research institutes and government agencies that issue the reports. Last year, the writer Elliot Marshall reported in the journal *Science* that many researchers at both the NIH and the CDC had concerns about the "loosey-goosey" estimates of the number of deaths attributable to obesity, particularly in the way that age was used to calculate mortality.[53] One CDC staffer, who did not want to be quoted on the record for fear of losing his job, said that many at the CDC felt the conclusions of this report were not open to question, particularly as one of its lead authors, Julie Gerberding, was the director of the CDC. Marshall stated that many people believe that the *JAMA* article's "compatibility with a new anti-obesity theme in government health pronouncements— rather than sound analysis—propelled it into print."[54] Glenn Gaesser also reports that the NIH basically ignored the alternative studies that challenged the link between BMI and higher mortality when writing its report about the dangers of obesity.[55] While one might not expect a researcher to cite all the evidence about obesity, the NIH report omitted a number of studies questioning the link between BMI and mortality when setting the threshold of those considered overweight.[56]

Standardizing Our Weights

Now some may question why this is a very big deal; after all, does it really matter if the government gets its weight standards exactly right?

Isn't it a good idea to lose weight, even if weight is merely a proxy for other, more serious problems? Actually it is a big deal, for the use and definition of terms such as "overweight" and "obese" have a number of important consequences. First, being classified as overweight has an immediate impact on the lives of millions of Americans: it can determine whether they can work at certain jobs, whether they are considered fit parents, or whether certain drugs or medical procedures will be paid for by insurance or tax money.[57] Our current standards wrongly compel doctors to tell their patients they are sick and convince millions that they should starve themselves with dangerous crash diets and other weight-loss strategies. The current designations of overweight and obese may cause all sorts of unfair, unhealthy, and unnecessary behaviors on the part of Americans who think they need to be thin in order to be healthy.

Even more problematic is that these "official" pronouncements about what constitutes a healthy body weight are being thrust upon the general public in a coercive manner. Although they don't have a clear scientific rationale, our current standards of overweight and obese affect the self-image of many, imposing a standard by which most of us don't measure up, particularly if we are female, poor, or a minority. And, by evaluating ourselves relative to weight standards defined by BMI, we fall under the power of the medical and science professions that tell us how we should think about our bodies and how we should behave. Our current standards of overweight and obese are affecting the very conception of who we are.

But the biggest problem with our current definition of "obese" is that is makes weight a central determinant of health when, in fact, the relationship between body fat and health is far more complicated than what can be found with a BMI, particularly for the general population. Everyone has his or her own ideal body weight. My grandmother, who lived to a vigorous ninety-eight years old, was technically obese for most of her adult life. What is an optimal body weight for one person may be far heavier or lighter than for another.[58] Even if it is possible to identify an "ideal weight" for any one person, there is no way to create a uniform standard that can be applied for a large population.

Nevertheless, our government and the public health community continue to emphasize that we should evaluate our health relative to how much we weigh and to advise millions of Americans, who otherwise would not consider their weight a problem, that they should lose weight. Yet this same government and health community is not providing any clear or safe guidance of how Americans should actually meet this thin ideal. Without any clear understanding of what is actually causing our weights to rise, the government's warnings about the dangers of body fat will only encourage people to take up unworkable or unhealthy diet plans, which often do more health damage than anything else. However, the campaign to shape our perceptions does not simply stop with making millions of us wrongly think we are overweight or obese; as we'll see in the next chapter, they also want us to change how we understand what this obesity means.

two

How Obesity Became an Epidemic Disease

In spite of billions of dollars spent and decades of research, scientists at the University of Chicago said Monday that the scientific community is no closer to finding a cure for the potentially fatal disease of obesity. Many obesity sufferers have expressed frustration over the medical community's inability to cure them. "I came down with obesity two years after I got married," 41-year-old Oklahoma City resident Fran Torley said. "I know it was hard for my husband to watch me suffer from this disease. When he caught obesity a year later, he got so depressed, he couldn't do anything but sit on the couch. Some days, we sit and watch television from dawn till dusk, hoping for news of a breakthrough."

"Scientists Still Seeking Cure for Obesity," The Onion[1]

In 2000, it began to spread. Although this obesity-related condition had been around for decades, the number of cases had always been small—in 1994, there were only thirty-three and, as late as 1999, the number was still under fifty. Then, suddenly, the number began to rise. In 2000, it doubled to 107, two years later it doubled again and, by 2004, the number had reached nearly 700. Although it was increasing with epidemic-like speed, the condition I'm referring to is not biological or medical in nature. By itself, it did not result in any deaths. But it is, perhaps, the only aspect of obesity that truly deserves to be called an epidemic. I am referring to the number of news media stories proclaiming obesity to be an epidemic disease.[2]

Until the late 1990s, America's growing weight received little notice from the media. As with most Americans, the media tended to treat obesity as a by-product of one's lifestyle, not a medical condition, and certainly not an epidemic disease. Between 1994 and 1999 only about fifteen stories a year mentioned both the words obesity and epidemic.

Then suddenly, in 2000, a torrent of stories began to appear. Nearly all the major newspapers started running headlines. Newsmagazines, such as *Newsweek*, *Time*, and *U.S. News and World Report* ran cover stories. ABC, CBS, NBC, and other television news networks aired special features. The word was spreading—obesity was a deadly disease of apocalyptic proportions.

Yet, as *The Onion* so smartly points out, there is a fundamental problem with this news coverage—as a disease, obesity is a flawed construct. Consider, for a moment, some of the awkward questions that arise when you call obesity a disease: is someone who is only slightly overweight, only slightly diseased? Can someone catch or "come down" with obesity? Can obesity really be "cured"? If these questions seem ludicrous, it is because obesity does not readily meet the criteria of a disease. According to *Stedman's Medical Dictionary*, a disease is "an interruption, cessation, or disorder of body function, system, or organ."[3] By this definition, if obesity is a disease, then we must assume that, at some level, body fat is pathological. Yet as we saw in the last chapter, there is no clear evidence about what level or even how, exactly, adipose tissue is harmful to our health. For some extremely heavy people, their body fat may disrupt their ability to function, particularly their ability to exercise, but for most obese people their fatness is not a disorder. Indeed, body fat on some parts of the body, such as the thighs, can actually be helpful to sustaining our health.[4] Even *Stedman's Medical Dictionary* does not call obesity a disease; it is simply known as "excess subcutaneous fat in proportion to lean body mass" or, at worst, "a *public health* problem."[5]

So, if obesity is not really a disease, then why did so many news organizations start running headlines and major stories in the late 1990s saying that it was? The answer to this question reveals, once again, who is the primary author of America's obesity epidemic—America's public health sector. Already we have seen how various doctors and public health groups have influenced the way obesity is defined, setting obesity at a very low weight threshold. Many of these same groups are also working to reshape how obesity is understood. Since the early 1980s, a small number of dedicated health professionals, government health officials, and lobbying groups have been working hard, with substantial assistance from the pharmaceutical and weight-loss industries, to promote the idea that obesity is a disease. Industry sponsored groups such as the American Obesity Association have made it their mission to expand the government's role in funding obesity research, to increase coverage for weight-loss treatments, and to put diet drugs and weight-loss surgery on the same level as any other necessary medical procedure. And, in order to do this, they need to change public perceptions—rather than being seen as a consequence of individual choice, Americans are supposed to perceive obesity as something that is beyond most people's power to control, in other words, a medical disease of epidemic proportions. Yet, as we'll see, calling obesity a disease not only distorts the reality of America's weight gain, it is likely to cause even more problems than it solves.

The Beginnings of an Obesity Epidemic

There are numerous popular explanations for the origins of America's obesity epidemic. Some people think that it came from a virus, others think that it came from the advent of high fructose corn syrup, and still others blame urban sprawl. While these theories may (or may not) explain our rising weights (we'll explore why Americans started gaining weight later in the book), none of them really explains the rise of *obesity*. In other words, none of the theories about why Americans started gaining weight also explain why this weight gain has been interpreted as a medical condition. If we want to know what really started America's obesity epidemic, we need to find out how the *idea* that obesity was a disease of epidemic proportions became popularized. Putting the issue this way leads us in a much different direction. For the idea that obesity is a disease did not arise from any new scientific discovery or particular health cataclysm; rather it came from something much more mundane— a PowerPoint presentation.

Our story begins with the first outbreak of news coverage on obesity in 2000. The most curious aspect of the hundreds of news stories that started appearing at this time was that nothing on which they were reporting was really news, in the sense of being new information. No new scientific discoveries had been made about America's growing weight—medical researchers and government officials had been discussing Americans' weight gains since the late 1980s. Nor were there any new major breakthroughs on the medical dangers of being over-weight. The major medical journals, government health agencies, and even insurance experts such as Louis Dublin had been issuing warnings about the health risks of obesity since the 1950s. The idea that obesity was both sharply on the rise and associated with many health problems was well known. It was just that nobody in the media was paying it much attention.

So why then, in 2000, did obesity suddenly become so newsworthy? To answer this question, it is useful to understand how "new ideas" become widely accepted. Scholars of "diffusion theory" have long recognized that fads, innovations, and trends often accelerate across populations in an exponential fashion, much in the same way that contagious diseases do.[6] One day a single person pierces his navel or rolls up his pant cuffs and then, suddenly, everyone is doing it.[7] The key for the spread of a new idea, like the spread of a disease, is having the right set of circumstances and a particularly good method of transmission. The HIV virus, for example, allegedly spread out of Africa in the early 1980s because of the international promiscuity of a single Canadian airline steward, Gaetan Dugas, the infamous "patient zero."[8] The same holds true for ideas—a new concept lies fallow for a time until a triggering event, particular circumstance, or the right person suddenly causes it to be embraced by a large number of people.

In the case of obesity, the "patient zero," the person who infected lots of people with the idea that it was an epidemic disease was a pediatrician named William Dietz. In 1997, Dietz left his job as a physician and nutritional researcher at Tufts University to become a director of the Division for Nutrition and Physical Activity at the Centers for Disease Control and Prevention. Dietz joined the CDC because he believed that obesity was a problem that needed to be addressed on a national scale, something he could not do from an academic post. Although government health agencies had issued warnings and reports on obesity for decades, it was still not a major concern within the health establishment or even within the CDC. Somewhat like the doctors portrayed in the movie *Outbreak*, the historical focus of the CDC had been the containment of communicable diseases such as malaria, smallpox, or AIDS.[9] Obesity, viewed by many as simply a consequence of lifestyle, was not seen as a disease transmitted across populations. Dietz, however, held a view that was becoming more prevalent within medicine: that obesity was strongly influenced by the environment and was a condition that people passively experienced, something that happened *to them* rather simply the result of their own choices. In other words, obesity was a disease.[10]

The challenge, for Dietz, was getting others to see obesity in this way and the key, he believed, was to communicate how much obesity was growing. For years, the CDC had been tracking the rise of obesity through its annual telephone surveys on the health patterns of the American population. Like much statistical data, the findings from these surveys were often presented in long, detailed tables. To show the changing rates of obesity in each state over a fifteen-year period, one would have to look at a series of 15 detailed columns across 50 rows, the equivalent of 750 different cells of numbers. Except for the most dedicated of health policy mavens, few would have the patience for combing through a mind-numbing sea of figures. If Dietz was going to demonstrate how obesity was on the rise and a growing problem, he needed a more effective method. In the spring of 1998, he and another CDC scientist, Ali Mokdad, came upon the idea of presenting the data in a series of maps and, in order to show the change over time, they would arrange them in a seamless PowerPoint slide show.

The CDC maps presented a different and much more frightening picture of America's recent weight gains than the tables. On each slide, a map of the United States was shown with different colors signifying different rates of obesity for a given year, starting in 1985 (obesity was defined as a BMI of 30 or more). States with the lightest blue hues had the lowest obesity rates (less than 10 percent), states with a darker blue had more obesity; and, when a state's obesity rates went over 20 percent, they became red.[11] The force of the presentation was not in simply showing obesity on a state-by-state basis, but in the dynamic of obesity's growth. As the slides progress from 1985, more and more states begin to ominously dim from light to darker blue. Then suddenly, in 1997, the first three "red" states dramatically appear, quickly followed by six more in 1998, and eleven more in 1999. Rather than simply showing a trend, the maps conveyed something far more urgent—a spreading infection.

Facing page: Three of the maps released by the CDC to show the rise in obesity. The maps depict the growing weight of the population as if it were an infectious disease, spreading contagiously across a geographic area. *BMI = 30, or ~30 lbs. overwieght for 5'4" person. BRFSS, Behavioral Risk Factor Surveillance System; CDC, Centers for Disease Control.

Obesity Trends Among U.S. Adults*

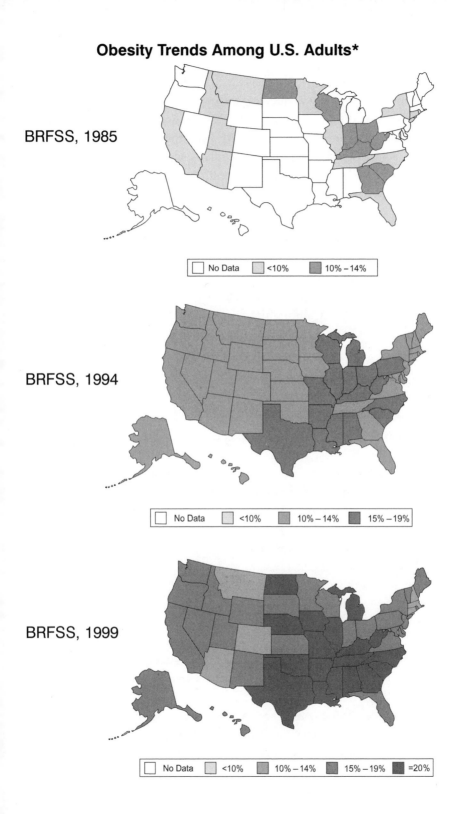

BRFSS, 1985

No Data   <10%   10% – 14%

BRFSS, 1994

No Data   <10%   10% – 14%   15% – 19%

BRFSS, 1999

No Data   <10%   10% – 14%   15% – 19%   =20%

As the redness moves from one state to others nearby, it seemed to demonstrate that obesity was infecting the population with a virus-like speed.

The PowerPoint slides completely changed the way many health professionals conceptualized obesity as a problem. Rather than simply being seen as a series of numbers, people viewed obesity in spatial terms, like an unfolding trend. "When we first began to use these slides in 1998," Dietz observed,

> invariably the audience responded with a growing murmur, then a gasp as the increase in the prevalence unfolded. Today these maps provide a good example of how effectively data can be displayed to illustrate a point. After people have seen the maps, we no longer have to discuss whether a problem with obesity exists. These maps have shifted the discussion from whether a problem exists to what we should do about the epidemic.[12]

Simply by virtue of the visual presentation of the data, the CDC maps could convince people that America's weight gain was, in fact, a real "epidemic."

The slides were effective not simply because of their visual power, but also because Dietz made the slides publicly available on a CDC website. Soon, obesity researchers, government officials, and academics across the country (myself included) were downloading the maps and using them in presentations. We were, in effect, carriers of the disease model, transmitting it across a much larger population. With the maps now being widely disseminated among the scientific community, the "obesity epidemic" was quickly becoming a broadly accepted characterization of America's weight growth. Articles started appearing in the major medical and scientific journals that began characterizing obesity as an "epidemic"—something that was new; prior to 1998 obesity rarely had been characterized this way. In 1999, the *Journal of the American Medical Association* devoted a special issue to obesity that included the maps and an article that Dietz coauthored decrying the obesity "epidemic."[13] Articles in the medical journals, in turn, shaped the coverage of obesity in major news publications, such as the *New York Times* and the *Washington Post*, which are always keen to report the trends coming out of scientific professions. These stories then got picked up by the major news networks, weekly magazines, and small town papers. The idea of an obesity epidemic spread like wildfire and was quickly becoming an accepted fact. And, it all started with a simple PowerPoint presentation.

The problem, however, is that the CDC maps are somewhat misleading. To begin with, the maps only show the percentage of people in each state with a BMI greater than 29; they do not show the spread of a disease. By using state boundaries, the maps also exaggerate the extent of obesity because the geographic size of a state doesn't relate to the size of its population—North Dakota is pictured as the functional equivalent of Pennsylvania even though it has a fraction of the Keystone State's population. The colors on the maps are also overly evocative, going from cool blues to hot reds as the obesity rates increase, thus giving the impression of increasing danger from an epidemic "hot zone." Finally, picturing the rise of obesity in this geographic way makes it seem like it is some type of spreading infection, like a virus that migrates from one state to another. In reality, weight gain has been most highly concentrated among certain portions of the population, particularly the poor and minorities. The reason the first "outbreaks" of obesity were in Mississippi, Alabama, and West Virginia was not because they were near some viral source but because these states are largely rural and poor.

Nevertheless, despite their misleading nature, these maps are still widely accepted and continue to be used to this day. They have been incorporated in countless scientific presentations on the obesity epidemic and were featured in the surgeon general's 2001 *Call to Action to Prevent and Decrease Overweight and Obesity*, the government's first major proclamation about the dangers of obesity. "Nothing," Dietz believes, "has been more effective at increasing the visibility of the obesity epidemic than the CDC slides."[14] And, he is right. By simply repackaging data in map form, America's recent weight gains have become widely interpreted as a rampant epidemic, spiraling out of control.

The Diseasing of America

Of course, the CDC maps are not entirely responsible for the idea of an obesity epidemic. The characterization of our growing weight as an epidemic is emblematic of a much larger trend in American medicine— the transformation of nonpathological physical states into diseases.

Over the past few decades, numerous physical states that, by themselves, are not necessarily harmful, have come to be labeled as diseases. The condition of high blood pressure has now become the disease of "hypertension," malaise is often diagnosed as "depression," unruly children are afflicted with "attention deficit disorder," a low sexual drive has become "erectile dysfunction," and so on. Today, it seems that any physical inconvenience, symptom, or correlate of a health problem has been elevated to the status of a disease.

To understand why this is occurring, it is useful to consider our current healthcare situation in a historical light. At the beginning of the twentieth century, health, like many basic necessities, was in short supply. Infant mortality was extremely high, infectious diseases were rampant, and the average American life expectancy was only forty-eight years. American health services were highly constrained by limited knowledge and resources. But as America's economy industrialized and its affluence increased, its population's health began to improve. Americans founded hospitals, established public health agencies, provided health insurance for many workers and their families, and endowed universities to train doctors and research diseases. These investments yielded fantastic returns. As the twentieth century progressed, most infectious diseases were eradicated and regular medical attention became commonplace. By the century's end, average life expectancy in the United States had increased by nearly thirty years and infant mortality plummeted.

This success, however, also created a new set of challenges. On the supply side, the health services infrastructure that had been created to eradicate polio, tuberculosis, smallpox, typhoid, and other infectious diseases lost its purpose as these conditions disappeared. Once their initial mission had succeeded, government health agencies including the CDC, medical researchers, and private health charities such as the March of Dimes needed new problems to tackle in order to justify their existence or, in the case of private companies, maintain their profits.[15] The CDC, for example, first branched into nutritional research in the 1970s, then started a center for chronic disease prevention, thus expanding its mission far beyond its original focus on containing insect-born diseases. On the demand side, the increasing affluence and health of the population meant that people began seeking treatments for ever more physical conditions. As we eradicated one condition after another, an expectation arose that medical treatments could do ever more to increase the quality of our lives. And in many ways they have—from surgeries to correct our vision to lotions that "correct" baldness, Americans enjoy a wealth of medical treatment options. Yet this supply and demand has also restructured our basic conception of health and medical care.

First, a host of new "diseases," "disorders," and other maladies has emerged. Some are genuine pathologies—as Americans started living longer, chronic illness such as cancer, heart disease, and Alzheimer's disease have become more prevalent. But, in many instances, the "discovery" of a new disease or disorder is prompted by the mere association with an illness: high cholesterol, being correlated with heart disease, became a health problem in its own right; hypertension, being correlated with stroke, became a "killer," and so on.[16] That is not to say that such conditions may not be symptomatic of some larger ills: high levels of "bad" cholesterol may indicate high levels of blood lipids, which can clog arteries and lead to heart disease. But in the rush to treat what are often the symptoms of real diseases, we end up applying the disease label to a host of conditions that are not genuinely pathological.

Much of this increase in the number and prevalence of diseases also comes from the various interests within the "health-industrial" complex. Academic researchers seek to identify new physical correlates of disease and mortality because it helps them to get published, funded, and tenured. Their findings, in turn, prompt government health agencies to issue warnings and expand their own programs. Drug companies and doctors then capitalize on these warnings by coming out with ever new products and treatments to keep the new "diseases" in check and fund researchers to find even more conditions that need constant medication. In our massive health-service economy, "market" expansion depends upon finding ever more conditions that can be treated as diseases, even if they are only ancillary to a real disorder. And, because this is done in the name of our health, it is largely unimpeachable.

The second consequence of our health system's success was that our system of medical care became highly oriented around treating symptoms rather than alleviating causes of disease. Unlike earlier infectious diseases, such as polio or influenza, the chronic diseases that claim most lives today are less amenable to medical cures because they often originate from nonbiological sources such as pollution or other toxins in the environment. Without an inoculation against cancer or antibiotics to eliminate heart disease, there is little doctors can do to prevent their patients from contracting these illnesses. What doctors can do, however, is to treat both the symptoms and the associated indicators of these conditions. They can offer radiation treatment and chemotherapy that kill cancer cells but don't cure cancer, or prescribe drugs such as Lipitor that lower cholesterol but don't cure heart disease. And the focus on treating symptoms is not limited to severe or life-threatening conditions. Some of the greatest expansions in medicine have come in the treatment of everyday maladies; thus, backaches are treated with Oxycontin, anxiety with Xanax, depression with Zoloft, impotence with Viagra, and so on. Today, nearly one in two American adults is taking some type of prescription medication. This cornucopia of pharmaceutical treatments is changing the very way we understand health. Living well and healthy means the absence of symptoms or painful conditions, often achieved with a constant regime of medication.

Ironically, as a result of the very success of our healthcare system, we are now spending more money on less serious conditions. As researchers identify even more esoteric health conditions to remedy and pharmaceutical companies devise more ingenious ways to treat ordinary discomforts, health costs will continue to rise even as our overall health tends to level off. These diminishing returns are most evident in the ratio between how much we spend on health care and our average life expectancy. In the fifty years between 1930 and 1980, healthcare spending in the United States as a proportion of GDP increased from 4 to 8 percent; during this same time, the average American life expectancy increased from 59.7 years to 73.7 years. In financial terms, a doubling of healthcare spending yielded us fourteen years more life. Since 1980, healthcare spending has nearly doubled again (we currently spend rough 15 percent of GDP on healthcare services) but life expectancy has only increased by three years.[17] Despite spending twice as much on health services, we are getting 75 percent fewer life years in return. As we become healthier and start living longer, we will continue to spend even more money on treatments for all sorts of new "diseases," even as our overall life expectancy ceases to improve.

The Obesity Disease Boosters

Which takes us back to the creation of an "obesity epidemic." The idea that a certain body weight should be classified as a "disease" is not driven by any clear medical facts; rather, the pressure to label obesity a "disease" comes from a range of interests, from high- to low-minded, across the healthcare spectrum. Weight-loss doctors use the disease model to promote their business—once you can label fat people as "sick," then it is easy to convince them and their insurers they need treatment and medication. Government health agencies, such as the CDC, are under continual budget pressure, and they sustain their budget allocations by convincing their primary "customer" (Congress) that the nation has a real health problem. Thus, they inflate the number of deaths and the severity of illness that result from increased weight. Academic obesity researchers and scientists often exaggerate or play up the dire impact of obesity in order to secure more research funding, heighten the importance of their own work, or advance their own political causes. Although these various groups do not always agree or have the same aim, they end up working in concert because they share the same strategy. In order to achieve their goals, whether it is some idea of public health or simply expanding their medical practice, they want to promote the idea that obesity is a major epidemic that threatens our very survival.

No one has been more active in this campaign than the American Obesity Association (AOA). Founded in 1995 as an advocacy organization for obesity issues, the AOA has made its primary mission to get America's governments and health insurers to treat obesity as a "serious, chronic disease." Already, they proudly boast an impressive list of accomplishments. The AOA claims to have convinced the Internal Review Service to make certain obesity treatments tax deductible; they have lobbied for more obesity drugs to be covered by Medicare; and they assisted the surgeon general with his 2001 *Call to Action* on obesity, which helped bring the idea of obesity into the national spotlight.[18] Most impressive, the AOA helped get the federal Centers for Medicare and Medicaid Services in the summer of 2004 to change their official position, which originally held that obesity did not qualify as a disease. This was a major decision. If obesity could now be considered a disease, it meant that any weight-loss procedure could potentially be considered a medical "treatment" and thus be subject to reimbursement, not simply by Medicare, but also by all the major healthcare providers who pattern their coverage after Medicare.[19] If the AOA has its way, anything from gastric-bypass surgery to diet programs such as Weight Watchers would be paid for by your health insurance.

Given all these achievements, it is important to consider, however, who exactly comprises the AOA. Although the AOA's name would suggest that it is an organization of obese people, it is anything but a grassroots society of ordinary folks. In fact, it has only a tiny membership base. It gets almost all its funding from weight-loss companies, including Weight Watchers, Jenny Craig, Hoffman-La Roche (makers of the weight-loss drug Xenical), and SlimFast, and weight-loss surgeons.[20] Many of the academic and health professionals who founded the AOA and now serve on its board—among them Dr. Richard Atkinson of the University of Wisconsin and Professor Judith Stern of the University of California, Davis—also have been paid consultants to many of these companies and themselves have professional stakes in advancing the importance of obesity as a disease. Despite all its health-related trappings, the AOA is really just a lobbying group for the weight-loss industry and obesity researchers. The campaign to get obesity classified as a disease is arising from the very groups who stand to benefit from an "obesity epidemic."

The AOA's campaign has been joined by a wide range of participants, some with very high-minded intentions. For example, one of the biggest proponents of America's "obesity epidemic" is Marion Nestle, a nutritionist from New York University and one of the leading critics of America's food industry. In numerous articles and interviews, she routinely sounds the alarm of the American obesity epidemic.[21] Yet, unlike many obesity researchers, Nestle herself doesn't stand to gain personally from labeling obesity this way—she is not on the payroll of any pharmaceutical company. Instead, she employs this language as part of a political effort against major food corporations, such as Coca-Cola and Frito-Lay. By claiming that obesity is an epidemic, Nestle can argue that the political power of Big Food is adversely affecting Americans' health. She notes, "Obesity is the most serious dietary problem affecting the health of American children . . . the blatant exploitation by food companies of even the youngest children raises questions about the degree to which society at large needs to be responsible for protecting children's health."[22] For Nestle, like many liberal critics, the idea of an obesity epidemic is a useful weapon in the battle against corporate political influence.

The idea that obesity is an epidemic disease is also reinforced by the professional cultures within the health programs of major research universities and the health agencies of the federal government. The scientists and administrators for America's health programs are largely trained within the same research institutions and same curriculum. These institutions instill particular ways of analyzing health problems, particularly with regard to larger populations.[23] Health outcomes are seen in aggregate trends rather than in terms of individual well-being. Thus, if a certain percentage of people with a physical condition contracts a disease or dies, then anyone with that condition is seen to be sick. For example, because obesity is statistically *associated* with so many health conditions, it is often inferred to be a cause of disease. The drug industries also work to reinforce this "diseasing" through their sponsorship of pseudoscientific health organizations such as the IOTF and their support of industry "thought leaders" who testify before government panels and lobby government agencies on behalf of particular views. Points of view or perspectives that are outside of the public health paradigm often do not get represented. Skeptics such as Dr. Glenn Gaesser, Dr. Steven Blair, or Professor Paul Ernsberger often express their frustration with getting alternative points of view acknowledged.[24]

This professional bias toward characterizing obesity as a disease was particularly evident in the response to the April 2005 *JAMA* article by Kathryn Flegal that radically reduced the estimated number of deaths due to obesity. Rather than embrace the findings as good news (after all, according to the new estimate obesity was no longer such a major killer), organizations such as Harvard's School of Public Health and the CDC went on the offensive. Harvard's School of Public Health, under the auspices of nutritionist Walter Willett, issued a press release calling the study "flawed" because of its methodology—although they were conspicuously silent on previous estimates that offered much higher mortality predictions that used even more problematic statistical methods.[25] They went on to host a one-day conference on May 26, 2005, in which the study was roundly criticized, mostly because they did not like its conclusions. The CDC issued a set of "talking points" to state health agencies that said, "despite the recent controversy in the media about how many deaths are related to obesity in the United States, the simple fact remains: obesity can be deadly." Scandalously, the CDC presentation went on to assert, "we know obesity causes about 2/3 of diabetes, 2/3 of heart disease, 20 percent of cancer in women, and 15 percent of cancer in men," when, in fact, there is absolutely no clinical evidence to make such a causal claim. In the name of sustaining its own political agenda, the nation's leading health agency was issuing statements about health that were patently false.

Once an idea emerges that a certain condition is a "disease," it is often difficult to express skepticism or alternative points of view because of the professional norms within the medical field. Health professionals base their expertise on the claim of superior knowledge in interpreting data and findings from scientific research. The power of the profession is based on the ability to make diagnoses, classify illnesses, and prescribe treatments.[26] Their credibility hinges on their claim to base their medical decisions on the objective standards of science.[27] However, this assumes there are objective standards to begin with, which, in the case of such a complex phenomenon as obesity, are elusive at best. Thus, the more a consensus can be forged around a particularly topic, such as the health problems resulting from obesity, the more the judgment of the health professionals sounds like truth.

Such professional norms are reinforced through organizations such as the North American Association for the Study of Obesity, the nation's leading organization of obesity researchers. In the fall of 2004, I attended their annual meeting at Caesar's Palace in Las Vegas. Amidst the various lectures and events sponsored by pharmaceutical and medical supply companies, obesity researchers, government health statisticians, molecular biologists, and doctors mingled with each other sharing their ideas and work. In virtually every presentation I attended, the data were interpreted to portray obesity as a major problem, no matter how weak the actual findings were. For example, one presentation highlighted all of the possible ways that obesity could be linked to cancer with only the most passing acknowledgment of the weakness of the data. Another presentation demonstrated that obesity greatly increased the likelihood of deaths from auto accidents and suicide, yet, once again, no one asked if these effects could be caused by other factors such as education or income. In more than a dozen conversations with participants, when I pointed out how the scientific evidence linking obesity to many diseases and deaths was weak, I was either attacked or simply given a befuddled look. It quickly became clear that the primary function of an organization like NAASO is to reinforce a particular view about body weight—after all, why be an obesity researcher if you do not think that obesity is a problem? Yet, as we saw in chapter 1, the idea that obesity is a health problem is largely an assumption without strong scientific backing.

Together, these various elements within America's health service sector are promoting the idea that obesity is a disease. Whether it is motivated by individual career goals, budgetary outlays, political agendas, or well-intentioned ideas of advancing public health, the nutritionists, health researchers, and government health workers are campaigning together to get insurance companies, the federal government, and the general public to think of obesity as a disease. Unfortunately, this campaign is not without its own harmful consequences and nowhere is this more evident than with diet drugs and weight-loss surgery.

No Different from Eyeliner, Except for the Flatulence

Over the past several decades, pharmaceutical companies have spent hundreds of millions of dollars in what the World Obesity Congress recently called the "race for the biggest windfall in the history of modern pharmaceuticals!"[28] The prize of this race is neither a cure for cancer nor a remedy for heart disease, but something much more lucrative—a safe and effective diet pill. Every year Americans spend upward of an estimated 45 billion dollars in weight-loss products and the pharmaceutical industry desperately wants a larger share of this market.[29]

From the perspective of the pharmaceutical industry, a diet pill is a nearly perfect product. Because the only way that diets are really successful is if people stay on them their whole lives, anyone who wanted to stay thin by using a diet drug would have to stay on the medication perpetually. Thus, if you can find a drug that safely helps people reduce their appetites or keeps them from ingesting fat, you could potentially have a customer for life. And, if you are curing a "disease," you can get Medicare or private HMOs to reimburse you, thus expanding your market even further.

In the race to find such a drug, pharmaceutical companies are exploring almost any type of compound that might produce weight loss. My favorite example of this was the recent discovery by Norman Levine, a dermatologist from the University of Arizona. Hoping to reduce the damaging effects of sun exposure, Levine was searching for the genetic sources of darker skin. At first, Levine thought he merely identified a gene receptor that controlled skin pigmentation but after a few tests, he realized that he had stumbled on to the pharmaceutical equivalent of a perfect storm. For the compound used to act on the gene receptor (called PT141) that darkens the skin also happens to increase sex drive and suppress appetite. In clinical trials, subjects were not only getting darker, they were also getting aroused as well as losing weight. Like scores of other promising treatments, this chemical equivalent of an amphetamine- and Viagra-drenched day at the beach is still in clinical trials and its side effects and efficacy remain unknown.[30] Palatin, the pharmaceutical company that licensed Levine's discovery, is only seeking FDA approval of PT141 as a cure for erectile dysfunction. Nevertheless, there is widespread anticipation that it will be used as an "off-label" weight-loss drug.

The case of PT141 is a good example because it also epitomizes the real nature of weight-loss drugs—they are largely cosmetic products. The greatest share of the market for diet products is not made up of people who are trying to lose two hundred pounds, but by people trying to lose only twenty.[31] The typical consumer of a diet plan is a white female with a BMI between 24 and 32. Such a person, as we saw in chapter 1, is under no health risk from her weight. Weight-loss companies make products for people who want to look thin, not people who are concerned about their health.

Although there is nothing necessarily wrong with selling a cosmetic product as long as it is safe, most weight-loss drugs, unlike eye shadow or blusher, come with potentially dangerous side effects. For example, Xenical (also known as Orlistat), one of the most popular prescription medications on the market, inhibits the body from absorbing fat. While this may keep some people from eating too much ice cream and French fries, it also results in cramping, diarrhea, and "bowel leakage."[32] Meridia (also known as Sibutramine), the other major prescription weight-loss drug, has been associated with various heart ailments. The soon-to-be-approved Acomplia (also known as Rimonabant), which has been touted as the new wonder drug, has been correlated with increased incidents of depression and anxiety in recent clinical trials.

The prevalence of such harmful side effects, however, is exactly why the pharmaceutical industry needs to support the idea of obesity as an epidemic disease; it is the only way to rationalize the cosmetic use of diet drugs. Consider the conundrum that drug companies and weight-loss doctors face with the Food and Drug Administration. When the FDA approves drugs for weight loss, they base their decisions on whether the benefits of the drug outweigh any of the health risks. If pharmaceutical companies want to get FDA approval for products that carry such intense side effects, they need to have a justification that goes beyond simple cosmetic appeal; they need to make a health claim about what will happen if the drug is not approved. For example, when the FDA recently approved Meridia, it did so partly because obesity could be considered a "widespread, chronic disease" and those who suffer from this disease deserve treatment, even if that treatment carries side effects.[33] Similarly, in the mid-1990s, the FDA approved the weight-loss drug Redux, in spite of its negative side effects, because of the putative link between obesity and mortality. Only later, it was discovered that Redux caused heart damage.[34]

In truth, current weight-loss drugs will do little to improve anyone's health, nor will they do much to alter anyone's weight. Most successful diet drugs are only able to produce, at best, a 10 percent level of sustained weight loss after a year and less after that. By our current standards, a 10 percent weight loss will do little to improve the "health" of an obese person and is unlikely to remove them from the category of being "diseased." In fact, because they convey virtually no health benefits, diet drugs are ostensibly no different than eyeliner or hair coloring—except that the latter don't have side effects like melancholy, flatulence, or heart failure.

Diseasing One's Self in Order to Be Healthy

On a bright September day in 2003 in San Francisco, California, the American Society for Bariatric Surgery organized the first annual "Walk from Obesity." The event was meant to "educate the public and healthcare professionals about effective treatments for obesity" and, as with other "walks for a cure," the participants, many of whom were former bariatric (in other words, weight-loss) surgery patients, professed the most well-meaning intentions. As Bryan Woodward, the march's organizer said, "We have walks for heart disease and walks for cancer, and the biggest killer for all of us is obesity, so why not have a walk to educate people about that disease?"[35]

Little did the walkers know what was waiting for them. Instead of being greeted with the usual applause and cheers that such Samaritans often receive, a group of large women, brightly clad in pink cheerleading outfits, heckled the marchers with such cheers as, "Staples are for paper, not for people! Rah! Rah!" and "2-4-6-8: we do not regurgitate!" According to the Bod Squad, as the protesters call themselves, the "Walk from Obesity" is less of a charity event and more of a cheap advertising gimmick for bariatric surgeons and their suppliers. (The walks are financed by surgeons and medical supply companies such as Auto Suture Bariatrics and Lap-Band Systems.) Even more disturbing, in their view, is the message that the walks convey—that body fat is something from which one can simply "walk away" and is sufficient grounds for intestinal "mutilation." The protesters believe the walk not only promotes a distorted view of health and body weight, but it also advocates a dangerous and unethical weight-loss treatment.

In lockstep with the drug industry's effort to promote the disease model of obesity are bariatric surgeons. Over the past decade, the number of weight-loss surgeries in America has skyrocketed. This year, more than 120,000 Americans are likely to get some type of bariatric surgery, with most of these being gastric-bypass surgeries, a procedure where a small part of the stomach is sectioned off and a shortcut is made to the small intestine. Bariatric surgery is one of the leading growth areas within American medicine and represents an increasingly lucrative market for surgeons trying to expand their practices. Most telling, it is currently the only general surgical procedure (in other words, the area of surgery covering abdominal organs) for which practitioners actively advertise—most general surgical procedures, such as an appendectomy, are in response to a particular incident and are not solely elective.[35] Outside of cosmetic operations, there are few surgeries that are as highly promoted as bariatric surgery.

Although such procedures have gained a lot of attention, largely from celebrities including Al Roker and Carnie Wilson, these are not simple or unproblematic processes. For elective surgery, they have an extremely high mortality rate. Based on current estimates, this year, more than one thousand Americans will die from complications directly resulting from weight-loss surgery and possibly thousands more will die from postsurgical complications including malnutrition, leaks in the digestive tract, liver and kidney diseases, cancer, and heart failure.[36] For those who manage to survive the initial surgery, life does not get much easier. At least 20 percent of patients need further surgery and almost all patients encounter chronic side effects ranging from minor ailments such as body odor and bad breath to more severe impairments including chronic vomiting, diarrhea, infections, and such digestive ailments as "dumping syndrome."

Perhaps the cruelest irony of all, however, is that these surgeries do not guarantee any weight loss or improvement of health. The National Institutes of Health (NIH) report that a majority of weight-loss surgery patients regain up to 10 percent of their weight after two years and that, for some procedures, nearly 30 percent of patients achieve no sustained weight loss at all.[37] The NIH goes on to report that nearly 30 percent of patients who have weight-loss surgery develop nutritional deficiencies such as anemia, osteoporosis, and metabolic bone disease. Although studies funded by the makers of medical supplies used in the surgery purport to find health benefits, other research found no positive effects from weight-loss surgery either on diabetes or hypertension.[38] Nevertheless, despite the many risks and the unclear health benefits, thousands of Americans will elect to receive some type of weight-loss surgery this year.

The case of bariatric surgery encapsulates much of the politics that are behind the effort to call obesity a disease. Bariatric surgery is not cheap—a typical gastric-bypass procedure can run well over twenty-five thousand dollars. Yet, Medicare and most private health insurance plans do not cover it because they do not yet formally consider obesity a disease (although this may change now that they have said that obesity is no longer formally "not a disease"). Nevertheless, in the absence of an imminent or deadly illness, most insurers still consider it to be an elective procedure and will not pay for it. So, surgeons wanting business and patients wanting operations are stuck—how can they convince major medical insurers to pay for the procedure?

One of the first ways they got around this was by playing with the language. In the 1950s, a bariatric surgeon named Howard Payne, who was looking to expand his practice, coined the term "morbid obesity" in reference to people with a BMI of 40 or more (a term that is widely used today). This special designation of a subclass of obese people allowed him to justify bariatric surgery, when most doctors viewed it as a radical and elective intervention. Using the justification of "morbid obesity," bariatric surgeons have won some recent concessions from the government, including a landmark decision by the IRS to make weight-loss surgery tax deductible. Now, in an attempt to expand their market, the bariatric surgeons are pushing the boundaries of what levels of body weight should be considered diseased. Some bariatric surgeons will now perform gastric-bypass on a person with a BMI as low as 32 (that would be about 240 pounds on a six-foot man) if they can identify other metabolic conditions such as hypertension or high cholesterol.

Yet, the case of bariatric surgery also reveals the problems in defining health relative to the pecuniary interest of the medical profession. Among general surgical procedures, bariatric surgery is unique in that it does not target a distressed or infected organ. Whereas all other general surgical procedures go after things such as an inflamed appendix or a sick gallbladder, bariatric surgeons target a *healthy* stomach and small intestine. Paradoxically, weight-loss doctors evaluate the various bariatric surgical procedures based on their capacity for creating "malabsorption," the ability to make the stomach and small intestine dysfunctional. The Orwellian logic behind this process is telling: in order to "cure" the imaginary "disease" of obesity, doctors will surgically alter a healthy organ and make it permanently sick to the point that it actually meets the technical definition of a disease. They are ostensibly treating an imaginary disease by creating a real one.

This is but the latest example of a long history of dangerous diet practices performed by American doctors. For more than a century, physicians have been using all sorts of hazardous and ineffective weight-loss treatments. From thyroid treatments in the early twentieth century to methamphetamines in the 1950s to liquid protein diets of the 1980s to fen-phen in the 1990s, American doctors have promoted a host of dangerous drugs and treatments for people wanting to be thin. Now, if obesity gets classified as a disease, they will promote even more dangerous and ineffective weight-loss products in order to be "healthy." But, as the case of gastric-bypass surgery demonstrates, in order to avoid being labeled as diseased, Americans may actually make themselves sick.

Obesity as Metaphor

The late Susan Sontag famously observed that we rarely see diseases for what they are but often view them as metaphors for something else: we attribute meaning to sickness that often goes beyond the actual pathology. Historically, diseases have been seen as representations of God's judgment or the manifestation of a person's inner character. Tuberculosis was often romanticized in the nineteenth century as an indicator of secret longing brought forth; cancer and AIDS were often thought of as punishments for inner moral failure.[39] Such metaphorical thinking is dangerous, in Sontag's view, because it inhibits people from properly understanding the reality of their own condition and often triggers inappropriate behaviors, such as seeking unproven treatments.

This is clearly the case with obesity. Even without the additional connotations of disease, we already think about obesity in largely metaphorical terms. Throughout American culture, body fat is viewed as an indicator of moral weakness. As with AIDS or even cancer, we attribute so much more to obesity than the reality of what is just a large amount of body fat. And, one reason we attribute so much meaning to obesity is because body weight is something that seems to be so far out of our control, particularly in a society that demands such a high standard of thinness.

With all the metaphorical baggage we already attach to obesity, it seems unlikely that labeling obesity as a disease, or even a disability, is going to clarify our thinking about the causes and consequences of our increasing body weights. Indeed, obesity does not meet the criteria of a disease specified by *Stedman's Medical Dictionary* nor is there clear evidence that obesity is causing hundreds of thousands of deaths each year or that body fat is independently responsible for diabetes, heart disease, or any number of other diseases.[40] Indeed, the 18 percent decline in the rate of cardiovascular deaths over the past decade belies the notion that obesity is a major killer. Although the media often picture extremely fat bodies when presenting stories on obesity, in truth most Americans are neither as threatened nor even as large as we are typically portrayed when the issue of obesity is brought up.

Now, many health professionals I interviewed privately acknowledge these facts, but nevertheless still think that calling obesity a disease can be a useful mechanism for getting people to adopt healthier habits in their lives. If people see their body fat as a disease, the thinking goes, it may scare them into eating better and exercising more. It may also move their health insurers and doctors to get involved in this process.

At first glance, this pragmatic approach seems reasonable. After all, people care a lot more about how they look than how much they exercise or eat right. And this is for good reason—strangers don't judge us by how often we go to the gym or whether we eat five servings of fruit and vegetables every day; they do judge us, however, by our appearance. If the social stigma of fatness is already out there, then why not harness it for a useful purpose? From this perspective, if people want to exercise or eat better because they are ashamed of how fat they are or they are afraid of dying from being too fat, then so much the better.

This, however, is a poor rationalization. Body weight is an inappropriate focus of concern from both a health and a policy standpoint; in fact, if the goal is to improve our health, focusing on weight very well may backfire. By lowering the thresholds of "overweight" and "obese" to such low levels, public health professionals have arbitrarily designated millions of Americans to be "diseased" when, in reality, their weight has not been proven to be a health danger.

Thus, we are encouraging Americans to be worried about their weights and self-conscious about their bodies without a safe or an effective mechanism to help most people maintain any substantial weight loss. For the vast majority of Americans who simply want to lose twenty pounds or less, weight loss is not simply a matter of cutting out bad food or exercising more; it is a struggle against nature itself. As we'll see, our bodies are naturally calibrated around a certain weight level and they will fiercely defend themselves to retain that level. Even if people start exercising regularly and eating a balanced diet, they may not lose any weight. Many of us are predisposed to gaining weight and our bodies will strongly resist any efforts to relinquish the weight once it is on. Our bodies, programmed to protect us against the next famine, are simply operating according to their design. If people think weight is a barometer of health and they fail to shed any pounds by eating better or exercising more, they may turn to solutions that are expressly unhealthy.

For all its self-proclaimed good intentions, the campaign to designate obesity a disease is unlikely to improve Americans' health; in fact, it might only make our health problems worse. As we'll see in the chapters ahead, Americans' recent weight gains come from a complicated interrelationship between genetic and environmental influences. Americans are caught between the government, doctors, and other sources telling them they are too fat and a physiology and culture and lifestyle that all but ensures weight gain. This is exactly what Susan Sontag warned us about. By labeling obesity as a disease, we are prevented from seeing our weight for what it really is—not a health pathology but a consequence that comes from our very way of life.

three

Why We Hate Fat People

Jennifer Portnick is not only friendly, smart, energetic, and attractive, she is also incredibly fit. This San Francisco aerobics instructor teaches classes six days a week, often back-to-back. And judging by the fact that her classes are often filled to capacity, it is safe to say that she is popular with her students. So it came as a big surprise when the Jazzercise aerobics company rejected her application to teach at one of their studios. Jazzercise didn't reject Jennifer for being technically unqualified as an instructor. Nor did they reject her for being unfit (she often teaches three classes in a row). They rejected her for one reason only—Jennifer, at 5'8" and 240 pounds, did not conform to the "image" of a Jazzercise employee, which was supposed to be very thin.[1] Like many other Americans, Jennifer was denied a job simply because of her weight.

America prides itself on being a land of equality, where all can succeed irrespective of their race, creed, sex, or other physical characteristics. We boast of our commitment to civil rights and equal treatment before the law. And yet there continues be one group that is systematically mistreated throughout American society—fat people. Size-based discrimination (or fatism, if you will) is one of the last bastions of socially acceptable bias in American life. In education, fat people have a harder time getting into top colleges, are subject to severe harassment and stigmatization by peers and teachers, and, in some instances, have been expelled from schools because of their weight.[2] At work, fat people have trouble finding jobs, and they are evaluated more negatively, are less likely to be promoted, and are paid less than their thin colleagues.[3] Fat people are denied insurance coverage for many medical conditions and are routinely mistreated by health professionals.[4] Fat people even have a harder time renting apartments.[5]

The derision of fat people is pervasive throughout American culture. In magazines, television, and film, fat people are often the objects of ridicule and disdain, stereotypically depicted as gluttonous, lazy, or impotent. One study, analyzing more than one thousand major television characters, found that only a small percentage of them were fat and that these characters were usually the butt of jokes or cast in villainous or tragic roles.[6] Meanwhile so-called reality television shows such as *The Biggest Loser* make fatness the central problem for the "contestants" to overcome, quite untroubled by the derogatory pun in the program's title.

Not surprisingly, the American public's attitudes toward fatness and fat people are also unstintingly negative—numerous studies have found that Americans, particularly white, middle-class Americans, exhibit strong prejudices against fatness and fat people.[7] For instance, more than a quarter of college students believe that becoming fat is the worst thing that could happen to a person.[8] A majority of college-educated adults think that obese people are weak willed and lazy.[9] Most alarming is the extent of fat hostility among the very people who profess to be most concerned about the obese: health professionals. One study found that more than two-thirds of doctors surveyed thought that fat patients were morally weak while another study found that nearly a quarter of nurses said that obese patients "repulsed" them.[10]

Such prejudices are influencing the way we understand our increasing weight as a health problem. Many Americans, including our political elites, are willing to believe the inaccurate or unsubstantiated health claims about obesity because they coincide so well with their own fat biases. If one already prejudges fat people as gluttonous or lazy, it is not very difficult to think that they are also sick. Indeed, this is actually the goal of such organizations as the American Obesity Association—to get people to change their negative perceptions of obesity: instead of thinking of our fat as a moral problem, they want us to think of it as "a serious, chronic disease."[11] Thus, if we want to know the real origins of America's obesity epidemic, we need to look beyond the political machinations of the drug companies and health researchers to call our fatness a disease and, instead, examine why we hate fatness so much.

This question, however, is more complicated than it first may seem. After all, from a cultural and historical perspective, our aversion to fatness is something of an aberration. Across most of the planet, fatness is generally still thought of as a good thing.[12] In Cameroon, for example, the inability to fasten a shirt collar because of a fat neck ("le cou plié") is considered a symbol of success.[13] Among tribes in Niger, the Middle East, and the Marshall Islands, adolescent girls are put into "fattening" rooms where they are freed from any physical obligations and plied with whatever foodstuffs they desire.[14] Chinese Buddhas are famously fat and happy, Indian film stars are often quite corpulent, and many African political leaders wear their girth as a symbol of their power. Although Western television images, global marketing, and improved standards of living are beginning to change these perceptions, most of the world continues to celebrate physical largess.[15]

So what is it about the industrialized West, and the United States in particular, that has come to make fatness such a target of contempt? Like many types of prejudice, the aversion to fatness is rooted in anxiety, specifically with regard to one's economic status and social position. White, middle-class Americans particularly loathe fatness because it seems to violate the American creed of temperance and self-reliance; thus fatness marks those who lack the requisite moral standing to be in society's upper echelons. In other words, if someone doesn't have the wherewithal to stay thin, then surely they do not have the fortitude or capability to succeed in business or society. Ultimately, as we will explore below, the anxiety over America's growing weight is rooted less in concerns with our health and more in fears of losing our privilege and social position.

Premodern Celebrations of Fatness

If we want to understand why Western culture reviles fatness so much, it may be useful to first consider why almost everyone else on the planet seems to celebrate it. And a good place to start is at the beginning of human history and our Paleolithic forebears. From the standpoint of someone in the Ice Age, body fat was an unquestionably good thing. Our ancestors had to endure brutally cold climates in which plant life and game were scarce. In this environment, calories were a precious resource to be guarded and maintained. Although one could try to hide the nuts, berries, or game one hunted, there was always the threat of other creatures stealing them. The safest (and warmest) place to keep food supplies was on the body. Being fat allowed our ancestors to keep warm, secure their resources, and ensure their survival.[16]

Yet humans are also social animals who survive by pooling their resources. Our inherently social nature thus gives our body size tremendous economic and political significance. After all, to be fat in isolation simply means having plenty of stored calories, but to be fat in a society of limited resources means that one has the political power to have command over a finite food supply. In this way, fatness itself has connotations that go beyond its pure biological function—it is also a visible display of one's authority and prestige. Like wearing flashy jewelry or expensive clothes today, body fat historically has been a marker, not just of wealth, but of social dominance.[17]

Nor did the value of fatness diminish with the advent of human civilization. Although the development of agriculture may have provided more regular meals, it did not eliminate the problem of food scarcity. If anything, early farmers had less food available than hunters.[18] Thus, even as humans became more technologically advanced, body fat retained its connotations of wealth and power. And this early importance is still with us today—in most of the world's languages, words used to describe physical largess are almost always synonymous with terms denoting wealth, prestige, or sex appeal. Among the Chinese, it is common to describe someone who has gained heft as "fa fu," which means fortune

The value of fatness is evident in the earliest known depiction of the human form, the "Venus of Willendorf." The twenty-five-thousand-year-old limestone statuette is notable not only for its age but for its conception of what archeologists commonly interpret as the idealized human form as enormously fat. Although the meaning of the figurine is subject to considerable speculation (some think she was a fertility goddess while others consider her an erotic image), it is clear that she was an emblem of political reverence.[19]

and happiness. Hindi speakers describe a corpulent man as "mota," which is often used as an adjective meaning wealthy. In most English dictionaries, the term "fat" generally denotes ideas such as "abundance, complacence, and well-desired." Just as we do not have words like "over-rich" or "over-beautiful," few cultures, until recently, have had a concept of "overweight."

The historic value of fatness is also evident is the Western artistic tradition. In the premodern West, fat was glorified through art, not just as an expression of plenty and health, but also as a connotation of political dominance, physical prowess, and economic abundance. Rubens's fleshy nudes epitomize the Baroque embrace of the sensual, itself a product of increasing prosperity and trade in post-Renaissance Europe. Breugel's scenes of health and cheer depicted fat subjects, while scenes of deprivation are shown with emaciation. Lillian Russell's heft and girth exemplified nineteenth-century ideals of feminine and maternal fecundity, which was valued at a time when infant mortality and infectious diseases still ravaged the rapidly urbanizing populations.[20]

Of course, this is not to say that people in the past did not concoct alternative or negative conceptions of body fat. History is replete with figures castigated or lampooned for their corpulence—Shakespeare's Falstaff and Dickens's Mr. Bumble were seen as healthy, oversexed, and mirthful but also greedy, gluttonous, and impotent.[21] This ambivalence toward fatness was particularly evident in the medieval Catholic Church, which fretted that corpulence embodied the "deadly" sins of gluttony and avarice.[22] Overeating, like many sins of the flesh, was considered immoral because it was associated with animal impulses and indicated a weakness of reason and self-restraint.[23] Gluttony was also dangerous because it was thought to foster other sins of the flesh. Just as eating the apple led Adam and Eve to sex, gluttony was the medieval equivalent of a "gateway drug" that would lead to other vices. A lustful, passionate body could only be tamed through a discipline of regimented activity and religious practice.[24] This is why the term "diet" derives from the Greek root *diæta* which meant "way of living" for each day, something originally designed for the life of the monastic ascetic.

Yet, when we think about these alternative views of fatness, it is important to understand them in their social and economic context. Typically, the authors of these alternative ideologies rarely condemned corpulence per se (indeed many of them, such as Thomas Aquinas, were quite fat themselves); instead they admonished uncontrolled appetites and overeating. And, this was politically relevant. For moral strictures against gluttony, such as in the seven deadly sins, may have been written for spiritual and medicinal purposes, but they were also distinct, and often subversive, political ideologies. Resisting the power of the ruling classes often meant resisting the symbols of their influence—one of those symbols being their girth. By condemning gluttony, marginalized groups could discredit one of the powers that ruling classes enjoyed—to eat more than everyone else.

Thus, it is not surprising that the medieval church embraced a moral code that condemned consumption. In their constant political struggle with the landed gentry of Europe, popes and priests primarily utilized moral codes and the fear of damnation to check the military and economic power of secular rulers.[25] Condemning the powerful and wealthy for utilizing their power and wealth was thus one of their primary weapons. A similar strategy was evident in other revolutionary ideologies: Protestant reformers and early American puritans condemned fatness as embodying the indulgences (sensual and otherwise) of the Catholic Church; French revolutionaries embraced a slender ideal in contrast to the bloated and inert aristocratic classes they sought to depose; and American progressive reformers in the early twentieth century advocated rigorous diets in opposition to the overindulged wealth and power of monopolist capitalism.

Thus, if we are trying to understand our own attitudes about fatness, it is important to recognize that, historically speaking, fatness has always had political connotations. On one hand, it was typically associated with power, health, and well-being. Political elites (kings, aristocrats, clergy, and early industrialists) were often fatter than the general population and the physical toil and deprivations of daily life meant that few common folk were able to sustain heavier bodies.[26] On the other hand, because of its association with wealth and power, the fat body was also depicted as the embodiment of gluttony, avarice, and other sins. If fatness epitomized prestige and power, thinness was a symbol of political transgression and resistance.[27] By the late 1800s, however, all these attitudes began to change.

How Fatness Lost Its Social Cachet

The factor that had the biggest impact on Westerners' perceptions of fatness was the industrialization of agriculture in the late nineteenth century. At the beginning of the 1800s, farming was not much different than it had been for centuries. Most of the population toiled on small plots growing food for local markets.[28] The diet of the average American or European was still comprised mostly of cabbage and salted meats. But as the century progressed, advances in scientific and industrial technology greatly improved agricultural productivity, particularly in America. Mechanical reapers, steam engines, steel plows, refrigeration, and new processes in fertilization and plant crossbreeding greatly expanded the food supply. With the advent of railways and steamships, cheap beef and pork as well new types of fruits and vegetables were available to the growing masses within the urban centers. New preservatives and packaging methods, such as canning, allowed foods to be stored for long periods of time.[29] By the century's end, food was not only becoming less costly and more plentiful, but a greater variety was available. The Industrial Revolution not only changed the way people worked, it also changed the way that they ate.

Now in many ways, the new abundance of food would seem to be the most logical explanation for why attitudes about fatness changed.[30] The value of fatness, like any commodity, is a function of its scarcity: when food is limited, body fat is rare; when food is plentiful, fat becomes common and less precious. But, such a simplistic economic explanation is not sufficient: although the rise in the food supply was undoubtedly important, it cannot explain why Americans started to embrace a thin ideal, primarily because body fat did not actually become more common. Between the 1890s and the 1920s, even as American culture became increasingly preoccupied with dieting and thinness, the average American body weight remained relatively constant.[31] Similarly, Americans became even more obsessed with thinness in the 1960s and 1970s, even though their body weights during this period were generally unchanging. Although the growth of the food supply may have invalidated fatness as a sign of wealth, it did not necessarily mean that thinness would become valued.

Rather, to understand why we started to become so obsessed with thinness, we need to appreciate the changing value of fatness and thinness as symbols, particularly in their relationship to class politics. The industrialization of the late nineteenth century also bred an emerging middle class and, with it, a particular middle-class apprehension of the body and bodily functions. The white, Anglo-Saxon Protestants who comprised most of the middle classes in America and much of northern Europe were particularly obsessed with bodily cleanliness, order, and control. Indeed it was precisely this obsession, according to Max Weber, that enabled capitalism's early development: the values of thrift, hard work, and self-discipline embraced by many early Protestant sects were well suited to the demands of capital accumulation and the rationality of industrial production.[32] Although Protestantism was a deep and multifaceted worldview, one of its central pillars was a deep fear of sensual pleasure. In contrast to the sensual indulgences of the Catholic aristocracy, Protestant reformers advocated a severe asceticism, trumpeting the importance of reason over passion and of self-control over bodily appetites. Among early Protestants, overt displays of wealth, sexuality, or luxury were frowned upon; temperance and modesty were spiritually prized.

The Protestant denigration of appetites and sensuality may have started as a dissident political movement against the opulence of the aristocratic and ecclesiastical classes in the sixteenth and seventeenth centuries, but by the late 1800s, it had become a hegemonic norm in much of the West. Protestant middle-class reformers, particularly women, began to flex their increasing political muscle by campaigning to codify their moral apprehensions into law. In the United States, this concern with private behavior took the form of crusades against alcohol, drugs, pornography, birth control, abortion, and homosexuality. In fact, many of the "blue laws" that we currently live under today originated with the Protestant reformers of the late 1800s.[33]

The Protestant, middle-class preoccupation with abstinence and self-regulation served many functions. It helped provide a more disciplined and productive workforce (which was the goal of many alcohol restrictions); it coincided with an ideology of delayed gratification and saving (which helped the accumulation of capital); and it justified the inequality of wealth and property among the rapidly urbanizing population. By emphasizing the importance of self-control over bodily appetites, the Protestant ethic made the individual morally accountable for his or her social circumstance. Protestants who believed in predestination desperately sought signs from God about their fates in the afterlife and clues to their own moral piety. Poverty and squalor were seen as portents of a latent depravity; wealth and status were seen to arise from piety and the restraint of bodily desire. Instinctual repression thus not only made one wealthy; it also made one righteous.

Hence it wasn't just that a plentiful food supply made fatness widely available, but rather that a plentiful food supply made eating a new target for a Protestant, middle-class preoccupied with bodily control. With scarcity no longer a limiting factor on one's diet, voluntary self-restraint was needed, as eating became seen as a decadent and dangerous yielding to appetite and passion.[34] The ideal of fatness was thus replaced with a new conception of physicality that better suited the concerns with rationality, efficiency, and self-discipline of an industrial age. Among the American and European middle classes, this meant slimming the idealized body from a sedentary girth to a mobile thinness: the fleshy cachet of people such as the actress Lillian Russell and "Diamond" Jim Brady gave way to the trimmer Gibson Girl and the slender boxer Jim Corbett.[35] Meanwhile body fat became infused with its more contemporary connotations: an indicator of a weak will and mind, a marker of sloth, and a badge denoting the failure of self-control and restraint.

Thinness also came to be a marker of social status, which was particularly important given the expanding and urbanizing character of America's middle class. As millions of Americans climbed the social ladder and flocked to new cities, traditional markers of social position, such as family name or pedigree, became less relevant. Instead, physical cues, including speech, manners, clothing, and the body became even more crucial as indicators of one's social position. Although a thin body did not necessarily signify a high social status (there were still plenty of thin low-status people), it became a necessary condition to indicate that one had the *moral standing* of a high-status person. As the philosopher Susan Bordo observes, fat had become "indicative of laziness, lack of discipline, unwillingness to conform, and absence of all of those 'managerial' abilities that confer upward mobility."[36] The well-to-do used their thin bodies not simply as a marker of their affluence, but as a testament to their moral fortitude.

Several new developments in the late nineteenth century assisted in spreading this new meaning of thinness. One of these was the development of an image-driven mass media. The growth of the railroads and the spread of compulsory education and literacy created a national market for magazines. Around the turn of the century, scores of new journals and weeklies emerged, distinctive not only in their targeting of women and the middle class but in their heavy use of images.[37] For the emergent middle class trying to ascertain proper standards of behavior (that is, how to behave like the wealthy and powerful), these periodicals and their illustrations were a crucial source of information. In turn-of-the-century magazines such as *Harper's Bazaar*, the *Ladies Home Journal*, and *Life*, the idealized middle-class person became increasingly slim. Women's periodicals, in particular, became preoccupied with thinness, featuring scores of articles, pictures, and advertisements that emphasized the importance of leanness, diet, and self-control.[38] Millions now had the same body images against which to compare themselves and, by the 1920s, a standardized, middle-class body ideal was beginning to emerge.

The middle-class preoccupation with thinness and propriety was also encouraged by a spate of new products and advertisements. Ads for diet pills, obesity belts, weight-loss tonics, and other devices bombarded readers with messages about the importance of thinness, and all sorts of new schemes and fads emerged about how and what foods should be eaten. The most curious and popular of these turn-of-the-century diet fads was one developed by Horace Fletcher. Dismayed by the eating habits of his fellow Americans and chastened by his inability to get life insurance because of his weight, Fletcher developed a new regime of dieting that focused on how to eat. According to Fletcher, each bite of food should be chewed at least one hundred times or until its taste was gone. "Fletcherism promised a ritual purification of the body," writes diet historian Hillel Schwartz. "Perfect chewing, like perfect fasting, made the body clean as it was light."[39]

Such body consciousness was also enhanced by the development of mass-produced consumer goods, particularly clothing. In the late 1800s, America's expanding railroad network created a new national market for direct mail products. Small industries, such as patent medicine and pornography, had already been utilizing railroads to ship their products, but in the late 1800s, clothing and retail distributors such as Montgomery Ward and Sears, Roebuck, and Company began to exploit train transport. Along with the growing department stores, these mail-order businesses heralded both a new way of buying clothes and a new self-understanding. Whereas before, most American clothing was custom made (either at home or by a tailor), the growth of commercial retail offered ready-to-wear clothing that was sized.[40] This created a new identity—people were now a size 8 or a size medium—their bodies standardized to a national market. It also fostered greater bodily awareness, particularly among middle-class women who were the primary consumers of ready-to-wear clothing.

Together, these forces helped to spread a new language about weight and body fat in the late nineteenth and early twentieth centuries. It was not just that terms such as "overweight" and "obese" became common; a whole new derogatory vocabulary emerged: terms including "pudgy," "tubby," "porky," and "jumbo" became commonplace and even such previously complimentary terms as "stout," "plump," and "fat" became infused with pejorative meaning.[41] These words did not enter the language unprompted. They mirrored the growth of the diet, fashion, and media industries and the expanding middle-class preoccupations with self-restraint, morality, and control. By the 1920s, these forces had come together to make thinness the physical ideal among America's middle class. Suddenly, people, such as the fashionable Duchess of Windsor, were beginning to believe that one couldn't be "too rich or too thin."

Although the idealization of thinness was largely suspended during the privations of the Great Depression and World War II, by the 1950s America's preoccupation with fatness began to rise again. Partly this came from the efforts of doctors and health researchers including Louis Dublin of the Metropolitan Life Insurance Company. Dublin's tireless promotion of the idea that thinness prolonged life made a big impact on the American health establishment and the general public.[42] His efforts were aided by the emerging pharmaceutical industry, which began to market a host of new diet drugs, such as methamphetamines.

The changing physical demands of everyday life also began affecting American attitudes about bodies. Prior to the 1960s, most Americans physically labored in factories, farms, and the home, whether it was guiding a plow, manning a lathe, or washing clothes. Pale skin, soft hands, and a supple figure historically had been signifiers of wealth and leisure because they were only available to the select few who could avoid the physical demands of most people's lives. However, with the rise of a more sedentary service economy and the emergence of labor-saving machinery and household appliances, most activities required less bodily effort. Increasingly, Americans could live their lives with relatively little exertion, something most actually came to do.

Just as an increase in the food supply helped make body fat less valuable, so too did an increase in physical ease make body softness less precious. In a world where exercise was no longer necessary, muscular tone was increasingly hard to come by, and, by its scarcity, became valuable. A firm and muscular appearance, one that could only come with the time and resources necessary for costly gym memberships and private trainers, became the marker of social privilege. The popularity of exercise gurus such as Jack La Lanne in the 1950s and Jane Fonda in the 1970s reflected this new growing preoccupation with a hard body, a symbol of both virtue and affluence.

The emphasis on muscular thinness was also aided by the rise of the youth-oriented fashion industry during the latter half of the twentieth century. Although the fashion industry's influence on body perception goes back to the 1920s, the idealizing of the youthfully thin body really took off in the 1950s and 1960s, arising largely from the newly emerging teenage consumer market. The size, buying power, and untapped product loyalties of the baby boom generation promised a tremendous market for American companies and youthfulness came to dominate many aspects of American popular culture. In women's fashion this was evident with such innovations as the bikini, miniskirt, and halter-top, which were all tailored to the young and revealed expanses of flesh. Thinness now signified not only wealth and status, but also youthful freedom, exuberance, and sexuality. With women's fashion revealing ever more flesh, magazines such as *Vogue* and *Cosmopolitan* began focusing on women's bodies as much as their clothes—by the late 1960s, they started featuring bodies themselves as fashion statements.[43] And, as the body became an increasingly malleable fashion statement, a younger, nubile, and even more elusive physical ideal inevitably emerged. By the 1970s and 1980s, teenage fashion models such as Brooke Shields and Kate Moss epitomized a bodily ideal that was becoming ever younger and more adolescent.

Enterprising companies stoked the demand for thinness with a range of products that could mold a youthful figure, including diet fads and drugs as well as new medical procedures including plastic surgery. Like an advertisement that promised to let customers "Have the body you've always wanted—without any of the hassles of diets or exercise!"—appeals to people's desire to be thin became a common part of the cultural landscape in the Me Decade of 1970s. These messages made grand promises to deliver the eternally youthful body, irrespective of one's age or natural characteristics. Magazines and television shows were filled with stories, products, and advertisements promoting the myth that the skinny body of the supermodel was within anyone's reach. A vicious cycle thus ensued: as more people exercised, dieted, and tried to lose weight, the ideal standard became thinner, younger, and more physically rare.

But while the rise of the middle class and the emergence of the fashion and diet industries may explain why thinness came to be valued as a symbol of one's social status, it still does not entirely explain why fatness came to be so hated. After all, just because we value a Mercedes, it doesn't mean we necessarily hate a Chevy. Rather, to understand our contemporary animosity toward fatness, we need to appreciate why it evokes the outrage of certain groups of people. And for this we need to look at the meaning of fatness in its contemporary political context.

Thin Like Me

"Obesity! Ugh. Those people are so gross. It's sick. How could they let themselves get that way?"

It is remarkable how often I've heard comments like this one when I tell people about the book I am writing. Most thin people I've met seem to have a pretty harsh view toward the obese. Over the past three years, I've heard scores of unsolicited invectives of disgust and contempt for fat people, particularly from educated, middle-class folks who otherwise pride themselves on being rational and fair-minded. Even more interesting is how they assume that I, as an affluent thin person, naturally share in their horror. Like a group of white folks surreptitiously sharing a racist joke, many thin middle-class people will easily convey their disdain for the obese if no fat people are around.

Although we have seen the logic of why thinness is valued, it does not sufficiently explain the vehemence against fat people. Clearly, the loathing of fatness comes from another source, and that source is fear. As with any type of prejudice, the animosity toward fat people originates in some much deeper anxieties over self and social status. For not only is thinness a convenient way for middle-class people to assert their moral superiority and boost their self-image, it also serves to rationalize the social inequalities that exist between various social groups.

Find this hard to believe? Listen closely to how Americans criticize fat people and you'll find rationalizations that are remarkably similar to those historically used to justify negative attitudes toward all marginalized groups in America. Fat people are thought to be gluttonous, lustful, greedy, lazy, weak-willed, and lacking any kind of self-control. If fat people are targets of our contempt, it is only because they have brought this on themselves with their unwillingness to take responsibility for their own actions.

The ideology that underscores this prejudice is an ethos of individualism and self-reliance.[44] As with blacks and the poor, fat people are thought to violate some of the most fundamental tenets in American political culture: that all people are fundamentally responsible for their own welfare; that self-control and restraint are the hallmarks of virtue; and that all Americans are obliged to work at improving themselves. These views derive partly from our liberal political tradition that emphasizes the importance of individual freedom and rights and the restraint of government power. And, as we've seen, they also come from America's Anglo-Protestant heritage that emphasized individuals' unique responsibility for demonstrating their worth before God. This individualism has also been accentuated by two hallmarks of American economic development—laissez-faire capitalism and entrepreneurship—which both celebrate the good that individual initiative promotes in the free market.[45] Whether it is the rugged frontiersman, the lonesome cowboy, or the Horatio Alger stories of the self-made man, American heroes are notable for their individual pluck, initiative, and isolation.[46]

The importance of this individualistic ethos continues to be evident in contemporary American attitudes toward the poor. Most Americans dislike welfare programs, not because they are opposed to helping others, but because they think that relying on government aid betrays a lack of self-reliance and individual responsibility.[47] In situations in which poverty is seen to be beyond the person's control (such as with children or the elderly), Americans are quite willing to embrace government spending. Programs including Head Start and Social Security enjoy wide support because they are seen to assist the "deserving" poor. Conversely, able-bodied adults are held responsible for their own condition and are thought not to be deserving of aid or government redistribution of wealth. This individualistic ethos thus serves as an important rationale for justifying the tremendous gulf between rich and poor in the United States: barring a few exceptions, if people are poor, they only have themselves to blame.

Nor does this individualistic ethos stop with the poor—it is also at the heart of many white Americans' racial attitudes.[48] Most whites know that it is no longer publicly acceptable to express racist stereotypes and, unlike a generation ago, most whites no longer publicly voice negative stereotypes of blacks, support segregation, or oppose interracial marriage. When surveyed, most white Americans strongly endorse the principle of racial equality.[49] But this does not mean racial bias has disappeared. Instead, according to many race scholars, whites now couch their racial resentment in rhetoric of individual responsibility. Blacks are not denigrated because they are fundamentally less intelligent, lazy, or some other stereotype; rather, blacks are denigrated because they fail to embrace principles of individual self-reliance and self-control. Like the poor, blacks are held accountable for racial disparities in income, employment, and wealth because of their own moral failure. Policies that promote racial equality, such as affirmative action, are discredited because blacks are believed to be unable to live up to the individualistic norms of self-reliance.[50]

The same individualistic ethos that underscores Americans' attitudes toward race and class is also at the heart of their antipathy toward fat people. As with their views of poor people and blacks, most white Americans see fat people as violating the tenets of discipline and self-control. In two national surveys I conducted for this book, more than 64 percent of Americans believe overweight people are "fat because they lack self-control" and more than 70 percent ranked individual laziness as the most important cause of obesity.[51] The University of Kansas psychologist Christian Crandall has shown that most Americans also believe that fat people are morally deviant, self-indulgent, and unwilling to correct their own behavior. Not surprisingly, people who express a prejudice against fat people also endorse a worldview that emphasizes traditional values, individual responsibility, and the notion that "people get what they deserve."[52]

Conversely, if someone is believed to be fat for reasons beyond their control, then the contempt quickly changes to sympathy and compassion. Experiments have shown that antifat attitudes diminish when people think that obesity is glandular in origin.[53] Americans dislike fatness because they think it indicates a person's unwillingness to be responsible and self-monitoring: as with the poor, if someone is fat, they only have themselves to blame. In fact, people who have strong antifat attitudes also tend to be more hostile toward minorities and the poor.[54] In the national survey I conducted, more than 80 percent of people who believed that blacks are "welfare dependent" or that the poor are "irresponsible" also believed that overweight people are fat because they lack self-control, much higher rates than the general population.[55]

Given the confluence of racial and class prejudice with antifat sentiments, it is not surprising that apprehension of body fat is strongest among middle-class whites. Whites are five times more likely to report feeling ashamed of their weight than blacks or Latinos, even though the latter two groups have much higher body weights on average.[56] Nor are antifat attitudes about others nearly as strong or prevalent among minorities as they are among whites.[57] The similarity between modern racism and antifat attitudes may also explain these racial differences.[58] As blacks or Latinos experience racial stigmatization in the same terms as the moral condemnation that is applied to the obese, it is logical that body size as well skin color have become intertwined as a part of their cultural identity.

But perhaps the greatest reason why fat prejudice is so intertwined with class and racial prejudice is because America's poor and minorities are much fatter, on average, than its middle-class, whites. [59] Nearly one in three African Americans and one in four Latinos are obese compared to only one in five non-Latino whites. Body sizes also vary consistently by education and income—27 percent of high school dropouts are obese compared to only 16 percent of college graduates; people below the poverty line are nearly 15 percent more likely to be obese than those not in poverty.[60] Indeed, the very highest levels of obesity are among people in both categories—nearly 50 percent of poor black and Latino women are technically obese (that is, have a BMI of 30 or above).

With obesity so prevalent among minorities and the poor, condemning fatness is an effective way of highlighting their "moral failure" and justifying their continued marginalization. After all, if poor black people are unable to control their weight, the reasoning goes, then it is surely another indication of their inability to exercise self-control in general. Thereby, they deserve whatever low social conditions they live in and should be subject to greater restriction in terms of their moral behaviors. In truth, the higher body weights of minorities and the poor have little to do with their own "moral weakness." As we'll see in future chapters, the logic of America's food industry almost predetermines that the poor will have higher body weights than the affluent. Meanwhile, genetic evidence suggests that people of non-European ancestry are more biologically predisposed toward weight retention. Yet, despite these facts, minorities and the poor are still blamed for weighing "too much" while thin, middle-class people can view their slenderness as a signal of their own superiority.

The Real Problem of Obesity

America is a society gripped by fear. We are afraid of crime, terrorism, drugs, environmental collapse, economic decline, moral erosion, and numerous other threats.[61] Much of this fear, however, is directed at the wrong things. For example, the economist Steven Levitt has shown that, despite all the hoopla over gun control, guns are much less dangerous, statistically speaking, for children than something far more benign: swimming pools. The average American child is one hundred times more likely to die by drowning in a pool than from a gun.[62] Nevertheless, most parents would be much more concerned about their children playing at a house where they think a gun might be than they would be about them playing at a house with a swimming pool.

A similar type of misperception is happening with obesity. There is perhaps no greater fiction in the United States than the idea that we are worried about being fat because of its implications for our health. While the media and public health establishment may be sounding ever more hysterical alarms over the growing weight of the population,[63] it is not because our obesity actually represents a verifiable health threat. Rather, it is because we are afraid of fat.

Compare how obesity is being handled as a public health issue versus another major killer, automobiles. Last year more than forty-three thousand Americans died in automobile wrecks, far more than the numbers estimated to have died from "weighing too much." Moreover, unlike the estimated figures with obesity, these are verifiable numbers. Yet, outside of a handful of environmentalists, few people are talking about an epidemic of driving in this country. We have no pejorative terms like "overdriven" in our language. Although we have numerous mechanisms for ensuring driver safety, we still allow increasingly dangerous vehicles including Hummers and SUVs to roam largely unrestricted despite the threats they pose to our collective health.

Given the general lack of concern about driving relative to its real impact on deaths, it seems highly implausible that we are worried about obesity because of its health consequences or its medical costs. In fact, in terms of our collective health or economic well-being, we shouldn't worry. Yet, it is obesity, not other, more demonstrable risks to health and mortality, such as driving, that are capturing the headlines.

This obsession with weight and obesity goes beyond the financial interests of the health-industrial complex described in chapters 1 and 2, and taps into something much more powerful: the racial and economic anxieties of America's middle class. One reason Americans so readily accept that obesity must be a major problem is because obesity is associated with those at the bottom end of America's social ladder. Thus, if obesity is growing, it surely must be a sign of American decline.

Indeed, it is precisely because it is such a powerful symbol that obesity has been adopted by so many different groups. Among conservatives, it is evidence of the growing moral degeneration of America: the fact that we are getting fatter only shows that we are getting lazier, and more lustful, and moving farther away from the Anglo-Protestant tradition that defined American greatness. Among liberals, obesity represents the increasing power of international corporations and food companies in making us heavy against our will. Among whites, it taps into latent racial fears that come with America's growing ethnic diversity—the growth of obesity parallels the increasing numbers of Latinos and African Americans relative to a shrinking white majority. And among the economic elite (the group in America most preoccupied with weight), obesity taps into a sense of social insecurity.

Ultimately, however, the reason that so many people think the rise of obesity is a cause for alarm is because of our own chronic feelings of helplessness. In an era of corporate downsizing, globalization, and mass marketing, Americans often report that more and more of their lives seem beyond their control.[64] Our bodies remain one of the last areas where we feel that we should be able to exercise some autonomy—a view that is only stoked by the diet, fitness, and cosmetic industries. Yet the fact that we continue to gain weight despite all our dieting, nutrition advice, and working out belies just how little control we may actually have. It is our anxiety with our own powerlessness and status much more than any health issue that is driving the perception that our growing weight is an epidemic disease. But this anxiety is only part of the story. Our fear and aversion to obesity also derive from something equally important in our culture—sex. And it is to this that we next turn.

four

Women, Fat, and
the Sexual Market

It's a free country. If you wanna be a big, obese blob of human go right ahead. However, what I will ask is that you fat chicks stop deluding yourselves and realize that you are very fat and cumbersome and greasy and smelly and that no amount of primping or make-up can help you. Am I picking on fat women? I sure am. Fat men don't try and lie about their size. Do you know what I think fat women should do? They should become the nicest, funniest people in the world. They need a redeeming quality. Fat women should dance around and laugh and fall down and amuse us.

Posting from the blog www.believeyourbeliefs.com

Although fat people in America encounter widespread disdain and discrimination, there is one group that bears the brunt of our fat bias: white women. The quote above, although extreme, typifies a cultural perspective in America that views overweight white women with unparalleled scorn. For men, being overweight can be interpreted in two ways—it can be a sign of power, mirth, and largesse or a sign of ineptitude and melancholy.[1] Among black and Latino populations, a large posterior on a woman can still be seen as a sign of strength and sexuality. But for white women in American culture, fatness has unstintingly negative connotations.

Nowhere is this more evident than in American popular culture. On television, just as there is a particular bias against fat people in general, there is an even more specific bias against fat white women. Not only do fat white actresses have a harder time getting work (only about one in nine white female television actresses is overweight), but they are almost never cast in romantic roles.[2] Overweight male characters or women of color are not forbidden heroism or romance but fat women invariably are.[3] To survey popular culture is to notice the particular

79

problem of weight for white women: there are no television shows called "Fat Actor," but actress Kirstie Alley's weight is reason enough for an entire series; the corpulence of black talk-show host Star Jones is inconsequential compared with the weight concerns of her white counterparts; the ample black actress and singer Queen Latifah can grace the cover of fashion magazines with no comment on her weight, while the see-sawing weight of white model Anna Nicole Smith fills the tabloids; even Oprah Winfrey's diet odyssey is the exception that proves the rule (it is hard to find any white female celebrities of equal stature who weigh as much as Ms. Winfrey does at her thinnest).

White women also find more fat prejudice at work. All things being equal, a fat white woman will earn far less and is less likely to be promoted than a woman with the same qualifications who is thin. Economist John Cawley found that a white woman who is sixty-five pounds heavier than average earns 6 percent less in annual income simply by virtue of her weight alone—such weight-based wage discrimination does not occur for women of color or for men.[4] Other research demonstrates that fatter white women were less likely to be affluent, irrespective of their background, and were more likely to be in poverty, differences that, once again, were not found for women of color or men.[5]

These biases are also evident in the attitudes of the general population. Not only are Americans more punitive toward fat white women than other groups; white women are also more punishing toward themselves. For example, most white American women see themselves as overweight, even if their weights are below the official classification of overweight (a BMI of 25), something that is far less common among men or women of color.[6] Compared to white men, "overweight" white women (women with BMIs of 25 or more) are also five times more likely to report feeling ashamed about their weight, are twice as likely to be dieting, and are four times more likely to get weight-loss surgery.[7] These differences become even more pronounced as one moves up the social ladder; white women with a college education were more than twice as likely to see themselves as overweight as those with only a high school degree, even when they are of the exact same body mass.[8]

This prejudice is taking an undeniable toll. The negative conception that many white American women have of their bodies results in poor self-esteem that affects their mental health. For example, heavier white women are more likely to be depressed and suicidal than thin women.[9]

They are also more socially isolated, less likely to find dating partners or marry, and more likely to be harassed and abused for their weight— problems that are far less common for fat men.[10] In an effort to meet a thin standard, millions of American women are engaging in unhealthy eating behaviors and self-destructive dieting. Thousands more are imperiling themselves with the eating disorders anorexia and bulimia, dangerous diet remedies and drugs, or weight-loss surgery.[11]

Given these facts, one cannot discuss America's obesity epidemic without noting the specific emphasis our society puts on white women's weight. Obesity may be officially characterized as a general health concern, but it is deeply entangled with questions of gender. As we'll see, the medical community and public health establishment treat obesity differently in men and women. Women are expected to adhere to a lower ideal weight, are given more stringent messages about weight and health, and face greater expectations about being thin. Yet, in many ways, this remains a puzzle. After all, the different expectations of women's thinness are not based on any medical or biological criteria; in fact, they often fly in the face of medical evidence because mortality is less correlated with obesity among women. So why do we punish white women so much more for being fat?

Over the past four decades, scores of feminist books and studies have tried to answer this question. From early classics by Simone de Beauvoir and Betty Friedan to more contemporary, postmodern theorists, a host of feminist authors have generally come to the same conclusion—our contemporary female beauty standards are the latest example of a long history of patriarchal subjugation of women and women's bodies.[12] In their view, weight prejudice is simply "the last bastion of sexism."[13] Although this account may be so common that it has now become conventional wisdom, it also leaves many unanswered questions. In particular, it doesn't explain why *thinness* has become the instrument of women's oppression or why thinness is embraced so fervently by women themselves.

A more fruitful explanation, I think, lies elsewhere. Rather than being a male conspiracy to keep women oppressed, our attitudes toward white women and fat arise from the interaction between the shifting economic position of women and our unchanging biological impulses. In liberal, Western societies, economic development has freed women from traditional domestic confinement, giving them more independence and greater sexual liberty; economic development, however, does little to change our more hardwired biological impulses toward mating and sexual attractiveness, which in men tend toward physical signals of youth and fertility. As I'll explain below, when social liberation meets human biology, a cultural ideal of female thinness arises as the currency of status and desirability. Paradoxically, it is the very increase in women's social freedom and sexual equality that has both increased the size of the sexual marketplace and generated a more stringently thin standard of white female beauty. This, in turn, is shaping understanding of obesity as a health issue. In other words, our attitudes about weight are driven not just by race or social status, but by sex as well.

The Traditional Perspective on Women and Weight

> Yesterday, there was a customer in my office. When he left, I mentioned to a [male] co-worker that he was attractive. My co-worker said, "You're not good enough for him. He likes skinny women." Of course, this made me furious. My co-worker said, "I was just being honest. He's the jerk, not me!" My co-worker doesn't understand, I wasn't angry because he said that I was "too fat" for the customer's tastes. I was angry because he said I wasn't "good enough."
>
> *Anna Vosburgh*[14]

Ask almost any white middle-class woman in America and she will tell you about the enormous pressure she feels about her appearance. In America, as in much of the developed world, white women are supposed to adhere to a singularly high standard of behavior and beauty. Their skin must be smooth, and wrinkle-free, their hair must be soft and luxurious, and their flesh must be firm and without cellulite. And, perhaps most important, they must be thin. Regardless of any natural cycle of weight gain that comes with aging, menstruation, or pregnancy, white women are supposed to maintain the nubile figure of an adolescent girl.

The most widely held explanation for this standard has come from a large body of feminist writings. For most of human history, many feminists note, women have been treated as men's property, their status usually no greater than any other object for barter or trade. Babylonian law, for example, viewed rape, not as a crime against a woman, but as a crime of property damage against a husband or father; in Judaic law, women were catalogued with sheep in statutes about property rights; and in classical Greece, women were viewed as underdeveloped and "misbegotten" men.[15] Even as late as the nineteenth century, the legal status of American women was little better than that of women in early history; the early republic denied women political enfranchisement, property or legal rights, or any legal protection from spousal abuse. Seen in this light, Western history has been continually marked by the disenfranchisement and repression of women.

From the feminist perspective, our contemporary norms of female beauty and weight are yet another instance in this recurrent pattern of female subordination to male interests, albeit through more discreet and subversive means.[16] Women may no longer be shackled by the same legal and economic restrictions of past centuries, but they still remain subject to various mechanisms meant to keep them disadvantaged. Today, however, these methods of subjugation are exercised more through cultural norms than through law. Female beauty standards are but one of many extralegal mechanisms by which a male-dominated society keeps women socially constrained. The goal of these cultural norms, according to philosopher Sandra Bartky, is to turn "women into the docile and compliant companions of men just as surely as the army aims to turn its raw recruits into soldiers."[17]

Of all the cultural norms that keep women shackled, few have the power, according to many feminists, of the "tyranny of slenderness."[18] Other aspects of female beauty may require clothes or cosmetics, but they are generally accessible. With enough resources, almost any woman can have a certain hairstyle, clothes, or makeup. But body weight is inherently restricted by genetics and heritability. If a woman is naturally stout or full figured, there is little she can do, save radically dangerous, expensive, and invasive surgery, to achieve the slender yet busty look of a fashion model. In fact, her body has multiple mechanisms to resist achieving the thin ideal. Healthy young females of our species typically carry at least 28 percent of their body weight as fat—a necessary protection for the demands of pregnancy, childbirth, and breastfeeding. Older women typically carry at least 35 percent of their body weight as fat. To reduce one's body fat level to that of a typical fashion model (say around 15 percent) is to struggle against millions of years of evolution, particularly for women over thirty.

According to these critics, the very unnaturalness of today's slender beauty standard makes it a very effective mechanism that men use to disempower women, particularly the middle-class white women who enjoy the greatest access to the halls of power. By establishing an impossibly low ideal weight, our culture puts white women in a position of perpetually policing themselves and their own food behavior. The mental discipline required to maintain a state of semistarvation in an otherwise food rich environment is not only monumental it often leads to a variety of damaging psychological consequences. Food becomes a topic of obsession, eating disorders and distorted body images arise, and feelings of depression, helplessness, and low self-worth grow.[19] Held to an unattainable standard of thinness, white women are forced to spend enormous energy and resources at maintaining their appearance and are undermined in self-confidence, mental health, and self-esteem.

Although feminist writings vary enormously in their analysis, this theme of weight and disempowerment is a dominant theme.[20] For example, in her best-selling book, *The Beauty Myth*, Naomi Wolf argues that our contemporary weight standards work precisely to inhibit women's strength and independence. A woman who is tired, depressed, and preoccupied with her weight is less likely to pose a significant challenge to the institutions and practices that keep women as second-class citizens. Striving to meet a preternaturally thin beauty standard absorbs time and energy that could be applied to addressing the political interests that women share including issues of equal protection, childcare, and public safety. "Dieting is the most potent political sedative in women's history," Wolf writes, for "a quietly mad population is a tractable one."[21]

The same argument can be found in Kim Chernin's book *The Obsession*. It was no mere coincidence, Chernin asserts, that thin female beauty standards arose at the same time women were becoming economically and politically formidable. As women emerged from their domestic confinement and gained some measure of political and economic power, new mechanisms were required to keep them distracted from the gross inequalities they faced in a male-dominated society. The standard of female thinness was concocted at the very same time that women were entering the public sphere, and as women became more empowered, the standard grew slimmer. The slender Gibson Girl became popular in the late 1890s, exactly at the same time that middle-class women were increasingly working for suffrage and legal equality.[22] Female beauty was slimmed further during the 1920s, right after women won the vote and experienced the sexual freedom of the Jazz Age. Conversely, female beauty ideals were more busty and full figured during the 1950s, coinciding with women's domestic retrenchment and the sexual repression that came in the wake of World War II.

And, it was no coincidence, these writers argue, that the 1960s and 1970s, the period of women's greatest social and economic empowerment, was also the time when female beauty standards became ludicrously emaciated. These decades proved liberating to women in many ways. The advent of the birth control pill allowed them unprecedented control over their reproductive lives and thus gave them much greater sexual freedom; federal legislation gave women new protections from discrimination in public facilities and the workplace; and the feminist movement mobilized millions of women to contest the sexist double standards in all dimensions of American life. The increase in female education, the opening of universities and professions, and the growth of the service economy also meant women were becoming more economically self-sufficient. Within these pivotal decades, women had gained an unprecedented level of freedom, economic power, and stature in American society. Yet this was also the time when the emaciated Twiggy emerged as a beauty icon, when anorexia nervosa became a widespread disorder, when diet organizations such as Weight Watchers and Over-Eaters Anonymous were founded, when diet books became best sellers, and when misconceptions about weight and health became firmly entrenched.[23] Just as women were gaining equal rights and status they were facing a cultural norm of weight that demanded them to be increasingly thin and youthful. Women were suddenly expected to adhere to an impossible skinny beauty standard.

Many feminist writers believe that the political purpose of the weight standard also explains why thinness is more demanded of white women. White, affluent women face the most severe beauty standards precisely because they are in the most advantageous position to challenge male power. Unlike minorities or the poor, who face racial and class barriers to political and social equality, affluent white women are only hampered by their sex.[24] It is also why eating pathologies such as anorexia and bulimia are concentrated primarily among young, white women of privilege—women with the greatest opportunities are also the ones who have internalized the thin ideal most strongly. From this stand-point, the formula is clear: the greater the female position of power, the greater the enforcement of a weight and beauty norm.

This feminist perspective offers a potent and compelling explana-tion for why women are judged so much more harshly for their weight. The coincidence between the rise of thin beauty standards and the rise of women's social and economic equality gives credence to the idea that patriarchal forces concoct new methods for keeping women disempowered and docile. One could be justifiably suspicious that thin-ness is yet another tool men use to keep women down. Indeed, some feminists might even suspect that the very idea of an obesity epidemic is another manifestation of the patriarchy at work.

But for all its intuitive appeal, this indictment leaves a lot of impor-tant questions unanswered. For example, many feminist writers of-ten assume that men want thin women as objects of sexual partnership and political subservience, but this assumption is rarely explained or substantiated—it is usually just asserted as fact.[25] Yet this argument flies in the face of common sense. Across the planet, there are enor-mous cultural differences both in regard to women's roles in society and standards of attractiveness. Ideas about women's rights, social position, and physical beauty are highly differentiated by ethnicity, social class, and religion. In most of the world's cultures, corpulence is a hallmark of feminine sexuality. Nor is it sufficient to say that self-starvation is simply the most effective mechanism for subjugating women. One can easily imagine other beauty standards, such as wear-ing powdered wigs or restrictive corsets, that would be just as effec-tive in keeping women physically preoccupied.

Moreover, none of these writers explain how this ideology of thinness is sustained. Many point to the media and the fashion and diet industries as the primary instrument of female subjugation and clearly they have a point. The barrage of emaciated supermodels and actresses undoubtedly propagates a thin beauty ideal throughout American culture. And, it is in the interest of the fashion and cosmetic industries to promote bodily dis-satisfaction as a means for selling their products—the more consumers feel unhappy with their appearance, the more likely they will purchase clothes, makeup, and other goods to make themselves look "better." But, blaming the media puts the cart before the horse. Any advertising executive will tell you that marketing follows trends more than it dictates them. The media, while undeniably important for informing and representing standards of value, still have a very limited power in dictating what those values should be. The success of a profit-driven enterprise such as *Vogue* or *Cosmopolitan* depends more on how well it taps into the existing preferences of readers than its ability to manufacture those preferences. The media promote a thin feminine ideal because a thin ideal has some resonance with the public. Ironically, to assert that women are so enthralled by the power of fashion and media presupposes that women have little capacity for their own independent judgment or to independently propagate their own thin beauty standards.

From the popular feminist account described above, it is clear that the thin female beauty standard is both disempowering to women and consistent with a long history of female subjugation. But it is still not clear, however, exactly what motivates *some* men to value thin women or why so many white American women readily accept this thin beauty norm. To explain the thin beauty standard, we need to look beyond a simplistic notion of male patriarchal domination. And in this search, two seemingly unrelated fields offer some interesting insights: biology and economics.

Evolution and the Sexual Marketplace

> There's another customer in my office with a very attractive, thin wife. This woman cheats on him, lies to him, and steals from him. A male co-worker was describing all this to me, but then added, "He's a lucky man, though. She's hot."[26]
>
> *Anna Vosburgh*

Size discrimination may affect women in the workplace, in education, and in health care, but among the scores of women I interviewed for this book, the area in which their weight was of greatest concern was their romantic relationships with men.[27] Fat white women are far less likely to marry, report far fewer dating partners or dating experiences, and generally report fewer close friends than thin women.[28] Moreover, thinness is important for white women's social standing; white women who are thin are not only more likely to marry, but are more likely to marry men of higher social status.[29]

There is a better explanation for the different fates of fat and thin white women than an oppressive patriarchy. It starts with some observations that have been made by sociobiologists, the people who try to explain human behavior from the perspective of evolution. Female beauty standards arise, not from some patriarchal conspiracy, but from largely unconscious, reproductive imperatives that differ dramatically by sex.[30] As with a peacock's plume, human beauty standards originate in the different goals of males and females in passing on their DNA.

To understand this view, let us consider human life relative to the demands of evolution. According to the theory of evolution, all life is fundamentally predicated upon genetic replication—those species whose genetic adaptations can be passed on will survive; those species who are unsuccessful at surviving and replicating will die off. Our bodies, lives, and instinctual behaviors all exist primarily to insure the continuation of our genes. The reproductive imperative, however, means quite different things for men and women. Unlike with males, female reproductive capacity is limited by pregnancy and nursing. Females thus have fewer opportunities to reproduce and invest a great deal in each of their offspring. Consequently, it is advantageous for females to seek male partners who are likely to be better providers for young (in other words, men of wealth and status). Males, on the other hand, replicate their DNA by trying to impregnate as many females as possible and by seeking female partners who are particularly fertile, as these are more likely candidates to produce their offspring. And while female fertility is marked externally, constrained by age and other physical characteristics, male fertility is determined by factors that usually have little to do with any external physical traits.

Because of these reproductive differences, each sex has evolved different criteria for evaluating potential mates. Females seek males who demonstrate power and the ability to provide. These traits are partially identified by certain physical characteristics; women tend to find tall and muscular men more attractive than short and skinny ones—but, more important, women seek other signs of status such as wealth and social position.[31] For example, it is a near universal trait that women find men with resources more desirable, something not shared by men in their evaluation of women.[32] Interestingly, this tendency is more pronounced among economically empowered females; in other words, rich women have an even stronger preference for rich men than poor women.[33]

Males, on the other hand, tend to focus more explicitly on visual cues: when assessing the potential attractiveness of mates, males tend to rely mostly on external, physical characteristics. When asked to rank the importance of looks in choosing a mate, men consistently outscore women by a large margin.[34] There is probably no better evidence of the male preoccupation with physical appearance than the fact that the pornography industry caters almost solely to men (both gay and straight).

Not surprisingly, the visual cues to which men respond are those traits that correspond with greater reproductive success: youth, fertility, and body proportion. In almost every culture around the globe, female beauty is associated with youth and from an evolutionary perspective this makes sense.[35] A young woman is not only typically fertile but also less likely to be pregnant by another male or breastfeeding a child, which prevents or inhibits ovulation. Beyond youth, males also are keenly attuned to women's body proportion, particularly the ratio between waist and hip—wide hips relative to a narrow waist are also a sign of reproductive success. This fact is often used to explain why, even though the weight of *Playboy* centerfolds and Miss America contestants has been going down over the past few decades, their waist-to-hip ratio has remained constant.[36] Numerous psychological experiments have demonstrated that men, regardless of their ethnicity or background, are more likely to find women attractive if their waist-to-hip ratio is great.[37] The importance of a narrow waist relative to wide hips may also explain the appeal of younger women; women tend to have an hourglass figure between the ages of fifteen and thirty-five, the time of their greatest fertility.[38]

Generally speaking, this evolutionary perspective seems to explain a great deal about the nature of female beauty standards. The youthful wide-hipped, fleshy female form has been the paragon of beauty and sexual attractiveness for most of human history—think of Rubens's nudes, for example. In many parts of the world, adolescent girls are still "fattened up" in preparation for marriage.[39] But although the evolutionary account may explain beauty standards in the undeveloped world, it flies in the face of the beauty standards of advanced, industrial nations such as the United States. Looking through the pages of such fashion magazines as *Vogue* and *Elle*, one does not see Rubenesque women with narrow waists and ample thighs, but rather pencil-thin, boyish figures. From a narrow evolutionary perspective, this vision of female beauty makes little sense. The emaciated figures that fill fashion magazines are not ones that signal maximum fertility (unlike the busty, curvy models in magazines aimed at men), because women with so little body fat are unlikely to either ovulate or sustain a pregnancy. Clearly then, some factor other than mere biology is driving Western culture's current preoccupation with female thinness.

That other factor, I believe, is the size of the sexual marketplace. If we want to explain why thinness is demanded of white, middle-class women in America but not of women of color or women in the undeveloped world, we need to look beyond mere instinct and instead focus on the *interaction* between instinct and the environment. Reproduction is also about competition to find the best possible mate. This means that beauty standards will not simply be determined by biology but also by social context. If one only has a choice of two or three partners, the competition among potential mates is not very severe; if one lives in a city of 10 million, choice and competition greatly increase. Economic development and urbanization therefore create a much different set of social circumstances regarding sex and reproduction that end up tilting female beauty standards toward thinness.

Perhaps the best way to understand this point is to compare the social role of women in the developed and undeveloped world. In most undeveloped societies, women are usually confined to the home, marry at young ages, have children early in life, and are generally less socially independent. Cues of fertility and status may be important for assessing partners, but in most parts of the world, the range of partners is limited. This all changes, however, with economic development. By increasing education and job opportunity and fostering urbanization, economic development typically frees women from domestic confinement and allows them greater social mobility. Readily available birth control and social mobility mean they are likely to put off childbirth for a longer period of time.

Modernity also makes many of our "instinctual" reproductive impulses obsolete. To begin with, youth and waist-to-hip ratio do not necessarily correspond with fertility: advances in birth control and reproductive engineering mean that younger women are not necessarily any more fertile than older women. Similarly, the existence of state protections for women and children as well as advances in health care mean that women can have greater confidence in the life-expectancy of their children (thus partially explaining the lower birth rate in more advanced countries). Women also have greater opportunities for economic self-sufficiency. In the most developed countries, the pool of available partners is much greater and the time of potential fertility much longer (by having fewer pregnancies, women in developed countries are ovulating more often). The presence of television, magazines, and other media in industrialized countries also provides a much wider range of social comparisons and often promotes sexual icons and ideals by which people compare themselves. One of the least recognized consequences of economic development is that it greatly increases the size and the scope of a country's real (and imagined) sexual marketplace.

Yet, even as economic development radically changes the social environment, the biological impulses remain. Women are still biologically programmed to find partners who are good providers and thus are less concerned with men's bodies and more attuned to cues of wealth and status when evaluating a mate. Men, on the other hand, continue to focus on visible female physical traits that indicate fertility, particularly youth. As the science writer Nancy Etcoff concludes,

> sexual preference is still guided by ancient rules that make us most attracted to bodies that look the most reproductively fit. Nor can we escape the jarring thought that women compete in the mating world for men whose brains are hard-wired to find nubile teenagers highly desirable and particularly beautiful.[40]

From the sociobiological perspective, the disparity in instinctual drives means that different beauty standards will continue to divide the sexes, even as a society becomes more egalitarian in other domains.

And this is where thinness comes in. One consequence of a larger sexual marketplace is that men and women will rely more heavily on visible cues as signals to potential "buyers"—in a large, mobile society, family name or local social connections are often no longer relevant as a means for communicating a person's social standing. Rather, in a big, crowded city, men and women must ascertain information about each other through immediate visual cues. This, however, has different implications for men and women.

Women, seeing that men are attracted to youth and fertility, will try to emphasize those qualities in themselves as means of getting a higher status mate. This increased competition greatly increases the pressure women will feel regarding their appearance. Not only are women thirty and older "competing" for male attention with women in their twenties and teens, but they are also are being compared with images of women in the media. Given how men are over-responsive to visual appearances, women rightly see themselves as being evaluated relative to actresses, supermodels, and media stars. Because women of all ages are now being compared with nubile, adolescent female icons, they will feel pressure to emphasize their own youthfulness.

Although women cannot reverse their age, they can affect something that is highly correlated with youth: body weight. This means that women will begin to assess themselves relative to their own thinness. Models in women's magazine are so thin as to be infertile because of the magazines' audience: women who are perceiving what they think men want (thinness) to the detriment of what they really want (fertility), although with breast augmentation this, too, is beginning to change.

The importance of thinness is also exacerbated by men's efforts to increase their own stature. "Women don't look for handsome men," Milan Kundera once mused, "they look for men with beautiful women."[41] There are numerous studies that show a man who is seen with a beautiful woman on his arm is generally rated as more intelligent, wealthy, and powerful than a man who is simply by himself.[42] Thus, in the sexual marketplace, men will seek "beautiful" (that is, thin) partners not simply for their appearance, but because their partners' beauty becomes a way of advertising their own social status. Think, for example, of "arm candy" (in other words, a young, beautiful woman on the arm of a powerful, distinguished man) and you get the point. This, in turn, also explains the greater pressure that educated, white women feel about their weight. When the sexual market sets the price of female beauty (and hence worth) at a marker of youthful thinness, then the pressure to maintain thinness among upper-class women, who are more driven to find high-status mates than lower-class women, becomes all that much greater.

In a class-conscious, economically developed society, a vicious cycle of thinning thus ensues: high-status women think they need to be thinner to attract a high-status man who wants a thin woman to demonstrate his higher status. From this perspective, the "tyranny of thinness" is not a conscious male effort to keep women disempowered but the by-product of sexual competition. Thinness becomes desirable as women gain greater economic and social equality, not because men are trying to keep them down, but because economic development expands the sexual marketplace whose currency is still minted in some deep, biological urges. This, in turn, produces beauty standards that differ dramatically by sex. For women seeking to attract a high-status mate, it means the distorted illusion of youth and fertility in an emaciated ideal; for men trying to attract more women, it means seeking the company of youthful and thin high-status females. This also creates different standards by race—for people of color whose social mobility and status are highly constrained by racism, there is less incentive to play the thinning game. Ironically, it is the very social and economic mobility of white women that makes thinness such a preoccupation.

Of course, this explanation too has its weaknesses. To begin with, trying to ascertain the biological basis of human behavior is a tricky business. Any attempt to read the evolutionary logic behind a social phenomenon can often seem like a post hoc rationalization because any cultural norm or pattern of behavior must be evolutionarily adaptive else it would not exist. Sociobiologists have a difficult time accounting for many human preferences and behaviors, such as homosexuality or altruism, which may be counterproductive to genetic survival. Consequently, evolutionary explanations for social phenomena always run the risk of being unprovable. This is particularly the case when one tries to read the genetic logic behind a complicated social phenomenon such as concepts of beauty or sexual attractiveness.

In addition, the sociobiological perspective does not allow for other factors such as politics or indigenous cultural practices to explain differences in human behavior. For example, this theory does not explain why so many men seek to lose weight (for that, see the discussion of Anglo-Protestant culture in the previous chapter). Human behavior is clearly influenced by instincts that evolved over time, but humans are also a self-transforming species capable of a wide range of self-constructed behaviors. Indeed, this capacity for self-creation is partly what defines us as human. Considering this, it remains unclear how much the "tyranny of thinness" is the result of these biological imperatives. Biology offers no systematic way to evaluate which human behavior or cultural norm makes more evolutionary sense than any other one.

Nevertheless, despite these caveats, I still think this is the most plausible explanation for why thinness is so demanded of middle- and upper-class white women in American society. And, ultimately, regardless of whether one subscribes to the feminist or the sociobiological explanation, the conclusion is still the same: white women in America bear the brunt of fat prejudice because of men's sexual prerogatives. The American cultural standard for what constitutes an attractive woman is determined primarily by what men find sexually appealing and what they think will heighten their social status. Whether it is driven by a Protestant cultural norm, a patriarchal imperative, or asymmetric reproductive impulses, size prejudice is the by-product of competition for status, power, and sexual attraction. From either perspective, attitudes about body weight and attitudes about sexuality are inexorably linked.

Sex and the Obesity Epidemic

Because American cultural attitudes about body weight are so intertwined with these sexual politics, any pronouncements about America's obesity epidemic will necessarily involve considerations that have nothing to do with health and a lot to do with the gender dynamics described above. In fact, it may be hard to disentangle them already. Consider, for example, the differences in how "overweight" gets defined. Women in the United States have, on average, a higher BMI (27.8) than men (26.8). This statistic is easily explained by the fact that women carry more fat on their bodies, a condition that is necessary given the particular demands of pregnancy and nursing. Yet, despite this fact, the official threshold of what is considered overweight or obese has always been lower for women than men. In the Metropolitan Life tables calculated by Louis Dublin in the 1950s, the "ideal" weight for women was nearly half a BMI point lower than for men, even though the data and methods used to make this calculation were flawed.[43] This was also evident when the 1998 NIH expert panel on obesity lowered the BMI threshold of what was considered overweight to a BMI of 25. Not only did this decision put millions more women into the "overweight" category than men, but it also employed the use of a statistic that is inherently biased against women. Today, the same BMI formula is applied to both men and women, despite the fact that, because men are taller on average, the formula automatically gives them a lower BMI. (BMI is a ratio of weight to height-squared, so the taller one is, the lower one's relative BMI will be.)

So even if one wanted to use BMI as an indicator of health (which is problematic), it would still be more appropriate to use different formulas for men and women. But, in most instances this is not done. For example, the 1998 NIH official report on obesity makes no mention of sex differences in using BMI to calculate a desirable weight, even though the relationship between weight and mortality is much different in women than in men (heavier women have far lower mortality rates than heavier men). Thus the very way the government defines "overweight" and "obese" is biased against women.

Not surprisingly, the American public shares this sexist view of what is "overweight." In research for this book, I conducted a series of experiments in which respondents in a national survey were shown a series of computer-altered illustrations of a man and woman at increasing body weights. In looking at the series of pictures, the respondents were to indicate at what point they thought the man or the woman in question was "overweight" and what point they thought each was "obese." The most striking finding is that women are identified as "overweight" and "obese" at body weight levels far below those of men. For instance, women are identified as "overweight" after only a 20 percent increase in the size of their figure; men do not get this label until their figure has increased by 35 percent. The same thing also happens with "obese": women get labeled as "obese" at size levels that are much lower than men.

These distorted body perceptions are also evident among women themselves. In a recent Roper poll, more than 70 percent of white American women reported that they would like to lose weight and, on average, these women say they would like to lose twenty-three pounds.[44] American white women are three times as likely as men to say that their weight is a problem and twice as likely to have gone on a diet in the past year.[45] It is almost a self-evident conclusion that a negative perception of body weight is a far bigger problem for white women in America than for men or women of color.

What is even more alarming is that the medical community is transmitting these distortions. In another national survey, I asked respondents if their doctor had either talked to them about their weight or

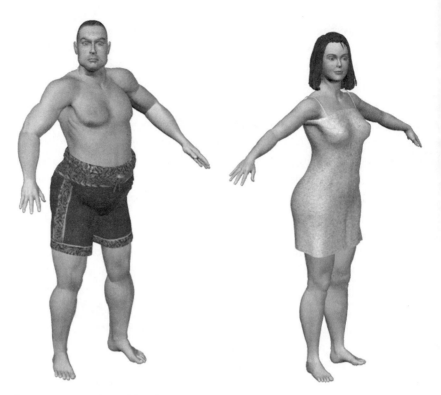

In a survey conducted by the author, eight hundred Americans were asked to pick out what they saw as "overweight" bodies from a series of computer-generated images of a man and a woman. These are the sizes that the majority of the sample considered overweight. Note the woman's depicted body weight is much smaller than the man's.

suggested they lose weight. Once again, dramatic differences existed between men and women: nearly 30 percent of women said their doctors had suggested that they needed to lose weight compared to only about 22 percent of men. An even more striking difference was among those who were in the official range of "overweight" (with a BMI between 25 and 29). Doctors had spoken about weight to more than 35 percent of the "overweight" women but to only 15 percent of the "overweight" men.[46] Of course, some might note that the differences in how doctors treat men and women only reflect the sex differences in weight. American women are, relative to their height, heavier than men and have gained more weight over the past two decades. (The average American woman is thirteen pounds heavier today than in 1970, the average American man only seven pounds heavier.) But these differences are not large enough to account for these different rates of treatment among doctors. After all, if anyone should be appreciative of women's biological need for more body fat, it should be doctors.

But perhaps nothing unmasks the fiction that obesity is an "epidemic disease" more than the fact that the overwhelming consumers of weight-loss products and diet plans are female. Consider the irony of this—although women generally have less disease and live longer than men, they are expected to be much thinner. In fact, by the same criterion that we currently label obesity as a "disease" (that is, its relationship to mortality), we could say maleness is a disease. After all, the average female life expectancy is seven years longer than for males and women have lower rates of many conditions such as heart disease. (This, of course, begs the question of whether there is an "epidemic" of maleness—something with which many feminists might agree.) Yet despite being healthier and living longer, women are far more preoccupied with their weights than men and women make up the overwhelming majority of gastric-bypass surgery patients and clients of programs such as Weight Watchers and Jenny Craig.

The sexist tinge to our weight concerns is also evident in many of these weight-loss programs. Consider, for example, the evangelical diet programs that are aimed specifically at women including Jan Christiansen's More of Him, Less of Me, Patricia Keml's Slim for Him and Gwen Shamblin's Weigh Down Diet. Shamblin, who has sold more than 1.5 million Weigh Down Diet books, advocates that women sublimate their hunger for food with a hunger for God. The diet plan, which calls for eating less and not snacking, is rooted in the concept that to overeat is to deny the abundance that God provides and to put one's own appetites above concern for God. But, if making her female readers feel guilty about their natural hunger isn't bad enough, Shamblin also condemns their fatness as a marker of shame. According to Shamblin, being overweight is God's way of "showing you he is jealous of you giving your emotions to food." Shamblin goes on. "Everday you are calling him ungenerous when you reach for more than he has given you." Then she tosses in an interesting sexual metaphor, "If you were married, but every night gave yourself to the man next door, it would hurt your relationship with your spouse. In all truth, you cannot love two masters: You can only love one and despise the other."[47] Shamblin gives her readers a choice: food or subservience to God (and husband). Eating becomes the equivalent of adultery.

Although these evangelical diet plans are based on guilt, they are also infused with a profound sexual anxiety. This is partly evident in their titles: "Slim for *Him*" or "More of *Him*, Less of Me" may refer to God but the sexist pun is undeniable. But, this is also evident in the diet plans themselves. Shamblin, for example, advocates submission not just to God but to one's husband; staying thin is important to please not only God but to keep one's husband from straying into sin. By Shamblin's reasoning, any woman who is not thin and made-up for her husband's sexual pleasure is, perversely, flouting God's will.[48] By dieting and getting "slim for him" the moralistic diet programs subsume women's appetites and their very metabolism to male sexual interest.

Of course, commercial diet plans are not alone in this coercion. Responsibility also lies with many of the same obesity researchers and public health advocates who are promoting the idea that obesity is an epidemic disease. A good example of this was at a recent meeting of the North American Association for the Study of Obesity. At a session that was reviewing the efficacy of diet drugs, Dr. George Bray, the dean of American obesity research, observed that the best target population for weight-loss drugs were people who were only slightly overweight. Why? Because weight-loss drugs only provide, on average, about a 10 percent weight loss. Bray noted, "For a 300 pound person, a 10 percent weight loss only gets them to 270 pounds, but for a 150 pound person, a 10 percent weight loss is significant."[49] But what Bray did not mention was that there are almost no 150-pound men who are trying to lose weight. Indeed, this group is almost entirely female and, at 150 pounds, is only trying to lose weight for cosmetic reasons. In short, the primary target of diet drug manufacturers and weight-loss companies, the people who are responsible for promoting the idea of obesity as a disease, is women. And, because women feel weight discrimination most acutely, they are also most likely to be concerned with their weight, be on a diet, and have unhealthy relationships with food and eating.

The experience of women offers a cautionary tale about our current campaign against obesity. For women, the war on fat is nothing new; American women have been battling their weight for more than a century now. The same messages that are being touted to the general public about the "problems of fat" have been directed at women for decades.

Yet, in the absence of a safe and effective mechanism for sustaining weight loss, the consequences of these efforts have been bleak. Despite all the punitive messages, not only have women continued to gain weight, but many have put their health in peril trying to achieve a mythical standard of an "ideal" body weight. These range from the health hazards of yo-yo dieting to the millions of women who suffer from anorexia and bulimia.

The dismal history of women and weight loss would suggest that before we go any further in trying to proclaim a problem with body weight, it is essential that we appreciate how such messages are likely to be interpreted. By repeating that fat is bad, unhealthy, and immoral, we are putting a great deal of pressure on Americans to focus primarily on their weight and to understand their weight as a barometer of their health and worth. Yet, given the fact that body weight is not a good indication of health and is a particularly difficult bodily trait to adjust, all we are doing is setting the public up to fail. As with the case of American women over the past several decades, admonishments about body weight are unlikely to curb the growth of obesity; they are only likely to generate a host of dysfunctional and destructive dieting behaviors as a result.

five

Fat Genes and the
Obesity Blame Game

In 2004, the U.S. House of Representatives passed a land-mark piece of legislation in response to America's obesity epidemic. The Personal Responsibility in Food Consumption Act (a.k.a., the Cheeseburger Bill) imposed explicit prohibitions on people suing restaurants and food makers for their obesity. The bill came in response to a series of lawsuits in 2000 against McDonald's and other fast-food restaurants; several heavy patrons sued them for making food that was fattening, addictive, and in extra large serving sizes.[1] Although the outcome of these cases is still unclear (after initially being dismissed by the courts, the cases have been reinstated on appeal), they were not without their effect. Not only did they prompt numerous state legislatures to pass similar "cheeseburger bills" but they also sparked a much larger, national debate on the central question behind America's obesity epidemic: who, exactly, is responsible for our growing weight?

The most popular answer to this question should come as no surprise: fat people themselves. According to a majority of the American public, the Bush administration, Republicans in Congress, conservative commentators, libertarians, and lobbying groups for the sugar, processed food, and restaurant industries, obesity is first and foremost a matter of individual responsibility.[2] If Americans are getting fat, they contend, it is largely the result of their own failure to make good choices. Indeed, this was the rationale behind the Cheeseburger Bill. According to Representative James Sensenbrenner, one of the bill's sponsors, the intent of this legislation is to say, "Look in the mirror because you are the one to blame."[3]

The appeal of this explanation is that is seems relatively straight-forward. To fight obesity, all we need to do is to get Americans to eat less and exercise more, a view that is also endorsed even by those who blame obesity on the food industry. For example, nutritionist and food industry critic Marion Nestle offers perhaps the only point many Republicans in Congress would support when she declares "to reverse the obesity epidemic, we must address fundamental causes. Overweight comes from consuming more food energy than is expended in activity."[4] Here, at least, seems one simple formula on which everyone can agree.

Except for one problem—it is not correct.

Although it is physically impossible to gain weight without taking in surplus calories, the simple calories-in/calories-out equation does not really explain why some people are heavy and some people are thin because it assumes that both factors are under our immediate control. Yet, for many people, their body weight seems to have a mind of its own, irrespective of how much they eat or exercise. Take me for example. Much like my father and grandfather, I'm the kind of person who never watches what he eats but has always been pretty thin. As a teenager, I was six feet tall and weighed 155 pounds and, until I was well into my twenties, I ate like a horse and never gained a pound. Conversely, my sister has always struggled with her weight and tends to be naturally heavy, something she shares with our mother and maternal grandmother. Regardless of what or how much they eat, some people just have a body that is naturally slender while others tend toward the other direction.

According to biologists, these differences are not the result of willpower, an appetite for fast-food, or watching too much television; instead, they are largely the consequence of our genes. The past two decades have witnessed a number of revolutionary discoveries about the genetic sources of body weight. Scientists have found that our genes not only determine our natural weight range, but they also determine our energy levels, feelings of hunger and satiation, and the ways our bodies absorb sugar and fat. We may gain weight by taking in more calories than we use, but the amount of calories in this equation varies largely in response to a preset genetic formula that is unique to each of us. Saying that we can control our weight is like saying that we can control our sleep habits or our disposition; in the short run we might be able to get by with less sleep or feign a cheery mood, but over the long haul we will inevitably revert to our natural tendencies.

These genetic discoveries have important implications for how we think of obesity as a health issue. Our current approach to the "problem of obesity" originates in an unrealistic set of assumptions about why we are gaining weight. All the policies, lawsuits, and arguments about who is responsible for someone's obesity are based on the simple calories-in/calories-out formula. They basically assume that we all use calories in the same way, that all calories' effects are similar, and, most important, that obesity is the origin of all our health problems.

When we look at the scientific evidence, we'll see that this whole approach to obesity is backward. Our body weight is not the cause of our ill health but merely the expression of metabolic processes that are meant to protect us in times of privation. In other words, our fatness is like our body hair or the shape of our ears—it is a natural part of our physicality that has a specific function. The real health problems that are associated with being heavy, including heart disease and diabetes, are not coming from our weight but from the same metabolic processes that determine our weight levels, such as our appetites and insulin levels. In our genes we can see the reality not only of why we are gaining weight, but what this weight gain really means.

The Case for Fat Genes

Most Americans do not place much faith in genetics as an excuse for being fat. Like the Republicans in Congress, most people think that body weight is first and foremost a matter of individual responsibility. In a recent survey, more than 65 percent of Americans agreed that the obese are heavy because they lack willpower.[5] Of course, most Americans realize that individual willpower is not solely to blame. In the same survey, 63 percent also agreed that obesity is caused by too much unhealthy food in restaurants and supermarkets. What few Americans do believe is that obesity is genetic: only 40 percent agree that obesity is something you inherit from your parents and only 18 percent agree that some obese people are simply "born that way."

Many public health experts share this view. According to the nutritionist James Hill "there is growing agreement among experts that the environment rather than biology is driving this epidemic."[6] The problem, Hill believes, is that genetics cannot explain the *changes* in our weights during past twenty years.[7] The American population has not undergone any radical genetic transformation since 1980 that would explain the tremendous increase in our weight. The human genetic makeup, varied and idiosyncratic as it may be in small ways, is generally the same as it was ten thousand years ago. If Americans are getting fatter, then surely it cannot be coming from genetic sources because our genes haven't radically changed in the past twenty years.

Many biologists, however, disagree. Instead, they argue that body weight is a highly complex phenomenon that is largely predetermined by one's genetic codes.[8] Americans did not start getting heavier because their genes suddenly changed but because their genes were doing the same thing that they have always done—protecting us from famine. Only now, this function is no longer suited for the type of world we have created.

Consider, for example, the statistics on America's weight gain. When talking about the rise in our weights, many public health experts like to cite the dramatically increasing number of obese Americans. For instance, between 1980 and 1994, the number of obese Americans increased by 55 percent.[9] While this seems like a large increase in obesity, it does not really reflect the amount of weight most Americans were gaining. Most Americans did not increase their weight by 55 percent; Americans gained, on average, only about seven to nine pounds, depending on their height. Thus, even as obesity rates were dramatically rising, most Americans were not gaining large amounts of weight.

The bigger problem with the statistics on obesity is that they mask an enormous variety in the weight of the population. Although the average American BMI has been rising over the past few decades, there is still tremendous variation across the population—some people gained lots of weight and some gained nothing at all. In fact, if you take a random selection of Americans of the same age and height, you will find that their weights differ by hundreds of pounds. Just as Americans demonstrate incredible variation by height, hair and skin tone, eye color, facial features, and nearly every other physical characteristic, so they exhibit tremendous variation in their weights.

These cross-sectional differences make the small increases in our average weight seem quite puny. And this dramatic fluctuation suggests that our body weights are highly individualistic and determined by something unique to each of us.

But if you really want to see proof of the genetic sources of weight, the best place to look is not in the national statistics but at a small group of Native Americans living in the Gila River Basin of southern Arizona, the Pima Indians. This tribe has the dubious distinction of being among the fattest people in the world. Nearly the entire adult population of Pima Indians is overweight and more than 75 percent are technically obese (a BMI over 30), a rate more than twice as high as the American population. The *average* Pima man weighs around 220 pounds, while the average Pima woman weighs in at about 200 pounds.[10] On the Pima reservation, a three-hundred-pound person is not an uncommon sight.

At first glance, it may seem that the Pima Indians' weight comes from the same factors now currently being blamed for America's obesity epidemic: a diet high in fat and sugar and a sedentary daily life. Prior to the 1940s, the Pima Indians tended to be lean and muscular, the consequence of a physically demanding agrarian life and a high-fiber, low-fat diet. With time, however, the Pima Indians adopted a more contemporary and mainstream American way of living. They started farming less, consuming more sugars and animal fats, and began working at more sedentary jobs. And, like many Americans, their weights began to rise.[11] While this lifestyle might have added a few pounds to an average American, it added scores of pounds to the average Pima.[12]

In the Pima Indians, many biologists see what they think is the true explanation for obesity: the *interaction* between our environment and our genes. Like other physical characteristics, such as height, body weight is largely predetermined by a genetic code—just as some people are born to be short and others born to be tall, some are born to be plump and others thin. But the environment matters, too. For example, even though our height is genetically determined, Americans have, on average, gotten much taller over the past century, a result of their better nutrition. The same holds with our body weight. Genes do not necessarily make people fat but they do make certain people more predisposed to being heavy if environmental conditions are correct. In the case of the Pima Indians, their genes give them an extremely high propensity for gaining weight. Although such genes were highly advantageous during the periodic famines that probably occurred throughout their history, when their food supply became much more fatty and sugary in the 1950s, the Pima Indians respond by adding high levels of body fat.

And, what is true for the Pima Indians is also true for much of the American public—our weight comes from the interaction of our genes and our environment. Scientists estimate that anywhere from 30 to 70 percent of our current body weight is attributable to genetic sources depending on one's environmental conditions. Indeed, for a small group of extremely obese people with leptin deficiencies genes are *the* primary force behind their extremely high weight ranges.[13]

But, herein lies the problem. Our weights may be written in our genes, but as far as obesity is concerned, it is written in a language far too complex for us to understand. This is because body weight is the classic example of what scientists call a polygenic trait, that is, a physical characteristic that comes from many different genetic sources. While some physical traits, such as eye color, are the result of a single gene, body weight and metabolism are the consequence of many genes, working in combination. In fact, there are more than seventy different gene locations that have been linked to differences in body weight.[14] Moreover, outside of a small percentage of people with specific genetic disorders, the particular combination of these seventy gene sets may actually be more important for shaping weight than any one particular gene set alone. This means that there are literally thousands of possible genetic formulas that influence our weight. While the media often reports discoveries of a "fat" gene, this is far from the case—what they should report is the discovery of one of many possible fat genes.

Now if all we cared about was whether we are disposed to gaining weight, the story might end here. But an interesting thing happens once you start examining all these different genetic sources of our weight—you begin to realize that weight itself is an expression of some much more fundamental metabolic processes. In other words, the most important thing about our genes is not *whether* they predispose us to getting fat (for some of us they do more than others), bur rather *why* our genes predispose us to getting fat. And by looking at this question we can discover the real culprits behind many of our current health woes. The same genetically determined factors that shape our weight (metabolism, appetite, and insulin resistance) are behind many of the diseases that are currently being blamed on our obesity. Once we consider the functions of our appetites and metabolism, we can see the problem with conflating issues of fatness with issues of health; it misses the fundamental processes that are at work. To better understand this claim, let us take a closer look at the ways our genes affect both our weight and our health.

Homeostasis and the
Set-Point Theory of Weight

When I was working on my doctorate in the early 1990s, I shared a large rambling house with six other graduate students. Funds being tight for all of us, we worked out a deal where we would pool our money, buy groceries in common, and share our meals. This generally worked out fine except for the occasional arguments about whether some people were eating more than their share. In the name of household peace (and being overinquisitive social scientists), we decided once to keep track of how much everyone ate. Much to our surprise, the biggest eater in the house was not any of the men or even the largest women. The biggest eater was the smallest of us—a very skinny, ninety-pound woman. Although small in stature, this woman was a gastronomical powerhouse. Despite being nearly half my size, she could eat me under the table. The difference, it turned out, was not in our stature but in our metabolism. While I was constantly lazing about, she was continually engaged with one task or another. Even while reading a book or watching television, she would persistently fidget. The incongruity between her voracious appetite and her tiny figure came largely from an intense metabolism that never seemed to let up. All the food that she was putting away was getting burned off in her continual whirlwind of motion.

I mention my old roommate because she typifies, in an extreme, one of the most important genetic factors behind our weight—the speed in which we utilize calories, that is, our metabolism. Our metabolic rate regulates how many calories our bodies use right away versus how many get stored in fat cells for the future. People with a "high" metabolism tend to be quite frenetic and burn off most of the calories they consume, while people with a lower body metabolism tend to be physically less active, exert less energy in a resting state, and store more of their calories as body fat. Of course, this information is not exactly new—people have been categorized by their metabolism for centuries. Galen, the second-century physician, grouped people by the four humors of sanguine, choleric, melancholic, and phlegmatic. These were not just descriptions of personality but also about how a person burned energy.[15] Today, we do the same thing, often describing people as "mellow" or "hyper," terms that make reference to their energy states.

In scientific parlance, these energy states are known as homeostasis: the point of balance between our weight and energy expenditure. According to the "set-point" theory of homeostasis, each of us maintains a particular but steady balance between our weight and our energy usage. Over the past half century, scientists have conducted numerous experiments probing this relationship and the cumulative evidence suggests that the human body fiercely defends itself relative to a particular weight range—if the body rises or falls below this range, it changes its metabolism to get back.[16] In other words, when a person's body weight rises above his unique set point, his metabolism speeds up and excess calories are burned off; when his body weights fall below this set point, his metabolism slows down and more calories are retained.

Perhaps the most famous demonstration of the set-point theory has come from Rockefeller University scientist Rudolph Leibel. In several experiments, Leibel closely monitored the metabolic rates of research subjects who were on severely restricted diets and exercise regimes. After months of constant observation (the research subjects lived basically like prisoners at the labs), Leibel found that the energy expenditures of the subjects varied greatly with their diets. When subjects were given more food, their metabolic rates dramatically increased—they tended to be more fidgety and burn more calories even when resting; conversely, when they were given a more restricted diet, their energy levels dropped, they acted more tranquil, and their metabolisms fell.[17] In a more recent study, researchers at the Mayo Clinic, using special underwear that recorded the posture and movement of subjects, found that obese people tended to be less physically active in the course of a normal day and generally burned around 350 fewer calories than lean people.[18] This was not because their fat made them sluggish (even after losing weight the obese subjects remained less active) but because they had a natural tendency toward languor. The evidence suggests, therefore, that how much you weigh is partly a function of how you burn energy—people who are frenetic tend to be leaner, people who are tranquil tend to be heavier.

The interesting thing about this homeostasis is not simply that our bodies are continually steered toward a particular weight range, but that this range seems to be largely hereditary. In the early 1970s, Douglas Coleman, a biochemist at Jackson Laboratories, first discovered that mice with a genetic mutation that made them obese had much different weight ranges than mice without the genetic mutations.[19] Later research found this occurring in humans as well. Studies of identical twins who were overfed for three months showed that the twins were far more similar to each other in the amount of weight they gained than to nonrelatives on the same diet.[20] Studies of the Pima Indians indicate that metabolic rates among family members were much more similar to each other than among the tribe as a whole.[21] In other words, your weight range is basically something you inherit from your parents. Some people are born with a high weight range (and are thus heavy) while others accede to a low one (and are thus thin).

The set point of our weight also explains why most people have little long-term success with diets—many people are trying to reduce their weight below the point to which their bodies are naturally inclined. It is an oft-stated fact that of the 60 million Americans dieting in any given year, only a very small percentage are able to keep their weight off for any period of time.[22] The problem for many dieters is that when they start losing weight, their bodies lower their metabolic rates and they begin to slow down, feel tired and hungry, and retain more water. To maintain a weight below one's set point requires constant monitoring of diet and continual exercise, which becomes increasingly difficult in a body that is both more hungry and tired as a result of weighing too little. In short, the set-point theory of weight suggests that substantial and sustained weight loss is going to be nearly impossible for anyone with a high weight range.

But, you are undoubtedly thinking to yourself, "if the set-point theory explains why Americans have such a hard time losing weight, then wouldn't it also say that Americans should not be *gaining* weight?" Indeed, this suspicion is well founded. According to biologists, our bodies are supposed to resist inordinate weight gain just as they resist inordinate weight loss. For example, in another famous study, Dr. Ethan Sims of the University of Vermont wondered how long it would take a group of men to gain 25 percent of their body weight. Using inmates from a nearby state prison, he conducted a simple experiment. The inmates were fed four large meals a day and relieved of any exercise. He found that it took the average subject nearly five months to increase his weight by a quarter and many could not even do this; in fact, many dropped out of the experiment because they were sick of eating so much. And, once the experiment stopped, almost all the subjects returned to their previous weights without dieting.[23] From Liebel's and Sims's experiments, it would appear that we resist weight gain nearly as much as we resist weight loss.

So why then are Americans getting fatter? In light of the set-point theory, three possible explanations have been offered. The first is that Americans have gotten heavier because they are getting older. With the aging of the baby boom, the age of the average American has increased dramatically over the past several decades. In 1970, the median age in America was only twenty-seven (in other words, there were as many Americans under twenty-seven as over twenty-seven); today, the median age is thirty-six and rising.[24] This aging may affect our cumulative weight in two ways. First, as we age we add more fat cells, thus giving us more bodily receptacles in which to store our excess calories.[25] This is why older people tend to be heavier, on average. Second, our set point of weight also increases with age. It is not merely one's imagination that it is easier to gain weight as one gets older. Our bodies tend to gravitate toward a heavier set point of weight, particularly once we reach our late thirties.[26] This means that middle-aged Americans will tend to get heavier and have an even harder time sustaining weight loss. Unfortunately, the data do not support this hypothesis—Americans of all ages have been gaining slight amounts of weight.[27] So the aging explanation is not sufficient.

A second theory is that America's increasing weight actually reflects the real set point of our weight.[28] Like the Pima Indians, our ancestors who survived the ice ages and food shortages over the past 100,000 years were the ones whose bodies could endure these changes in calories, that is, they could store excess calories whenever they were available.[29] Until a few decades ago, most Americans engaged in a lot of physical activity during the course of their day and were limited in the amount of calories they consumed between meals. This type of lifestyle might have meant that people were keeping weights that were below their bodies' natural program. With the removal of many physically demanding activities and the increased availability of calories, many people's bodies may simply be following a genetic program that is storing as many calories as possible in anticipation of the next famine. In other words, it may not be that our modern sedentary life and high-calorie diet are making us fat as much as an earlier lifestyle of limited calories and lots of exertion was keeping us thin. Yet, once again, this is largely speculative and given how sluggish and tired people are when they keep their weights low, it seems somewhat implausible.

I think the real answer to this mystery can be found in the statistics on who is gaining weight. Although the average rates of obesity have been on the rise, this growth has not been evenly distributed across the population—some people are getting far heavier than others. Indeed, when one looks at who has gained the most weight, it is those who were already heavy. Over the past twenty years, the rates of people who are "morbidly obese" (with a BMI of greater than 40) has quadrupled from 0.5 percent to 2 percent of all Americans, an increase that was twice as great as that for ordinary obesity.[30] The fact that most of America's weight gain has occurred among people who were heaviest to begin with suggests that obesity is rising mostly for those who are biologically susceptible to being fat.

If the "set-point" theory of weight is correct (and there is good reason to believe it is) then obesity is not simply a matter of individual choice. We do not choose our metabolic set point; we inherit it. My old roommate could never gain weight because anything she ate was quickly burned off, a condition she had had since she was a child. Conversely, for many heavy people, keeping a low body weight is tantamount to living in a state of never-ending hunger, fatigue, and listlessness. Under such biological pressure, it is extremely hard to sustain thinness. Many of us are simply programmed to be heavy and some, like the Pima Indians, are programmed to store as many calories as they can.

The set-point theory also shows that obesity is not simply a matter of a "toxic environment" either. Because people burn calories at different rates, one cannot say that the practices of the food industry are universally making us heavy; rather, they promote weight gain for those people who are susceptible to caloric retention. A large percentage of Americans have not gained any weight over the past two decades despite living amidst fast-food, suburbs, and superhighways. The people who are gaining the most weight are doing so because their set points are very high and their weight ranges are broad. This presents a problem for health advocates who want to impose uniform restrictions of the production or advertising of food products. A snack tax, for instance, would mean that some people would have pay more for what they eat even though they are at no risk for becoming obese. Unlike restrictions on tobacco, which only affect smokers, punitive restrictions on food would affect everyone, and this is not fair.

The science on genes and metabolism reveals the problem with making thinness a goal for the entire population, much less making obesity a scapegoat for our social and health woes. Some people are simply not going to be thin, no matter how much effort they spend dieting and exercising, just as some people are not going to be fat no matter how much they eat. This fact dooms almost any policy that makes body weight its central focus—not only are we expecting a significant portion of the population to struggle against their own biology, but we are often trying to do so in a way that punishes the rest. These problems are only compounded when we consider the second way that genes affect our weights—our appetites.

Feeling Full

In the early 1990s, the geneticist Jeffrey Friedman discovered the biological equivalent of El Dorado—Voltaire's famous lost city of gold. For decades, biologists had long known that mice with a certain *ob* gene were far more likely to be obese than mice without the gene. Not only were the obese mice less active, but they would feed constantly as if they were starving. What no one could figure out though was why. This was a seen as a crucial question because if you could unlock the genetic secrets behind appetite, many believed, you could also develop pharmaceutical remedies for people who suffered from weight problems. For example, if a man had a homeostatic weight range of, say, 250 pounds, the only way he could be thin was if he could moderate his hunger, which would usually be voracious if his weight went below this threshold. In our appetites, many believe, are the keys to this world of thinness.

After years on such a quest, Friedman found the missing link; the obese mice were not producing a hormone called leptin. Leptin is one of the crucial ways the body communicates to the brain about its energy-input needs. As a body adds fat tissue, it produces more leptin, which signals to the brain to eat less; as a body gets thinner, it produces less leptin, which the brain takes as a cue to seek more calories, thus triggering feelings of hunger.[31] Friedman believes that leptin is one of the central mechanisms our bodies use to regulate and maintain our weight. For example, in some extremely heavy people, researchers have found genetic mutations that reduce their leptin production. Whereas a normal person produces a lot of leptin, which then regulates hunger and metabolism levels, many severely obese people do not. Without this leptin, life is a state of constant hunger.[32]

The discovery of leptin had many important consequences for the science of obesity. First, it demonstrated another way that our genes shape our weights. By revealing the connection between genes and appetite, Friedman also showed that feelings of hunger and the ability to control those cravings are not simply a matter of willpower; they are a matter of heredity. People with leptin deficiencies experience life as a state of perpetual starvation—every waking moment brings an urgent desire to eat. Asking someone in this state to exercise "self-control" is like asking someone who has been awake for three days not to sleep; the physical desire is simply so great that it wears down any capacity for rational autonomy.

Second, leptin may also explain why Americans started gaining more weight. According to Friedman, over time, our bodies may become less responsive to leptin signals as the amount of leptin in our bloodstream increases and the leptin sensors in the brain become less sensitive.[33] Since bodies with more fat produce more leptin, a heavy population might also be a more leptin-insensitive population. A reinforcing cycle may occur between weight and leptin sensitivity—our increasing weight might be making us less sensitive to the signaling cues that we are full and thus prompting us to overeat and gain more weight, which, in turn, makes us even less sensitive to our leptin signals.[34] This could also explain why our set points are rising as we get heavier.

But the most important implication of Friedman's discovery was that it seemed to open the door for a brand new way of "treating" obesity. In the decade since Friedman's breakthrough, researchers have discovered numerous other body chemicals that regulate our weight and appetite. It is now clear that our body has several types of hormones and peptides that continually send information to the arcuate nucleus in the brain, the master control center of our appetite and metabolic rates. This part of our brain is responsive to both short-term and long-term cues about our bodies' energy needs. For example, a hormone that is produced in the stomach called ghrelin varies considerably according to the time of day: our ghrelin levels tend to be higher when we awaken and around meal times, which trigger sensations of hunger.[35] In short, Friedman's discovery has shown that just as our weights may have natural ranges, so, too, our appetites and feelings of hunger may be naturally determined. Some people may be biologically hard-wired to be always hungry or "big eaters" while others may feel contented after only a few mouthfuls of food.

Following Friedman's discovery, many scientists and pharmaceutical companies began focusing on developing appetite controls as a means of solving the obesity "problem" in America. Rather than trying to eradicate obesity through some difficult change in our environment or by making fat people suffer through a perpetual state of hunger and dissatisfaction, a more effective method could be to eliminate those feelings of hunger that make us eat so much in the first place. If we could take a pill, shot, or nasal spray that eradicated our appetites, the thinking goes, we would be unlikely to gorge on the snacks, fast-food, and sodas that are putatively making us so fat. Indeed, the media hoopla that generally accompanies the latest magic pill to "cure" obesity (such as Rimonabant) is inevitably based on the idea of eliminating our hunger cravings and addictive food behaviors.[36]

Like so many other aspects of obesity, however, this, too, is an illusion. Appetite-suppressing wonder drugs are unlikely to solve the "problem" of our weight; in fact, all they seem to do is worsen our health problems because of what they are forced to do—tamper with our body's core system for survival. To understand this, let us go back to Friedman's discovery. Soon after he discovered the link between obesity and the leptin hormone, newspapers proclaimed that the cause of obesity had been revealed and that a scientific "cure" was on the way. Amgen pharmaceutical paid Friedman and his associates more than 20 million dollars for the patent rights in the hope that millions of people would be lining up for leptin treatments to control their appetite and weights. Leptin, however, proved to be a disappointment. As with so many scientific discoveries, what researchers found with laboratory mice was far different from what worked for humans in the world.

Although leptin treatments were effective for a fraction of the obese population, it turned out that many overweight people already had high levels of leptin in their blood and their brains did not respond to leptin injections. Treating obesity was a much more complicated issue than simply increasing leptin in the bloodstream.[37]

Nevertheless, the allure of thinness and the market potential for a weight-loss pill has inspired scores of other researchers and drug companies to focus on other biological regulators of our appetites. Not only have most of these appetite-suppressing drugs been disappointments, but many have also caused significant health problems. The most notorious example of this was fen-phen. In the early 1990s, a widely publicized research study showed dramatic weight-loss results when two existing but little-used drugs, Pondimin (fenfluramine) and Phentermine, were taken together as appetite suppressants. Although the drugs were never approved by the Food and Drug Administration to be taken in conjunction or for long use, doctors and American Home Products, the company that produced Pondimin and other drugs, actively promoted their consumption. In just a few years, fen-phen use soared and by 1996 more than six million Americans were taking it or Redux (a similar drug) to lose weight. But soon, many patients were reporting a number of unwanted side effects and in 1997, researchers at the Mayo Clinic discovered that fen-phen caused heart valve damage and other pulmonary problems in a high percentage of users. Although American Home Products removed Redux and Pondimin from the market, the move came too late. Hundreds, and possibly thousands, of people had done irreparable damage to their hearts and pulmonary systems by taking the drugs.

Looking to fill this market hole that came with the withdrawal of fen-phen, Abbot Laboratories released Meridia (also called Sibutramine) which is currently the only major prescription medication approved as an appetite suppressant.[38] Although Meridia surged in popularity in the late 1990s, since this time its use has declined. This is at least in part because it has been associated with high blood pressure and other cardiovascular problems. It is also currently subject to a class-action lawsuit and Abbot is under investigation by the Food and Drug Administration for not reporting numerous Meridia-related deaths. Beyond its potential dangers, the other problem with Meridia is that it has not been very effective—few people taking Meridia have been able to sustain anything more than a few pounds of weight loss after two years.[39]

The difficulty in finding pharmaceutical mechanisms to control our appetite comes from what the medications are trying to do. Appetite is part of the body's core system for sustaining its own existence. Without a regular and dependable supply of energy, our bodies quickly begin to malfunction. Because it is so crucial for our survival, our bodies have developed numerous, overlapping mechanisms for the body to communicate to the brain its various energy needs. If one of these mechanisms should fail, then there are numerous other safeguards in place to ensure that we continue to acquire and store the energy necessary to keep us alive. The difficulty in controlling our appetites comes not only from the complexity of our metabolic system but also from its redundancy.

Consequently, if you are going to suppress this powerful survival mechanism, you are going to need very strong medications, which also means you are likely to generate a host of other physical consequences. For example, many appetite suppressants act on neurotransmitters in the brain, neurotransmitters that also control many other body processes. Thus, not only are there several appetite "switches" that must be turned on and off, but many of these switches also regulate other core aspects of our bodies. Not surprisingly, when you begin to tinker with these brain systems, you often end up with numerous side effects ranging from hair loss, eye irritation, or skin problems to heart failure and suicidal depression.

The complicated interrelationship between our appetites, drugs, and health reveals, once again, the flaws in our current strategy of focusing on weight as a means to health. As I've noted throughout this book, all the warnings about our growing weight are based on the hazards that our weight is supposed to have for our health and well-being. Doctors, government health officials, and nutritionists continue to make our fatness the centerpiece of their campaign for getting us to be healthier. Yet, not only are many of our bodies naturally resistant to weight loss, but the most promising pharmaceutical remedies for weight loss may actually cause more health problems than the weight itself. The focus on a "magic pill" is indicative of our generally misguided approach in which we are prioritizing weight as the primary (original) cause of our health ills, when, in fact, weight may be much farther out along the causal chain between diet, genes, and health than we realize. To better understand this point, let us turn to the third way that our genes affect our weight, insulin.

Are All Calories Created Equal?

A calorie is a calorie is a calorie. That is, if you believe most of America's obesity experts, Americans are getting fatter because they eat more calories than they burn off. Obesity researcher James Hill calls this the energy gap and estimates that it could be as low as one hundred calories per day. No difference is really seen between these calories—in Hill's eyes they are all the same. According to his calculations, if Americans could only close this energy gap, by exercising a little more or eating a little less, then the obesity would stop increasing.[40] Since dieting is so hard and ineffective, Hill suggests getting people to exercise more. His group, America on the Move, has as its goal to get Americans to take two thousand more steps a day.

Despite their good intentions and the health benefits of exercise, such efforts are unlikely to do much for our weight. And the reason is because their fundamental premise is flawed. To begin with, Hill assumes that caloric intake has no effect on metabolism. Yet, as we saw above, if you start consuming fewer calories, your metabolism will slow down and make it harder to lose weight.

But, even more problematic is the fact that all calories may not be created equal. A hundred extra calories may have a different effect on our weight and health depending on where they come from: in other words, a hundred calories from a candy bar, Wonder bread, or a Mountain Dew is a far cry from a hundred calories from brown rice, red beans, and broccoli. Although there are numerous diet theories that focus on the effects of particular types of foods on weight, the evidence is not yet clear about how they might work. We do not know for certain whether extra calories from fat have a different, long-term effect on our weight and health than extra calories from carbohydrates. There is good evidence, for example, that calories from trans fats (such as hydrogenated oils) increase problems associated with heart disease. Similarly, there is also a growing body of evidence that calories from refined carbohydrates may have a particular effect on our weight and health, largely because of how they affect a central component in our metabolism: our insulin levels.

Over the past decade, there has been a lot of attention in the medical and scientific communities to the way our bodies deal with the sugars that are released by carbohydrates, what is referred to as our glycemic index. Certain types of foods have high "glycemic loads," that is, they have the types of carbohydrates, such as refined wheat and sugar, that are easily turned into glucose, which causes blood sugar to spike. When blood sugar rises, so do insulin levels in the blood. Insulin is used to transport the glucose to cells and give our bodies the energy they need. For example, when you eat foods with a high glycemic load, you may experience a spike in energy and alertness, commonly known as a sugar rush. The problem with such foods, of course, is that this sugar rush is quickly followed by a sharp drop in blood sugar, which lowers energy and increases hunger, thus prompting people to look for another high glycemic "fix." A diet high in refined carbohydrates ostensibly makes us sugar junkies and, over time, may contribute to our insulin resistance, that is, when our body tissues become less responsive to absorbing glucose and require more insulin to get the energy they need. Insulin resistance then forces the pancreas to work harder producing more insulin, which can exhaust it and lead to type 2 diabetes.[41]

According to Dr. Gerald Reavan of Stanford University, insulin resistance may be *the* most important metabolic factor relating to weight, diet, and health and there's good evidence to believe he is right.[42] When people are more insulin resistant, their pancreases secrete not just more insulin but also higher levels of triglyceride (the fat modules that are carried in the blood) and lower levels of HDL or "good" cholesterol. This, in turn, can lead to numerous health complications. For example, people who are insulin resistant are 50 percent more likely to develop heart disease than those who are not. Insulin resistance, according to Reavan, is the key factor in both keeping our energy in balance and in reducing our susceptibility to metabolic syndrome and host of health complications that arise from this.

Once again, here is where our genes come into play. The evidence suggests that our susceptibility to insulin resistance is largely determined by heredity. In fact, some researchers have estimated our genes determine as much as half of our insulin resistance.[43] The genetic tendency for insulin resistance is particularly strong among people whose forebears came from regions with few grains such as the Americas and Africa, which partly explains the higher rates of type 2 diabetes among

Native and African Americans. Reavan notes, "the results of these studies of individuals, families, and large population groups all suggested that genes play a major role in the development of insulin resistance, and that people of non-European ancestry are more likely to have the offending genes."[44]

But if insulin resistance is really something we inherit, then our current understanding of the relationship between our weight, diet, and health is misplaced. Right now we typically think of obesity as a primary cause of insulin resistance. According to the NIH and surgeon general's reports as well as most popular medical authors, obesity is a major risk factor for nearly every metabolically related disease. For instance, it is a well-established fact that as one's BMI rises above 25, the incidence of insulin resistance and type 2 diabetes steadily increases.[45] Because of this fact, it is common to think that being too heavy either causes or exacerbates the problems of insulin resistance. This is why the surgeon general and numerous other health professionals worry so much about our caloric imbalance—the way to prevent diabetes, heart disease, and any other metabolic condition is to lose weight.

This view, however, is based only on the *association* between obesity and insulin resistance. No one has demonstrated that obesity *causes* insulin resistance.[46] All we really know is that insulin resistance is simply more prevalent among people who are heavier. In fact, we just may have the whole causal relationship backward—rather than obesity causing insulin resistance, it might be that insulin resistance is causing obesity. There are a number of plausible reasons for why the causal arrow may run in this direction.

First, by itself, insulin resistance contributes to weight gain. This is because of what insulin does. When our bodies take in food, our insulin levels rise to handle the increased energy. Part of the insulin's function is to move the glucose into tissues for immediate usage, but insulin also transfers the extra glucose into fat cells for storage. If our bodies become insulin resistant, they need more insulin in the bloodstream to get the necessary energy to our cells; with more insulin in our system, our bodies become even more insulin resistant and an upward spiral of insulin resistance ensues. But it is not just our muscle or other tissue that is getting more energy from all this extra insulin; our fat cells are also getting more glucose. This is why weight gain is one of the most common complaints among diabetics receiving insulin treatments—

when they inject the extra insulin into their bloodstream, they increase the amount of energy being stored as fat.[47]

Moreover, from an evolutionary perspective, it makes sense to think that insulin resistance promotes weight gain as a way of protecting the body against future famine. In many parts of the world, such as the arid Southwest where the Pima Indians live, humans have endured prolonged periods of drought and famine. The people who survived in such a precarious food environment were those whose bodies must have been naturally calibrated to store as many calories as possible in fat cells. They developed what the geneticist James Neel calls the thrifty gene.[48] According to Neel, this explains the evolutionary logic of such conditions as diabetes. Among groups like the Pima, one of the best ways their bodies could store calories was by minimizing the amount of blood sugars that were immediately absorbed as energy, in other words, by increasing insulin resistance. This is partly why the Pima Indians have such high rates of diabetes—their bodies use insulin resistance to resist absorbing blood sugars immediately and to promote saving calories for the next famine. For the Pima, insulin resistance is an evolutionarily adaptive trait.

Finally, if obesity was a causal factor behind insulin resistance, then we would expect to find uniform levels of insulin resistance at different points along the weight scale. Yet, we do not. Just as there are millions of obese people who are not insulin resistant, there are millions of thin people who are. Even more revealing is the fact that weight loss, particularly if it is achieved without exercise, does not reduce insulin resistance and, in some cases, may exacerbate its effects. In fact, trying to lose weight may be one of the worst things you can do for metabolic syndrome—people who go on diets to lose weight typically have higher rates of heart disease, type 2 diabetes, and hypertension than people who have never dieted.[49] If obesity causes insulin resistance, we would expect to see uniform benefits from weight loss, but these do not occur.

As with the discoveries regarding homeostasis and leptin, the research on insulin resistance should totally change the way we think of our weight as a health problem. If insulin resistance is the fountainhead of our metabolic illnesses, then, rather than emphasizing weight loss as a means to combat heart disease, diabetes, and other metabolic syndromes, we need to focus on the factors that directly affect our blood sugar, such as how much we exercise and what we eat. We know, for example, that people who exercise more, irrespective of their body weight, are less prone to insulin resistance.[50] This is because the regular usage of muscles seems to facilitate the transference of sugars from the bloodstream. Similarly, we also know that the refined carbohydrates so prevalent in many snack foods and sodas also cause our insulin levels to shoot up in the short run.[51] Over time, such elevated insulin levels may reduce our insulin sensitivity and contribute to the formation of many diseases. The key to our health is not in simply reducing our calories in order to be thin, but in reducing those calories that inflate our insulin levels.

Genes and the Obesity Epidemic

Too often, we tend to think of obesity as the first link in a causal chain of disease—obese people have health problems because they are fat. Yet, as we've seen, the causal relationship between our metabolism, weight, and health is far more complicated than this. In fact, there is strong evidence that our appetites and metabolism are the first links in the causal chain. After all, these are the factors that determine our weight and, by themselves, determine our susceptibility to many diseases. If we want to be healthy, we need to stop worrying about how much we weigh and instead turn our attention to how our diet and exercise patterns influence the way our bodies function. Our weight is largely tangential to the more crucial relationship between our biology and our way of living.

Which leads us to the problems with our current approach to obesity. One of the greatest illusions of America's obesity epidemic is that anyone can be thin if they want to—all they need to do is eat fewer calories and exercise more. Like any myth, this statement has a grain of truth. For most people, restricting calories will result in short-term weight loss. But this grain does not a mountain make. The problem is that few people can keep this weight off and that weight loss, by itself, doesn't necessarily make someone healthier. As we've seen, our bodies are designed to stay within a certain weight range and have numerous mechanisms for keeping us there. Our attempts to "fix" these mechanisms with appetite suppressants have not only been unsuccessful, but in fact, over the past fifty years such appetite suppressants have arguably caused much more harm than good. By putting forward a simplistic formula about how to be healthy, we are encouraging people to think that health and wellness are equivalent to being thin. They are not.

Rather than try to fight our biology and suppress its very functions, it would be far better to listen to what our increasing weight may be telling us. Fatness is not a disease or a bodily dysfunction; it is a protective mechanism that evolved to survive fluctuations in our food supply. Judging someone's health by how much they weigh is like judging a camel by how much water it has in its hump—in conditions of privation, our extra weight, just like the water, may be exactly what we need to survive. Our weight is merely an expression of this adaptive mechanism at work. The problem arises from the interaction between these adaptive mechanisms and our current environment. In other words, we are suddenly like camels who find themselves living in a rain forest— we are in a situation for which we are ill adapted. If you continually flood the body with refined carbohydrates, the same biological mechanisms that safeguard it in times of want (such as insulin resistance) are going to slip into dysfunction. So the real question we should be asking is not why are we gaining so much weight, but why are we eating so many refined carbohydrates and exercising so little? In the next two chapters, when these questions are addressed, we'll see that the real source of our metabolic problems is not our fatness, but something more fundamental to our very way of life—the free market and the virtually unlimited array of choices it offers.

six

Food and Weight Gain:
Super Sized Misperceptions

One of the surprise movie hits of 2004 was a low-budget documentary, *Super Size Me,* in which the director, Morgan Spurlock, recorded what happened when he ate nothing but McDonald's fast-food, three times a day, for a month. Within two weeks of starting his McDonald's diet, Spurlock's health started to decline—his cholesterol and blood pressure shot up and his doctor started to worry if he was doing long-term damage to his liver. In addition, Spurlock seemed to have a negative psychological reaction to his new diet—he became moody, depressed, and agitated. Like any addict, Spurlock's moods elevated and crashed between each McDonald's "fix." And, most important from the film's perspective, he gained twenty-six pounds. The film offers Spurlock's own personal degeneration as a metaphor for America's obesity epidemic—Spurlock went from a model of health and fitness to an overweight lout, due in large part to the nefarious efforts of McDonald's to super size his value meals.

Audiences ate it up. The film, which went on to become one of the highest grossing documentaries of all time, seemed to strike a nerve in the popular consciousness. Many Americans are growing increasingly suspicious that the foods we are eating are making us fat. Many, including Spurlock, lay the blame squarely on the shoulders of America's major food and restaurant companies. From obesity experts such as Kelly Brownell and Marion Nestle to best-selling writers such as Eric Schlosser (author of *Fast Food Nation*), numerous critics are accusing the major food manufacturers and restaurants for plying an unsuspecting public with too much fattening fare. Others, including writers Greg Critser and Michael Pollan, take a broader perspective and see McDonald's merely as a middleman. They blame the U.S. government for subsidizing corn, which, in turn, allows food makers to flood the market with inexpensive sweeteners and food additives.[1] In their view, the only reason that McDonald's is able to super size your meal is because the government makes it so cheap for them to do so. Then there are those who blame obesity on the government's nutritional recommendations. According to this theory, Americans started to gain weight in the late 1970s because they were following the government's advice to substitute dietary fat with carbohydrates.[2] Ironically, it was the very effort to eat better that has contributed to our growing weight.

At first glance, these charges seem to encapsulate the real political story of obesity in America. Much like the allegations leveled against Big Tobacco a decade ago, the indictment of Big Food suggests that corporate interests, political lobbying, and bureaucratic ineptitude have taken precedence over America's health. Americans are getting fat because a handful of major food companies is shaping government policy and bending consumer preference so that we eat more.[3] Given the billions of dollars that McDonald's and other food companies spend on advertising each year and the political influence of the food lobby, these accusations are quite understandable. But while these charges have some elements of fact, they are much like the proverbial blind men trying to describe an elephant; each depicts an aspect of the problem, but misses the much larger picture regarding our diet, weight, and health.

In fact, Americans are not consuming more carbohydrates and trans fats because McDonald's is super sizing our dinners. Nor is our diet changing because Uncle Sam is subsidizing corn. Rather, Americans are eating poorly because of a much more fundamental change in *how* we eat, specifically, the rise of snacking. In fact, the amount we eat and drink between meals accounts for nearly all the growth in our consumption of carbohydrates and fats over the past thirty years. Perhaps the biggest source of America's recent weight gain and sugary diet is not so much the value "meal" but the simple snack.

The reason that Americans snack so much is because the free market has finally caught up with American food culture. As America's agricultural sector industrialized and consolidated, it began creating products that both eliminate the need for cooking and promote individualized eating. This, in turn, has redefined the American meal, both freeing us to eat when and where we want, but also giving food new purposes. With snacking, food is no longer about sustenance or even sociability; it is about amusement and self-medication. We now eat to relieve our stress, to alleviate our boredom, or to simply make ourselves feel better. Food, in short, has become our drug of choice. And the types of foods that are best suited for these psychological tasks are the very ones that cause us so many health problems, that is, sweets, fats, and refined carbohydrates. In other words, the ultimate source of the changing American diet goes beyond McDonald's, corn syrup, or the food pyramid; the ultimate source is the American way of life.

Did the Government's Dietary Recommendations Make Us Overweight?

Given all the misinformation and concern about why Americans have started gaining so much weight, a good place to begin this discussion is to see how well the major allegations stack up against the evidence. Not only will this help us sort through all the charges and counter-charges about what is making us fat, but it will also allow us to piece together a much better picture about the changing American diet. So let us start with how exactly our eating behavior is changing and there is no better place to begin than with the food pyramid.

In a 2001 article in the *New York Times Magazine*, the science writer Gary Taubes sparked a furious debate by making a controversial accusation: the dietary recommendations of the U.S. government may be the unrecognized source of America's obesity epidemic.[4] According to Taubes, this all began in the mid-1970s when a consensus emerged around the health risks associated with dietary fat. Saturated fats, particularly those in red meat and dairy products, were found to raise cholesterol levels; higher cholesterol, in turn, was linked to clogged arteries, heart attacks, and heart disease. These connections led the U.S. government to label dietary fat as a primary nemesis of American's health. In numerous reports from the surgeon general and the National Institute of Health, fat was declared to be the single most unwholesome part of the American diet.[5] Subsequent governmental nutritional recommendations (that is, the food pyramid) advocated cutting back on whole milk, red meat, and other fatty foods.[6] And the American public responded. Over the next two decades, Americans cut their fat consumption, gorged on "fat-free" snacks, and started eating more of the pasta,

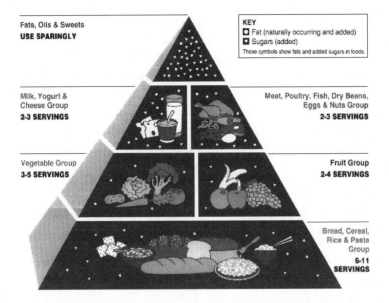

Fats, Oils & Sweets
USE SPARINGLY

KEY
☐ Fat (naturally occurring and added)
▼ Sugars (added)
These symbols show fats and added sugars in foods.

Milk, Yogurt &
Cheese Group
2-3 SERVINGS

Meat, Poultry, Fish, Dry Beans,
Eggs & Nuts Group
2-3 SERVINGS

Vegetable Group
3-5 SERVINGS

Fruit Group
2-4 SERVINGS

Bread, Cereal,
Rice & Pasta
Group
6-11
SERVINGS

The old food pyramid, according to some, encouraged the growth of obesity by emphasizing consumption of carbohydrates and recommending a reduced amount of dairy and red meat. Credit: U.S. Department of Agriculture and the U.S. Department of Health and Human Services

rice, and other carbohydrates that comprise the base of the Food Guide pyramid.[7] In response, food companies developed a large array of fat-free products (which were typically high in sugar) and Americans' overall intake of carbohydrates grew. Taubes suggests that it was exactly this switch to refined carbohydrates that has driven the obesity epidemic. The reason we're gaining weight is precisely because we're eating what we're told.

Taubes's claim was controversial, not only because he took on the nutritional orthodoxy, but because he was also suggesting that the U.S. government was responsible for the increase in obesity. He also seemed to be giving scientific credence to the controversial claims of low-carbohydrate diet gurus such as Robert Atkins. But while Taubes's charge has some elements of fact, it does not tell the entire story, particularly as to why Americans started gaining weight.

Consider, for example, the claim that Americans started eating less fat. At first glance, the evidence seems to support this proposition. According to the most reliable data on the amount of food produced, which comes from the U.S. Department of Agriculture, the *proportion* of fats in the American diet has decreased by nearly 5 percentage points over the past thirty years. This was driven by a 20 percent decrease in the consumption of beef, pork, eggs, and whole milk.[8] Less reliable data on individual eating patterns confirms this: Americans have replaced the beef and whole milk staples of their diets with other types of meat (most notably chicken and turkey) as well as with skim milk.[9] According to a CDC report, between 1971 and 2000 the percentage of calories from dietary fat decreased from 37 percent to 33 percent for men and from 36 percent to 33 percent for women. There was also a slight decrease in the proportion of calories from protein, which dropped from 16.5 percent to 15.5 percent in men and from 17 percent to 15 percent for women.[10] All in all, the evidence indicates that the *proportion* of fat and protein in the American diet has decreased while the percentage of carbohydrates in the American diet has increased.

But while the *proportion* of fat in the American diet went down, the total *amount* of calories from fat did not. This was because of an overall increase in the amount of calories Americans were consuming. Americans are actually getting as many calories from fat and protein today as they did in the early 1970s, but it only looks like a decrease because they're getting so many *more* calories from carbohydrates.[11]

The difficulty in knowing how the American diet has changed is that precise measures on food consumption are very difficult to come by and tend to be flawed; nevertheless, from the limited data available, all the evidence seems to indicate this upward swing in our total calories. The most accurate data on American eating habits comes from measures of food produced. In the past three decades, the per capita availability of food has increased by nearly 20 percent. In 1970, the amount of calories produced per person per day in the United States was about the same as it had been since the turn of the century—roughly 3,000; today it is nearly 3,654. Once the food supply is adjusted for spoilage, waste, and cooking losses, the amount of food calories produced per American increased from about 2,200 in 1970 to more than 2,700 in 2000.[12] And this holds for nearly every major food group. For instance, over 250 more per capita calories of grain (wheat and corn) are produced today than in 1970. Similarly, there have been large increases in the production of poultry and in table fats (such as olive oil) as well as in sweets and sugars. The only decreases in food production have come in animal fats, mostly from red meat, whole milk, and lard.

In addition, we also have fairly good evidence that Americans are *consuming* all of this extra food that is being produced. According to CDC estimates, men are consuming 168 more calories per day and women 335 more calories per day than they did in the early 1970s.[13] According to the U.S. Department of Agriculture, men have increased their average calories per day by 268 while for women it has increased by 143.[14] Although these individual surveys of food intake suffer from problems of under-reporting (which would explain the discrepancy with the food-produced data), each demonstrates that Americans, on average, seem to be eating anywhere from 5 to 10 percent more calories today than they did a generation ago.

And what have Americans been eating so much more of? Nearly everything it seems except for red meat and whole milk. In fact, Americans are eating slightly more of almost all major food groups and much, much more bread, sugar, cheese, vegetables, fruits, poultry, and frozen potatoes (in other words, French fries).[15] To put this in perspective, by one estimate, the average American is eating roughly forty pounds of white bread, thirty-two gallons of soda, forty-one pounds of potatoes, and over two gallons of vegetable oil *more* a year than they did a generation ago.[16]

So, Americans may have started eating a lower percentage of fats, but they did not necessarily start eating "less" fat. They may consume less beef and whole milk but they are eating more ice cream, cheese, and hydrogenated oils. And, most important, they started getting many more calories from refined carbohydrates. This was not, however, the advice they were given—the government did not advocate adding more sugar to one's diet, eating more potatoes, or consuming more bread. So why then did Americans start eating so many more carbohydrates in the late 1970s? To this, another group of critics feels they have the answer: government agricultural subsidies and the rise of high fructose corn syrup.

Are Agricultural Subsidies Promoting Obesity?

Naturalist Michael Pollan takes a different approach to explaining the rise in obesity—the declining cost of food made possible by rising farm subsidies. This argument follows a simple economic logic: Americans are eating more because food has become so much cheaper. In 1929, Americans spent roughly 38 percent of their income on food; today, Americans only spend about 11 percent of their income on food.[17] Compare this with the 20 percent the Japanese spend or the 55 percent Filipinos spend and one has an easy answer to why Americans weigh more than the people of other nations: American food costs so little.[18] And why is food so much cheaper in the United States? The primary reason, as Pollan and Greg Critser argue, is changes in U.S. agricultural policies during the early 1970s. Americans have gotten fat because the U.S. government is subsidizing the production of food in general and corn in particular.

Now at first glance, this claim seems to have some merit. The federal government spends tens of billions of dollars each year trying to regulate and maintain farm prices of five major staples: wheat, corn, soybeans, cotton, and rice.[19] Ninety percent of all farm subsidies go to these staples and, of the big five, none gets more money than corn. The federal government spends more than five billion dollars a year in a variety of corn subsidy programs, including direct payments to farmers as well as ethanol programs. In the past thirty-five years, American corn *production* has risen by nearly 20 percent and individual corn *consumption* has risen by a whopping 178 percent.[20] This year, over nine billion bushels of corn will be produced in the United States—that is more than 1,680 pounds of corn for every man, woman, and child (although the majority of this goes to animal feed, ethanol, storage, and export).[21]

Corn has been the focus of so much recent attention in regard to obesity, not simply because it is so heavily subsidized, but because it is ubiquitous in so many foods. Cornstarch is used in most breads and pastries. Corn syrup, starch, and oil are in many prepared foods ranging from French fries and peanut butter to beer and soy milk; corn-based additives are in a majority of processed foods. Look at any label of a food item on a supermarket shelf and one is likely to find cornstarch, corn-derived sugar, or some other corn-based additive in the ingredients. Corn also passes to humans in indirect ways, such as being the primary feed for lot-raised beef, pork, and chicken. In fact, corn is often indicted as contributing to obesity because it has allowed for the drop in beef prices, because lot-fed cattle are so much cheaper to raise than range-fed cattle.[22]

And then there is high fructose corn syrup (HFCS). This corn-derived sweetener has replaced cane and beet sugar in most sodas, candies, cookies, and sweet snack foods. Nearly all sweetened, processed foods manufactured in the United States now contain HFCS or corn-starch.[23] HFCS represents 40 percent of *all* added caloric sweeteners in the American diet.[24] It has seen the single largest increase in consumption of any food type in the past thirty years. Since 1973, per capita production of HFCS has increased by 4,000 percent.[25] Americans currently derive about 9 percent of their *total* calories from fructose and most of this comes from HFCS.[26] In other words, on average, each American man, woman, and child consumes more than sixty-two pounds of HFCS a year!

Pollan and Critser believe that these increases in HFCS show how government agricultural subsidies are causing the obesity epidemic. After all, America's obesity rates started increasing dramatically in the early 1980s, the same time that HFCS started entering so many processed foods. As Michael Pollan argues, "Cheap corn . . . is truly the building block of the 'fast food' nation. Cheap corn, transformed into high fructose corn syrup, is what allowed Coca-Cola to move from the svelte 8-ounce bottle of soda ubiquitous in the 70's to the chubby 20-ounce bottle of today."[27] Greg Critser, in his book *Fat Land*, comes to a similar conclusion: "High fructose corn syrup from the growing surpluses of U.S. corn had made it easier and less expensive to make frozen foods. TV dinners and boxed macaroni and cheese were downright cheap. At fast-food stands portions were getting bigger and getting cheaper and cheaper."[28] According to this line of reasoning, the U.S. government by encouraging the production of cheap corn (and high import quotas on foreign cane sugar) has flooded the food market with HFCS and greatly contributed to America's growing weight.

But while the increase in HFCS consumption has important implications for our health, the accusations about agricultural subsidies are off the mark. The assertion that government subsidized cheap food is enabling the marketing and overproduction of fast-food, soda, and junk food belies a great deal of ignorance about the economics of food production. To begin with, food has not gotten cheaper over the past two decades. The U.S. Department of Labor reports that the consumer price index of food rose, in constant terms, from 39.2 in 1970 to 157.3 in 1997. In 1970, Americans spent an estimated 340 billion dollars on food; by

2000, food expenditures rose, adjusting for inflation, to an estimated 572 billion dollars.[29] Although the percentage of income Americans spent on food declined during this time, it was not because food was getting cheaper; it was because American incomes, on the whole, were rising. For poor and working-class Americans, whose incomes have not risen as much during the past two decades and who also have the highest rates of obesity, food has stayed relatively expensive (more on this below).

Moreover, the cost of the actual food (that is, the farm value) is only a small part of what consumers pay for the food at the supermarket or at a restaurant. In the United States, only about 20 percent of the retail cost of food is, on average, from the farm value of the food itself. For many processed foods, the farm value is less than 10 percent of the retail cost and for many products using HFCS it is less than 1 percent.[30] This is less because the food is so cheap (commodity prices are actually kept artificially high by government subsidies, which act primarily as price supports) but that other components of food production are so much more expensive. The greatest expense for food manufacturers is labor, which is twice as high as the farm value of the food on average (roughly 40 percent) and much higher with respect to fruits and vegetables. The simplistic argument that cheap corn prices drove down the cost of soda during the 1980s ignores the falling costs of energy and transportation and, most important, labor during this time. If the price of corn were to affect consumption of HFCS, it would need to rise by nearly 1,000 percent, something that would not happen even if government agricultural subsidies were not in place.[31]

Once one looks at the reality of costs associated with food manufacturing it is clear that a much bigger source of America's cheap food is the very low American minimum wage. Labor expenses represent the lion's share of food costs, and decreases in the cost of labor had a much larger impact on food prices than changes in the farm value of the food. For instance, in 1968, the value of the minimum wage (in 1996 dollars) was $7.92, by 1980 it had dropped to $6.48 and by 2004 it was at $4.41—a drop of more than 40 percent.[32] Considering that a significant portion of the food industry's labor force works for minimum wage, this decline probably had a far greater effect on the price of food than government agricultural subsidies. If one still wants to believe that cheap food caused the rise of obesity, then a much better strategy would be to increase the value of the minimum wage than to eliminate government agricultural subsidies. America's agricultural policies may be criticized for the monetary payments they provide to large agribusiness and nonfarmers, but they should not be condemned for contributing to America's weight gain.

So yes, Critser and Pollan are correct in noting that Americans are consuming much more corn and HFCS today than they did in the 1970s, but this is not because government has made corn so cheap. Americans would probably be consuming just as much HFCS even if the subsidies were not in place—after all, potato farmers get no subsidies but American potato consumption has increased by 17 percent in this time. In truth, the bigger problem with agricultural subsidies is not that they make corn cheap; it is that they have furthered the consolidation and industrialization of American agriculture. This, as we will see, has led to much larger changes in the way food is produced, marketed, and distributed and a more fundamental alteration in America's food culture. This brings us to the third, and most popular, explanation for the rise in Americans' weight: the value meal.

Are Increasing Portion Sizes to Blame?

Although America's food industry may not suffer from a lack of critics, few have been more forceful, persistent, or notable than Kelly Brownell, a psychologist and director of the Yale Center for Eating and Weight Disorders, and Marion Nestle, a professor of nutrition at New York University. [33] Brownell and Nestle have written books, made headlines, and been lauded by *Time* magazine as America's "obesity warriors" for their efforts to tie Americans' growing weights to the way a handful of large food companies market and sell their products. If America's obesity epidemic has a single cause, it is, in their eyes, from the corporate malfeasance of its food makers.

According to Brownell and Nestle, Big Food (meaning the major food companies including Kraft, General Mills, PepsiCo, Coca-Cola, ConAgra, Tyson Food, Mars, Sara Lee, Heinz, and IBP) has created a "toxic environment" that is causing Americans to get fat. These companies disguise or label food as "healthy" that is really filled with sugars, fats, and little nutritional value. They have targeted children with thousands of commercials featuring cartoon characters and celebrities encouraging them to eat unhealthy foods. And, most important, they have packaged foods in larger sizes, which, in the name of value, encourages Americans to eat more than they otherwise would. Brownell writes, "Portion size increases conspire to drive up food intake and appear to contribute to increasing obesity. Food companies claim to 'provide people what they want' and take no responsibility for manipulating portion sizes in ways that increase overall eating."[34]

From Nestle's perspective, the biggest problem with these super size portions is that most of us are poor estimators of how much we need to eat. In fact, she claims the food industry has completely warped what Americans now see as a recommended serving size. Most Americans think a serving size is between two and three times larger than the official USDA designations.[35] Super sized portions also encourage us to eat more by influencing our levels of hunger and satiation. For example, nutrition researchers have demonstrated that when people are given larger portions of food, they will eat more before they feel satisfied.[36] Partly this is because we get pleasure from food—the satisfaction of eating, particularly foods high in sugars and fats, resonates in our brains—and partly this is because we often feel compelled to "clean our plates" in order not to be wasteful. Considering the millions of value meals served at fast-food restaurants every day, Americans allegedly are being lured into consuming more calories than they might otherwise do. Nestle concludes, "Taken together, advertising, convenience, larger portions, and the added nutrients in food otherwise high in fat, sugar, and salt all contribute to an environment that promotes 'eat more.'"[37]

Once again, at first glance, Brownell's and Nestle's charges seem to have a lot of merit. Over the past forty years, America has transformed from a society where most people prepared their own meals from scratch to one where most meals are either prepackaged or eaten outside of the home.[38] One need only look at the growing number of fast-food restaurants, the ever increasing portion sizes in those restaurants, or the size and type of foods available in supermarkets to believe that food companies are responsible for America's weight gain. Today, Americans spend about half their food dollars at restaurants or on take-out meals, a rate double that of a generation ago and on any given day, half of all Americans will get at least one meal from a restaurant.[39] The result, according to the Brownell and Nestle, is that America is growing obese.

Yet, once again, these charges miss the larger picture. To begin with, there is little indication that America's mealtime behaviors are being manipulated by the nefarious machinations of a few profit-hungry food conglomerates cajoling them into eating larger portions. Yes, Americans are consuming more calories, but it does not seem to come from super sizing their meals. In fact, larger portion sizes at meals seem to have very little to do with the increase in calorie consumption within the United States. For example, Nestle's argument on portion size contributing to obesity rests almost entirely on data about the manufacture of foods, she has no data on whether people are actually consuming larger portions during meals.[40] If you look at the real data on how Americans eat, you'll see that the preoccupation with portion sizes misses the real culprit behind America's weight gain—snacking.[41]

A generation ago, most Americans limited their daily food consumption to three meals and if they did eat between meals it was likely to be a piece of fruit or something easily consumed.[42] Today, the average adult eats the equivalent of four meals a day and children eat close to five, much more than in 1970.[43] According to the calculations of Harvard economist David Cutler and his colleagues, in the mid-1970s, men consumed about 2,080 calories per day and women consumed roughly 1,515 calories per day.[44] The biggest meal for both sexes was dinner, followed by lunch and then breakfast. Americans only got about 13 percent of their calories from snacking, a relatively small percentage. Today, men and women are getting almost 25 percent of their daily calories from snacking, the caloric equivalent of a full meal a generation ago. The average American male consumes more than 500 calories a day from snacks, the average female more than 346 calories a day. Even more interesting is that the calories from dinner have actually declined over the past several decades.[45] Men and women are actually eating smaller dinners on average than they did thirty years ago. Although Americans may be eating out more and restaurants may be serving larger portions, Americans are not eating larger meals.

What Americans are doing more of is snacking and drinking high-calorie beverages. Americans spend more than 38 billion dollars a year on snack foods, more than what they spend on higher education.[46] Of course snacking itself does not necessarily lead to weight gain or health problems, depending on what is eaten. But Americans are snacking more on foods that are high in calories and low in nutritional value such as cookies, chips, and candies. Over the past twenty years, sales of high-salt, high-calorie snack foods have skyrocketed, while that of fruits and vegetables (excluding potatoes) has only increased marginally.[47]

Nowhere is the prevalence of high-calorie snack food more evident than in the accelerating growth of soft drink consumption, particularly by children. Since the late 1970s, Americans' soft drink consumption has increased by more than 130 percent.[48] The average American drinks more than forty-four gallons of soft drinks a year and soft drinks comprise about one-fifth of their dietary sugar.[49] This increase is particularly sharp among children. Soft drinks have now replaced milk for most children as a dietary staple and are the third most common *breakfast* food.[50] The typical American teenage boy has at least three soft drink servings in a day—the equivalent of twenty teaspoons of sugar.

It is drinking and snacking, more than anything else, that have been responsible for changing the way we eat. And upon reflection, this makes sense. In the hoopla over obesity and the large value meals served in restaurants, most critics seem to forget that American culinary culture has always been distinguished by large portion sizes. As food historian Harvey Levenstein notes, "To nineteenth-century observers, the major differences between the American and British diets could usually be summed up in one word: abundance. Virtually every foreign visitor who wrote about American eating habits expressed amazement, shock, and even disgust at the quantity of food consumed."[51] What was not consumed was generally saved. Products including Tupperware and plastic wrap were developed precisely in response to the bounty of leftovers that were coming from the large American dinners. To suddenly blame the food industry for serving larger portion sizes is to ignore the fact that many Americans have been eating large meals for centuries.

Thus, while the super size portions in American restaurants may seem like a convenient target, they do not explain why Americans are eating more. If we want to understand why Americans are eating so much between meals, and why, in particular, we are snacking on so many fatty and sugary foods, we need to look at the more fundamental processes that are shaping how we eat. In short, we need to understand the logic of food production in the United States.

The Logic of Snack Food

At the front of my refrigerator sits a tube of Pillsbury chocolate chip cookie dough. The package has been ripped open and little bite size chunks have been taken out. Although it supposed to be baked, in my house it rarely is. The time and energy required to spoon out and cook the dough is far too great a hurdle. The dough is simply eaten raw, a quick shot of both fat (about seven grams per tablespoon) and sugar (about eleven grams per tablespoon). If there is anything that epitomizes the change in American food culture during the past thirty years, it is probably this little package.

Throughout most of American history (and indeed throughout most of the world), the widespread snacking that we know today simply did not exist. The cookies, chips, soft drinks, candy bars, and most of the other popular snack foods ubiquitous in the contemporary American diet were not common until after World War II and did not become pervasive until the 1970s. Outside of the very rich, most people were highly constrained with regard to when and where they ate. Americans occasionally may have eaten between meals, but their choices were often highly bound by season and geography. Even the historically favorite American snack, the apple, was typically only consumed in summer and fall.[52]

The absence of snacking largely arose from the inconvenience and cost of preparing most foods. Until the late twentieth century, food was not only expensive and limited in supply but was time consuming to prepare. Outside of a handful of fruits, nuts, and vegetables, most foods require extensive amounts of labor to be made palatable: wheat needs to be ground into flour and then baked into bread, meat needs to be slaughtered, cleaned, and cooked, and so on. Without refrigeration (a relatively modern convenience), it is difficult to sustain anything but dried, pickled, or salted foods for long periods of time, and, except for a few seasons, there are few fresh fruits or vegetables across all regions of the globe that are available for quick consumption.[53] Consequently, most food has traditionally been consumed in groups (in order to gain efficiencies in scales of production) and at set times (to help coordinate the group). The consumption of snacks, soda, or other foods, in isolation and at other times of day, was not common until the 1960s. But around this time two important changes began to radically change the way Americans ate.

The first was the entry of women into the paid workforce. Prior to the 1960s, most American women did not work outside the home and spent much of their time preparing meals. Today, this situation has reversed and more women work at paid positions outside the home than at any time in history.[54] The change in women's work status has greatly increased the value of food preparation and the market for preprocessed foods. Although major food companies have marketed various products to relieve women of the time and labor of making meals for a century (for example, the Van Camps canned pork and beans of the early 1900s or the TV dinners of the 1950s), these efforts really took hold in the 1960s and 1970s, at the same time women's participation in the workforce started to rise. Suddenly supermarkets became filled with precooked and processed foods that were increasingly packaged in individual-sized packages. Precooked dinners are now one of the largest growth areas within food retailing. Not surprisingly, with the growth of more processed foods, the amount of time spent preparing meals has plummeted: the average time mothers spend preparing meals at homes has declined by more than 50 percent in the last two decades.[55]

The restaurant business has undergone a similar change, remaking itself with families and working mothers in mind. Before the era of fast-food, most restaurants catered to an adult clientele. Parents with young children rarely ate out and, when they did, it was often without their kids.[56] But as families became more pressed for time, restaurants, particularly fast-food chains, realized the different requirements that came when children were customers. Food needed to be cheap, fast, and tasty for kids. Many restaurants also began to add special amenities for children such as playgrounds and "kids meals" with toys as an additional lure. So the changing role of women in the economy has led to a much larger change in the way food is sold and prepared.

The other big factor that has altered American culinary culture has been the industrialization and consolidation of American agriculture. A century ago, when America was a predominantly rural country, most food was produced by small farms for local markets. The American diet was largely seasonal and locally determined. But industrialization and agricultural policies changed this. Over the past fifty years, farms started getting larger, food collection and processing became increasingly mechanized, and companies started making standardized and branded products such as Oreo cookies, Kraft cheese, or Stouffer's frozen dinners.

Although many Americans still honor the ideal of the family farm, in reality, small family farms are only a fraction of the agricultural economy. Large agricultural businesses (less than 8 percent of all farms) produce about 70 percent of all the food in the United States.[57] The top twenty food manufacturing firms control more than 50 percent of all food processed in the United States.[58] The top ten food manufacturers sell more than 150 billion dollars worth of food annually.[59]

Yet even with this consolidation, selling food is still a tricky business. The agricultural sector is a classic example of what economists call "perfect competition," that is, it is a market where there are large numbers of buyers and sellers, where market entry is easy, where buyers and sellers have lots of information, and where firms produce a homogeneous product. Under such conditions, profits tend to be reduced to their lowest levels. In other words, if you are an onion farmer, it is very difficult to charge more for your onions than what it costs to grow them (and thus extract more profit) because some other onion farmer can easily undersell you with a virtually identical product. Food producers must also deal with the problem of spoilage: most fresh meats, fish, dairy, and produce rot after short periods of time.

The only way agricultural businesses can extract more profit from their efforts is by "adding value." One way they do this is by adding as much time to the "shelf life" of the food as possible. For example, if you are Pepperidge Farms and you want to sell cookies to the entire country, you need to make sure your Mint Milanos won't go stale within two weeks. The best way you can do this is by using preservatives to enhance or retain the food's flavors. This partially explains why saturated oils and high fructose corn syrup have become so common in today's foods; they are much heartier preservatives than either unsaturated fats or sucrose. Moreover, once a large portion of preserved foods are being made, new outlets can be found for selling them. Businesses that did not traditionally sell groceries, such as drug stores, clothing retailers, and even bookstores now stock all sorts of chips, cookies, sweets, and other snack foods largely because they do not have to worry about spoilage.

Another way that food companies add value is in the way they package the foods. Foods that require no preparation and are easy to consume are going to be much more appealing. One of more recent innovations in food packaging has been the development of individual servings that can be eaten alone, virtually anywhere. For instance,

Frito-Lay and Seven-Eleven recently started serving chips and candies in plastic cups. These so-called go-snacks are designed to fit in car cup-holders for easy consumption.[60] From ice-cream bars to potato chips, from fruit juice boxes to peanut butter and jelly sandwiches, more and more types of foods are handheld.

Food companies also add value by making foods of consistent quality. Starbucks can charge two dollars for a few cents worth of coffee beans and hot water because of the additional value of their labor in grinding the beans and serving it right away. But while almost anyone can do that, Starbucks can also transform the two-dollar cup of coffee into a four-dollar "grande mocha latte" partly because of its reputation for providing a uniformly good product. Another added value is familiarity. In an uncertain world, the consistent experience provided by food producers such as Starbucks, McDonald's, or Häagen-Dazs is perhaps the most valuable asset.

Finally, the most important way that companies can add value is by making food tasty. Of all the reasons why we choose the foods we do, none is more important to us than taste. And what exactly makes food taste good? We are drawn to the kinds of foods that trigger primordial response nodes in our brain, that is, foods that are sweet, salty, and fatty. We are hardwired to respond differently to various taste sensations—sweet foods trigger pleasure centers in the brain, bitter foods trigger negative responses.[61] One reason why fatty and sweet foods taste so much better is because those sensations signal to the brain that the foods have lots of calories.

In short, the economic logic of food production in the United States leads to making foods that are fun, easy to eat, tasty, and longlasting. This is what I call gas station food—the type of food products that can be sold and eaten virtually anywhere. These types of food have become the fastest growing sector of the food industry. Not only are they changing what we eat, but they are also changing the very meaning of eating itself.

The Freedom of Snacking

Until quite recently, food was among the most communal, hierarchical, and illiberal areas of American life. Whereas the American ethos may be based on life, liberty, and the pursuit of happiness, the American meal was constrained by social roles, ideological demands, and a communal orientation regarding what, where, and when one ate. For example, up until the 1970s, those who prepared the meals, typically women, determined what most of us ate. Although these women might have been influenced by the marketing efforts of large food companies, their own ethnic or religious customs, or even government sponsored nutrition guidelines, they were the primary arbiters of their family's diet.[62] The preparation and labor required for meals also meant that people ate at certain times and in certain places. Lunch was regimented by work and school schedules, and dinner was typically at a specific time each day. There was no freedom in the regime of eating.

The emergence of tasty and savory prepackaged snack foods has undone all this. Snacking has no prerequisites of cooking equipment, heat, or cutlery. It supersedes all culinary conventions and allows the individual to be the sole judge of when and how food should be taken. It allows the individual the fullest liberty in satisfying his or her own hunger, irrespective of the demands or constraints of society. Snacking has liberated eating in America, giving our meals the individualistic tenor on which this country is based.

But, in doing this, snacking is also changing the function of food. Historically, food has primarily been a means of satisfying our physiological needs; we eat to get the energy we need to stay alive. Food has also served as a way to keep us socially connected. Sharing meals is one of the central ways any society maintains its cohesion. Consequently, eating is very bounded by cultural practice: we eat in accordance with specific rules as a means of reaffirming our collective identity, as a family, a religion, or a people.

However, with the rise of snacking, food is beginning to take on a new function—as a means to satisfy our individual, psychological needs. Much of this comes from the dietary content of the snack food itself. Most snack foods have ingredients that act like opiates on the brain. Chocolate, for example, contains cannabinoids that are basically like a mild narcotic.[63] Most sodas contain not only high levels of sugar, which provide spikes of energy, but also the stimulant caffeine. Dietary fats may also have a tranquilizing effect. When the body consumes calorie dense foods such as fat, the adrenal glands receive signals to reduce the anxiety provoking stress hormones, thus making us feel calmer.[64]

Rich foods like ice cream or cookies really are "comfort" food—they literally act like a sedative on our adrenal system.

The candies, cookies, and sodas that comprise the snacking diet are not just nutrients; they are ostensibly drugs affecting mood, disposition, and psychological well-being. In fact, many food makers now are packaging and marketing foods precisely for their psychological functions. The heavily sugared and caffeinated soda Mountain Dew, typically advertised with teenage boys frenetically engaging in skateboarding or some extreme sport, offers youth and energy. Godiva chocolate, with ads that border on soft-pornography using filtered images and muted lighting, promises orgasmic delight (which physiologically speaking is not that great an exaggeration). And, Grandma's Cookies are, by their very name, meant to evoke a feeling of love and comfort. Food is now sold not just for its nutrition or taste but for its mood-enhancing qualities.

While chocolate, coffee, and other intoxicating foods have been around for centuries and packaged snacks since the 1920s, their prevalence has exploded during the past three decades. And the omnipresence of snacking choices is fundamentally changing our relationship to food. Eating in America today is no longer about simply getting nutrition. Nor is it simply to bond with one's family or to affirm a religious faith. Instead it is an amusement and distraction. People eat foods such as ice cream, chips, or cookies to reduce stress, to alleviate boredom, and to feel secure, outside of any shared social ritual. Eating has become a form of self-medication and for some, with binge-eating disorders, a compulsive and dysfunctional behavior. While shared meals sometimes can fulfill these psychological functions, their structured time and social character make them ill-suited for therapeutic tasks. Indeed, for many people, there are few events more stressful than a Thanksgiving meal with the family. Snacking, given its individualistic nature, is much better suited to address specific psychological needs.

Herein lies the dilemma we face with regard to our diet. On one hand, free-market forces are changing the nature of food production, giving us more highly saturated snacks that have psychotropic properties. On the other hand, the very elements in the food that give them their psychological power (refined carbohydrates and fats) also wreak havoc on our bloodstream. As we saw in chapter 5, our bodies are not well equipped to handle large amounts of refined carbohydrates, salts, and fats. Snack foods are creating a conflict between satisfying our individual desires and maintaining our health. Because many snack foods play a dual role of both nutrient and opiate, they pose a new and thorny political problem. By their convenience and solitary consumption, they allow for the individualized pursuit of happiness, something we hold to be extremely important; with their refined carbohydrates and trans fats, they act like a drug and may be at the root of many health pathologies. Thus, to some degree, our health woes are increasing from the democratization of our eating behavior.

Eating Well

In our preoccupation with whether or not McDonald's is making us fat, we are losing sight of a much more important issue. The real health problem with our changing diet is that it is flooding our bodies with all sorts of sugars and fats. Consider the movie *Super Size Me*; Morgan Spurlock could have made this film without any reference to obesity. He could have simply shown how eating five thousand calories a day of food dense in refined carbohydrates and fat has negative health consequences and causes a number of physical side effects including his raised cholesterol and blood pressure, sleeplessness, and depression. Indeed, the film clearly shows how flooding your body with excessive carbohydrates can cause so many health woes. Even though the real source of his health problems were not in the twenty-six pounds he gained, he continued to make his weight the center of the film's attention, which explains its appeal to its educated, middle-class audience.

This is the one of the biggest problems with calling our weight gain an "obesity epidemic." By worrying about our weight, we are focusing on the wrong target. Our changing diet is not a problem because it is making us fat; it is a problem because it has greatly increased our consumption of refined carbohydrates and saturated fats. And while it might be natural to conflate eating such foods and gaining weight, there is an important distinction. As we saw in chapter 1, we are not getting diabetes, cancer, and heart disease because of how much we weigh; we are getting these health problems partly because of how and what we eat. Moreover, a diet high in fats and carbohydrates will not necessarily make someone fat but it can affect their cholesterol, blood pressure, and general metabolism.

So why are we more worried if McDonald's is making us fat than if Coca-Cola, M&M's, and Ben and Jerry's ice cream are flooding our metabolism with too many sugars and fats? The answer to this question speaks to the dilemma that underlies our diet and health. Ultimately, the real problem with the American diet involves the changing food culture and the erosion of the traditional meal. If Americans want to start consuming fewer carbohydrates and fats, they need to figure out how to reconcile their own natural appetites and desires with a way of living oriented around satisfying them as best as it can. In other words, we need to come to terms with the paradoxes of our own freedom. As we'll see in the next chapter, this is not merely a dilemma of how we eat; it is also a problem with how we move.

seven

Sloth, Capitalism, and the Paradox of Freedom

Imagine a diet that allows you to eat unlimited amounts of meat, cake, pie, butter, eggs, bread, *and* sugar without putting on any excess pounds. Sound like a dream? For many Americans it is, but for one group—the Amish—such a way of life is a reality. Certain Amish communities have very low rates of obesity despite having a diet that is extremely high in calories, sugar, and fat. What explains the Amish's secret? According to some researchers, it is an extraordinary amount of exercise. The Amish reject most modern technologies and live a physically demanding, agrarian lifestyle. In an Amish community, the typical man gets about ten hours of vigorous exercise and about forty-three hours of moderate exercise per week, the typical woman about three and a half hours of strenuous and thirty-nine hours of moderate exercise weekly.[1] Even though the Amish diet consists of three full meals a day of rich and hearty foods such as ham, eggs, cake, and milk, their obesity rates were under 4 percent, four times lower than the general American population.

Many would like to believe that the Amish hold the key to explaining our recent weight gains. They assert that, contrary to the claims expressed in the previous chapter, Americans are not getting fatter because they're eating so much, but because they are exercising so little. From a historical perspective, such claims seem to make some intuitive sense. Obesity was not prominent in nineteenth-century America because most Americans lived like the Amish do today; they engaged in steady, manual labor and burned hundreds of calories through the course of their physically active day. But, the technological advances of the past hundred years have greatly altered our physical existence. Seated work at computers and in offices has replaced labor on farms and in factories; modern appliances have replaced the manual task of washing clothes and dishes; microwave dinners and fast-food have replaced cooking; driving has replaced walking; and television and video games have even replaced such amusements as playing sports.

In fact, many researchers think declining exercise patterns are *the* primary factor behind America's rising weights. Dr. Steven Blair of the Cooper Institute in Dallas concludes, "the evidence suggests that declines in physical activity are more likely than increases in food intake to be the explanation for the recent increase in obesity."[2] And, he is not alone in this assessment. Economists Tomas Philipson and Darius Lakdawalla estimate that 60 percent of America's recent weight gains have come from labor-saving technologies.[3] Several European scholars also have argued that low exercise is the primary source of obesity across the Atlantic.[4] The President's Council on Physical Fitness and Sports ultimately concluded that "Inactivity might be a far more significant factor in the development of obesity than overeating."[5]

Yet, it is difficult to know what to make of these claims because they often seem to be motivated as much by politics as by fact. In a time when food manufacturers and restaurants are facing more lawsuits, taxes, and regulations, it is clearly in some groups' interest to blame obesity on Americans' changing exercise patterns rather than their diet. For example, the Corn Refiners Association, the lobbying group of the manufacturers of high fructose corn syrup, argues that there is no such thing as "bad food"; instead they suggest that the focus on fighting obesity should be on "promoting physical activity."[6] Steve Anderson, president of the American Restaurant Association, says the real cause of obesity is "our sedentary society."[7] The food and beverage industry has funded research that, not surprisingly, supports this idea: a study subsidized by the National Soft Drink Association found that exercise is a much bigger contributor to obesity than food.[8] Similarly, large food companies including PepsiCo, Mars Candy, and Cargill have been important sponsors of organizations such as America on the Move, a group that emphasizes physical activity in response to weight gain.

While some of these efforts may be motivated by a genuine concern with the nation's health, many are little more than political smokescreens. This is particularly the case with the food and beverage industry. Facing charges that they are making Americans obese, many companies have worked very hard to shift the public concerns with obesity away from eating and toward exercise. They have lobbied Congress and government health agencies to designate lack of exercise as a primary source of obesity. They fund groups, such as the Center for Consumer Freedom, that attack public health researchers and organizations, calling them nannies and the "food police." They support researchers who exonerate food and blame television, suburbanization, or technology for causing our growing weight. Such political machinations, however, may be doing us a disservice. First, they are wrongly blaming our growing weight on our inactivity. There is little convincing evidence that physical inactivity is directly responsible for America's increasing weight. At most, inactivity has an indirect effect on our weight by making us susceptible to snacking—the more time we spend driving and watching television, the more likely we are to eat unhealthy, fattening snack foods. Second, in all the hoopla over obesity, we have lost sight of the fact that exercise itself is a major determinant of our health, not just a weight-loss measure. Because we too often conflate weight with health, we forget about the importance of exercise. Hence, thin people too often think they are healthy merely because of their slimness, just as fat people think they are ill because of their heft. Instead of obesity, inactivity may be the real chronic health problem that America faces.

America the Slothful

It is easy to see why inactivity is such a popular target in America's obesity wars—by almost any measure, America is not a very physically active country. Take, for example, voluntary exercise. While a small portion of Americans work out frequently, most still do not. According to data from the CDC, more than half of American adults do not get the old minimal amount of recommended exercise (thirty minutes of vigorous activity a day, four days a week) and one in four Americans never exercises voluntarily.[9] Researchers at the National Center for Health Statistics offer even lower estimates: less than one in three Americans engages in a minimal recommended amount of exercise, 30 percent exercise a little, and 40 percent of Americans do not exercise at all.[10] And the bad news doesn't stop there. For not only are these numbers based on the *old* recommendations for physical activity (the new recommendations call for at least an hour of vigorous activity, five days a week), they probably underestimate Americans' inactivity. Most Americans, particularly sedentary ones, tend to overstate how much they exercise, often by three times as much.[11]

Nor are Americans very active in other aspects of their lives and the reason comes from our very progress and technological advancement. Compare, for example, the daily life of an American fifty years ago with one today. In 1955, physical activity was, for most Americans, more of a necessity than a leisure pursuit.[12] Few people "worked out," ran marathons, or did aerobics because ordinary living and working required more energy. Most men worked in factories, farms, or in other physically demanding occupations. Most women labored cooking meals, cleaning homes, and taking care of children without the benefits of modern appliances. After spending hours washing clothes and dishes or working on an assembly line or in a field, few Americans had the energy or interest in exercising at the end of the day.

Technological advancements changed all this. Mechanical and electronic innovations (plus the growth of the service sector economy) moved American jobs away from physical labor to mental and interpersonal skills. Even many manual jobs, such as farming, logging, and factory work, are less physically demanding because of mechanization. Technological wonders have also entered the American home. From self-cleaning toilets to robotic vacuum cleaners, American households have become filled with labor-saving devices. The average American now spends an hour a day less on household chores and meal preparation than a generation ago; translated into energy expenditure this means that, on average, Americans are burning about 20 percent fewer calories in household work than their parents did.[13]

Of these new technologies, none have had more impact on our physical lives than cars and television. In love with automobiles since they were first invented, Americans' romance with cars has blossomed well into the twenty-first century. Americans are now using their cars more than at any time in their history. Since 1970, the percentage of Americans driving alone to work and using the car for minor tasks has increased by 15 percent, while biking and walking has declined by 25 percent.[14] Today nearly nine in ten Americans gets to work in a car with an average commute time of more than twenty-four minutes each way.[15] American adults spend, on average, about two hours a day in their cars, more time than they do reading books or playing with their children.

Cars have also defined the shape and nature of America's communities, particularly the suburbs. Fifty years ago, a majority of Americans lived in dense, large cities. These urban areas were designed around pedestrians: virtually all streets had sidewalks, many houses had front-porches and stoops, and most neighborhoods were within walking distances of shops and workplaces. But in the past half-century, this urban landscape has been radically changed. Today, more than 50 percent of Americans reside in suburban communities and most of these suburbs, particularly the ones built after 1960, are designed around the automobile. Not only are many suburbs placed near highways, but they also have wider streets, put greater distances between homes and shopping areas, lack sidewalks, and contain houses whose facades are dominated by formidable garages rather than open and welcoming porches—all of which favor driving at the expense of walking.

The "drive-in" design of most suburban communities greatly inhibits physical activity. For many American suburbanites, the idea of walking or biking to the supermarket, post office, their jobs, or even school is not only ludicrous, it is simply unfeasible given the distance and lack of sidewalks. This is borne out in a national study of 200,000 people in 448 counties, which found that people who lived in sprawling areas tended to walk much less in their daily routine.[16] Because most Americans now live in suburbs, most Americans drive even small distances. Although 25 percent of all Americans' trips are under a mile in distance, 75 percent of those trips are made by car.[17] Even more telling is the change in how our children get to school. Today, only 18 percent of children ever walk or bike to school; a generation ago, nearly 80 percent of kids did.[18]

The past forty years has also witnessed another significant change in the American physical lifestyle—television. Since 1960, the hours the average American spends watching TV has tripled; there is at least one television in 99 percent of American homes, and more than 50 percent have more than two.[19] According to the Nielsen surveys, the average American currently watches about thirty hours of television a week and the average household has a television turned on for nearly seven hours a day.[20] To put this in perspective: Americans spend, on average, about six times as many hours watching television as they do exercising. Television viewing is particularly high among children. Roughly 80 percent of American children under sixteen watch more than three hours of television a day and the average American child watches about twenty-eight hours of television a week and about fifteen hundred hours in a year.

The sedentary nature of our leisure time has also been compounded by the advent of computers and video games, whose prevalence coincides almost directly with the rise in Americans' weights. According to one study, on any given day, 30 percent of American adults under the age of sixty-five will be on the Internet, spending, on average, three hours a day on e-mail, playing games, shopping, or simply surfing for information.[21] Meanwhile, video games have become the most popular form of entertainment in America, particularly among people under thirty-five. The average American child spends nine hours a week playing video games and nearly 87 percent of American children play video games regularly.[22]

In short, the affluence and ease provided by our technology has made America a very physically inactive place. Not only is our work and home life not physically demanding, but our living spaces and leisure time require little exertion.

These facts have been seized upon by a variety of public health advocates who are using obesity as a justification to advance their own agendas. For example, some of the biggest alarms about obesity have come from urban planners, who claim that the automobile-oriented design of our metropolitan areas is making us fat. In a well-publicized study of more than twelve thousand people in metropolitan Atlanta, a group of urban planning researchers found that the more time a person spent driving, the greater their likelihood of being obese.[23] From the researcher's perspective, obesity was the direct result of the car-oriented design of metropolitan Atlanta. With its numerous drive-thru restaurants, shopping malls, suburbs, and great distances between places, Atlanta's sprawl was not just creating more congestion and pollution, but also more obesity, which was viewed as a major life-threatening condition.[24] And it is not just Atlanta. Cities including Houston, Dallas, and Charlotte are supposed to be among the fattest in the nation because they are the least conducive to physical activity—their workers have long commutes in cars that are alleviated only by convenience stores and fast-food chains that line their many highways.[25] Meanwhile, dense, walking cities such as New York are celebrated for the way they putatively keep their residents thin.[26]

Similarly, public health advocates have reported finding strong linkages between television watching and body weight that show, not surprisingly, that the more TV you watch, the heavier you are likely to be.[27] For example, a recent study of more than fifty thousand women found that for every two hours per day that a woman watched television, the likelihood of her being obese increased by 23 percent, a pattern that has also been found with men.[28] The effects of TV on body weight are supposed to be particularly strong among children. Numerous studies have reported that the more time kids spend in front of a television, the more likely they are to be overweight.[29] One of the most interesting reports came from a New Zealand study that tracked the television viewing and health of one thousand children born between 1973 and 1974. Having monitored the television habits of the children, the researchers went back and checked to see how much they weighed as adults. They found that by age twenty-six, nearly 20 percent of their body weight sample could be accounted for by whether they watched more than two hours of TV a day as children.[30] In other words, how much television a person watched as a child seemed to be a very good predictor of how much they would weigh as an adult.

But Are Cars and Televisions Really Making Us Fat?

From the research cited above, you might reasonably conclude that all our television watching, suburban living, and car driving is making us fat. After all, Americans, among the world's fattest people, also drive more, watch more television, and are more suburbanized than any nationality. Putting two and two together, it is easy to think that our inactivity is to blame.

Well, think again. Although it is true that Americans are not very physically active, we do not have any conclusive evidence that this inactivity is the primary source of our rising weights. In fact, the case against inactivity is actually quite flimsy.

To begin with, there is a problem of evidence. We do not know if inactivity is the reason why we started gaining weight in the early 1980s because there are no reliable studies that have tracked the physical activity of Americans over this time.[31] We simply do not have any accurate information on whether Americans are more or less active today than they were twenty-five years ago. In one respect, what little data we do have seems to suggest the opposite—although Americans may be less active in the course of their normal day, they are voluntarily exercising more than ever. According to recent Gallup polls, over the past several decades, the percentage of Americans who exercise has actually increased to more than twice the number from a generation ago.[32] Studies of Americans' daily time usage indicate that the average number of minutes Americans spent in leisurely and discretionary physical activity increased from twenty-seven minutes per day in 1965 to forty-seven minutes per day in 1995.[33] Over the past three decades, memberships in gyms, athletic clubs, and exercise studios have risen by more than 90 percent and nearly 34 million Americans belong to a health club (although gyms actually rely on members not using their facilities as a means to make a profit).[34] While it seems perfectly clear that our lives are less physically demanding than they were in the 1950s, it is not necessarily the case that we are cumulatively burning fewer calories.

Another problem with the charges against inactivity is that it is extremely difficult to determine the exact relationship between activity and weight, particularly when other factors including eating behavior are taken into account. Consider, for example, the research cited above that links television, suburbanization, and body weight. Although this research finds an association between these factors, it is unclear whether television viewing and suburbanization are causing the rise in weight or whether they are simply proxies for other factors. There is a lot of evidence to suggest the latter. For instance, a recent study by researchers at the Bassett Research Institute found that much of the connection between juvenile obesity and television watching resulted from snacking behavior. Children who watched TV during dinner and while snacking were less likely to eat fruits and vegetables or drink milk and were more likely to consume snack foods high in refined sugar and fat.[35] In other words, the weight is not coming from how much time kids spend watching TV; it is from what they are doing while they watch TV, snacking.

We could say a similar thing about cars and suburbs—are cars and suburbs making us fatter because they keep us from walking, or because they encourage us to eat? Once again, there is a strong case to be made for the latter. Think about how American driving culture has changed. Fifty years ago, few Americans ate in their cars. But starting in the 1960s, restaurants started offering "drive-thru" service for people who wanted to eat on the go. Recognizing this change, carmakers followed suit by offering vehicles with more amenities for eating. Most automobiles not only come with numerous cup-holders but many now have built-in tables and food storage compartments and some even have refrigerators. Food makers have also designed more foods to be consumed outside of the dining room, with everything from candy to pizza now sold in ready-to-eat packages or go-cups to fit in a car's cup-holders. We simply do not know if driving more makes people fatter because they not walking or if, in driving so much, they are simply consuming more food in their cars.

Another difficulty with blaming inactivity for our fatness comes in the actual way we burn calories. The overwhelming majority of calories we use are not for physical exercise but for simply maintaining our body functions and in processing the food we eat. The average person expends about 60 percent of their daily caloric intake through basal metabolism— that is the energy burned to keep the body alive—and about 10 percent of their calories to process food.[36] So even if we were completely inactive, we would still burn anywhere from 1,300 to 2,500 calories a day depending on our body weight.[37] And, as we saw in chapter 5, much of this also depends on a person's distinctive metabolism: while I might burn 2,000 calories a day in a sedentary state, another man with my height and weight may burn 2,300 calories. Unless someone is a lumberjack or a professional athlete, it is highly unlikely they will be burning more than a few hundred extra calories through exercise, and these differences may be less than those in people's basal metabolism.

This leads us to the biggest problem with blaming inactivity for our growing weight—the calorie differences between exercise and eating. As we've already seen, the American food industry has made it very convenient, cheap, and easy for us to eat large amounts of calories, particularly from refined carbohydrates. To consume about three hundred calories, all one needs to do is eat a seventy-cent bag of potato chips, a Snickers bar, or six Oreo cookies. To burn off three hundred calories through exercise, however, the average person needs to walk vigorously for about three miles. Given our food-rich environment, ordinary people would have to start becoming much more active to compensate for all the new calories they are consuming, particularly from snacking. According to Dr. Roland Weinsier at the University of Alabama, for Americans to begin losing weight through exercise, the current USDA exercise guidelines would have to be increased by almost 200 percent. In other words, Americans would need to start exercising at least two hours a day, six days a week for their weights to start going down.[38]

So America may be a sedentary country, but it does not necessarily mean that our inactivity rather than our diet is causing our weights to rise. Just because obese people are less physically active, on average, than nonobese people it doesn't necessarily mean that their inactivity is the primary source of their weight. Indeed, the relationship may be just the opposite—obese people are less active because their weight inhibits their physical exertion. For someone who is three hundred pounds, walking a mile is a lot more work than for someone half that size. And, for the country as a whole, it is much more likely that inactivity is making Americans heavier primarily by making them more susceptible to snacking: the more time a person spends lounging in front of the TV or waiting in traffic, the more they are likely to consume snack foods. From a weight standpoint, perhaps the worst you can say about our inactivity is that we are not exercising enough to compensate for all the extra calories we are taking in.

The Health Consequences of Inactivity

Now, for some this might come as a great relief. After all, if inactivity is not making us fat, then we don't need to worry about how little we are exercising, right? We can finally do away with all of those expensive gym memberships, awkward-fitting workout clothes, and neglected treadmills.

Perversely enough, this is exactly the logic behind much of the anti-obesity rhetoric coming from America's public health establishment. Although researchers, doctors, and health officials concerned with obesity almost unanimously recommend increasing physical activity, they almost all do so with the expressed goal of promoting weight loss. For example, the surgeon general's 2001 *Call to Action* on obesity focuses on assisting "Americans in balancing healthful eating with regular physical activity *to achieve* and maintain a healthy or healthier body weight" (my italics). Similarly, the CDC report that estimated 400,000 deaths attributable to obesity actually stipulated that the causes of death were "poor diet and physical inactivity" but assumed these were problematic because they made people obese.[39] Like Louis Dublin's "ideal weight" tables for the Metropolitan Life Insurance Company, they simply assumed, as many obesity researchers do, that the adverse effects of inactivity arise from their effects on body weight.[40] In the overwhelming majority of studies that detail the harmful consequence of obesity, exercise and physical fitness are not taken into account. Weight is almost always viewed as a consequence of inactivity.

But when it comes to our health, inactivity and weight are very separate issues, and there is a growing body of evidence that suggests the health problems of inactivity far exceed those associated with mere body weight. In fact, physical activity may be one of *the* most important determinants of our health. This was revealed in a fascinating thirty-year study at the University of Texas. In 1966, five Texas undergraduates agreed to stay in bed for twenty days and then had their heart and other physical states tested. As expected, they had poor heart rates and other signs of physical deterioration. Thirty years later these same five men were put on a six-month exercise program and then given the same physical tests as before. The results were quite revealing—the fifty-year-old men were in far better physical health than their younger, but bedridden selves. The twenty days in bed was worse for their aerobic capacity and heart rate than the subsequent thirty years of aging.[41]

The importance of exercise is also evident for many of the deaths and diseases that are currently being blamed on obesity. Over the past decade, scores of new studies have shown that health may be far less related to weight than to physical fitness. One of the leaders in this research effort is Steve Blair. For more than twenty years, he has closely followed the fitness levels, weight, and mortality of more than twenty-five thousand men: he concludes that men who are heavy and fit have far healthier hearts than those who are thin and sedentary.[42] During his study, men who had a normal weight (a BMI between 18.5 and 25) and were unfit had twice as much risk of death as those who were obese (a BMI greater than 30) and fit. Meanwhile, he found no difference in the mortality risk between obese and nonobese men who had the same level of cardiovascular fitness.[43] According to Blair's research, a significant portion of the deaths that we are currently attributing to obesity may actually be the result of too little exercise.

The importance of exercise is also evident in research on many "obesity-related" diseases; in fact, many of the ailments that are currently being attributed to obesity may actually be the result of inactivity. Take, for example, cancer. A recent study of nearly seventy-five thousand post-menopausal women found that women who walked briskly for 75 to 180 minutes a week were 18 percent less likely contract breast cancer than women who got no exercise, benefits that occurred regardless of their weights.[44] Similar findings occur for diabetes. Several studies have found that regular exercise also significantly reduces the likelihood of diabetes and the mortality rate from diabetes, once again, regardless of body weight.[45] More incredible, a recent study of diabetics actually found a lower mortality rate among those who started exercising and eating properly but who did not lose weight; in fact, those diabetics who actually lost weight had a significantly *higher* mortality rate.[46]

The same trend holds true for heart disease. Research published in the *New England Journal of Medicine* reports that among older men, physical fitness was a better predictor of mortality than smoking, hypertension, heart disease, and body weight.[47] Another study of women found that regardless of race, age, or body weight, the incidence of heart disease dramatically decreased as physical fitness improved, even when that physical fitness was simply walking a few hours a week.[48] These are but a few examples of an increasing body of research that shows exercise has a strong association with most major diseases independent of a person's body weight.

Upon some reflection, none of this should come as that great a surprise. If you think about our bodies from an evolutionary perspective, the greater importance of fitness relative to fatness is self-evident. For someone in the Ice Age, fatness matters little to health; indeed a Paleolithic fat person was more likely to survive in winter or through famine. Fitness, however, was another matter all together. Our ancestors lived in a strenuous environment of limited food and climatic hardship that surely required constant exertion. Over time, the human body evolved relative to these demands and came to function best with regular usage. And this evolutionary legacy is still with us. Although most Americans live in an environment that requires relatively little physical exertion, their bodies are little different from those that survived numerous ice ages and physical hardships.

Why We Worry More about Fatness than Fitness

So, why then, if exercise has so many benefits for health independent of weight, are we so much more focused on fatness than on inactivity? Why is inactivity generally mentioned only in relation to its effect on our weight? In many respects, we have already seen the answers to these questions in early chapters: Americans conflate fitness and weight because of their cultural ideas about body size. Although most Americans value bodily fitness as a marker of social prestige, they value thinness more. And for good reason—in a culture in which obesity is so demonized, being fit yet heavy does little to remove the stigma of a large body size, particularly for women. For instance, if a woman is incredibly fit but still bulky or heavy, she is still likely to face size discrimination. The emphasis on female fitness is primarily concerned with being thin not necessarily being healthy. Because of our cultural obsession with thinness, any discussion of exercise inevitably becomes connected to issues of weight while concerns about health fly out the window.

The conflation of obesity and fitness also harks back to the whole medical culture surrounding the idea of obesity as a "disease." Since the 1950s, Americans have been told by such people as Louis Dublin and his Metropolitan Life actuary tables that being too heavy is a threat to mortality. Little mention was ever made by Dublin or, until recently, most studies in medical journals about the health consequences of exercise. This was not because the importance of regular exercise was not recognized (doctors have known about the health benefits of fitness for some time); rather it was because body weight is so much easier to measure than fitness. One can easily calculate body weight with a simple scale, but to measure fitness one needs a heart monitor, treadmill, and other devices. Moreover, most Americans are also horrible estimators of their own fitness levels and generally exaggerate their own activity. So when epidemiologists started calculating the mortality risks or the incidence of diseases in large survey populations, they used BMI as an indicator of fitness because it can be easily gauged and is more reliable than the self-reports of people's own exercise levels.[49] Over the long haul, however, our limited biometric tools have helped to contribute to the conception that obesity is a "disease" whereas inactivity is generally ignored or unmeasured.

Another reason why we are less concerned with our inactivity is due, in part, to the profits of doctors and drugs. After all, there are numerous drugs and surgeries that can be prescribed to "treat" obesity but there are virtually no products that can be passively consumed to "treat" inactivity. Physicians can get reimbursed for prescribing drugs and performing surgery and drug companies actively market their products to physicians (unlike most fitness companies). Notwithstanding the late-night television infomercials hawking the "eight-minute" workout, fitness and exercise require active participation on the part of the "patient." Although a 12-billion-dollar-a-year fitness industry and a much larger sports equipment and clothing industry do make exercise a commodity to be consumed, Nike shoes and Gold's Gym memberships are only as beneficial as the efforts made on the part of the buyer. Moreover, it is important to remember that much of the profits garnered by the makers of sports apparel comes from their fashion relevance rather than their utility for exercise.

Moreover, since one can exercise through walking, running, gardening, or other noncommercialized activities, there are few direct profits that can be made for large industries when doctors recommend being more active. On the other hand, many weight-loss treatments involve either prescribing particular medicines, such as Xenical, or gastric-bypass surgery that make the patient a passive recipient of "treatment." And, because body weight is so easily measured, the "success" of the treatment can be readily gauged. Because obesity is something that can be "treated" by a doctor, it is given much more medical attention and becomes seen as a greater health hazard.

Together, these forces have come to create a standard by which our health and fitness is seen primarily in relationship to our weight. In reality our fitness should be, by itself, a far larger concern of public health, particularly based on the evidence that shows how little Americans exercise (despite the increases, most Americans still aren't exercising very much) and how much exercise influences our susceptibility to disease. However, when it comes to focusing on how we address our inactivity, we can begin to understand why we might rather concern ourselves with weight, for the problem of inactivity is a problem of what it actually means to live well.

The Paradox of Physical Liberation

> When the bread and butter problem is settled and all are rendered secure from fear of want, then the mind and soul will be free to develop as they never were before. We shall have a literature and an art such as the troubled heart and brain of man never before conceived. We shall have beautiful houses and happy homes such as want could never foster or drudgery secure.
>
> *Eugene V. Debs*

From Plato to Marx, philosophers and political activists since the beginning of civilization have pondered over the stultifying effects of bodily labor. Historically, physical drudgery has been recognized as one of the greatest impediments to true freedom in body, mind, and spirit. For instance, Aristotle believed that liberation from physical toil was a prerequisite for cultivating a good life. Alexis de Tocqueville believed that the continual drive of American technology and innovation would allow its citizens to enjoy "more leisure and less drudgery of life, [so that they] may devote their energies to thought and enlarge in all directions the empire of the mind."[50] Socialists, including Eugene Debs, and communists, including Karl Marx, railed against industrial capitalism precisely because it sapped all the physical energy from workers and inhibited them from realizing their true potential. Feminists such as Betty Freidan saw the burdens of labor as being particularly acute for women: the drudgery of housework and child rearing was the primary yoke of female domestic confinement.[51] Across the ideological and epistemological spectrum, the physical toil of daily existence has been viewed as the primary enemy of human freedom.

If these august thinkers are correct, then the innovations of the past decades should be ushering in a golden era for American civilization—the liberation from physical toil should not only be relieving our bodies but enlarging our minds, expanding our spirit, and ennobling our character. On the physical side, the necessary requirements are definitely there—the physical challenges of almost every aspect of the average American life have been greatly reduced. Cars have freed us from walking, computers and other machines have relieved us of physical drudgery, and appliances have diminished the time and effort of much housework. Technology has also opened up career opportunities for women and reduced many of the physical demands traditionally associated with women's social roles. In terms of simple exertion, American life has definitely gotten easier over the past few decades. But has it gotten better?

With regard to our weight and, more important, our health, it is difficult to know whether the freedom from physical demands is improving our lives. Consider the technologies listed above. Automobiles may have greatly increased our mobility, but they have fundamentally altered the nature of our habitats and reduced the walkability of many American communities. Television and computers may have opened a world of information and may provide a seemingly endless variety of entertainment options, but they have dramatically reduced our face-to-face social contacts.[52] And finally, as we've seen above, both of these technologies have made us more susceptible to eating and snacking on foods that are unhealthy for us. From the donut enjoyed on the morning commute to the carton of ice cream enjoyed during the late show, much of America's newfound leisure time is accompanied with sugary and fatty foods.

Thus, if America's growing weight is telling us anything, it is that we are not coping well with the physical license that is coming from sedentary leisure time. This is the lesson of the Amish. The fact that the Amish are thin and healthy is not simply because they exercise so much but because they have embraced a rigid, illiberal behavioral code that greatly restricts their range of behaviors. This highly constrained way of life forces them into activities that they might not otherwise choose, particularly if given the option to shirk. It is the very lack of freedom that keeps them healthy, well fed, and thin. But, for the rest of America, the solution to this paradox of exercise, liberty, and health is not so clear. America's core political principles are based on maximizing individual liberty and letting the free market work unencumbered to satisfy human needs in the most efficient manner possible. We are, in many ways, the antithesis of the Amish. Much like our snack foods, our labor-saving conveniences are all about expanding our choices and freedom. Thus, even if we want to improve "the public's" health, we need to figure out which freedoms we are willing to curtail. As we'll see in the next chapter, it is our inability to face this dilemma that explains the dysfunctional way we are trying to deal with our weight, diet, and activity as a matter of public policy.

eight
Obesity Policy:
The Fix Is In

Arkansas governor Mike Huckabee has seen the light. In 2003, this former Baptist minister was diagnosed with diabetes and, without a drastic change in his life, he was facing possible organ failure, blindness, and loss of limbs. Admittedly, he was, in his own words, "a poster child for everything that was wrong" with the American lifestyle: he never exercised, carried lots of stress, and ate a diet high in fats, sugar, and salt.[1] He also weighed more than 280 pounds. The diabetes, however, came as revelation and soon after being diagnosed Huckabee made a life-changing conversion. He became an avid runner; switched his diet to lean meats, fruits, and vegetables; and, after participating in a weight-loss program at the University of Arkansas, shed more than 105 pounds.

Not merely content with his own new health, Huckabee now wants to convert his fellow Arkansans. And the central focus of his crusade is weight. Last year, he launched "Healthy Arkansas," an initiative to get the residents of his state to shed their title as one of the nation's most obese states. In his weekly radio addresses, Huckabee extols his fellow Arkansans to lose weight, eat less, and exercise; he also tours the country continually promoting the Arkansas plan. For Huckabee, the word of weight loss has become akin to gospel.[2]

In these efforts, Governor Huckabee is not alone. Obesity is a hot political issue and nearly every politician, it seems, wants to do something about it. Since 1998, almost every state in the union has adopted or has considered policies to promote weight loss: .twenty-five states have eliminated or are trying to ban candy and soda from school vending machines; the New York state legislature is considering a bill to tax junk food, video games, and DVD rentals; Iowa's schools are giving away fresh fruits and vegetables for students to take home; Colorado is encouraging employers to let their workers walk during meetings; California is considering legislation that would force all restaurants to post the caloric contents of their foods; and so on. The federal government is also jumping into the fray. Already, the Department of Health and Human Services has spent several hundred million dollars in its "VERB: It's What You Do" media campaign, which encourages teenagers to be more active; the Food and Drug Administration is revising food labeling guidelines to reflect actual portion sizes; the Department of Agriculture claims to be revising the "food pyramid" to incorporate recommendations to combat obesity; and the Centers for Disease Control and Prevention are launching several initiatives to combat obesity. Within the next few years, state and local governments will spend nearly a billion dollars on anti-obesity programs.

From the preceding chapters, it might seem like these efforts are for naught: after all, if obesity is not a cause of death and disease, then simply making Americans thin will not necessarily make them any healthier. Yet, despite their faulty premise, these proposals are not entirely misplaced. In the name of weight loss, most anti-obesity proposals actually end up focusing on some of the real contributors to many chronic diseases, namely our problematic diet and lack of exercise. In their efforts to make Americans lose weight by eating better and exercising more, some obesity researchers argue, these policies may greatly improve our health.

Unfortunately, such an optimistic rationalization falls short. The problem with our anti-obesity programs is not simply that they focus on the wrong goal (getting us to lose weight); rather they do not address the real source of our health problems. Because few Americans want to limit their liberty and freedoms, our anti-obesity proposals will end up being like most diet plans; they will promise much, but deliver little and some might even cause great harm. Yet, they are worth examining in some detail because they show how difficult it is to formulate policies that try to change how we eat and exercise. If you want to know why it is so hard to change the way we live, then a good place to begin is how we are trying to curb our growing weight.

Schools and Junk Food

By far, the biggest concern with obesity in America is with regard to our children. Over the past twenty years, juvenile obesity has risen nearly twice as fast as in adults and, today, anywhere between 15 and 37 percent of American kids are thought to be at an "unhealthy" body weight depending on who is doing the estimating.[3] Because juvenile obesity is the single biggest predictor of adult obesity and is associated with diseases such as type 2 diabetes, it is often viewed as the first line of attack against America's weight gain. As the pediatrician Nancy Krebs proclaims, "We've got to stop obesity [in kids] because we can't treat it once it occurs [in adults]."[4] Juvenile obesity is also seen as an appropriate venue for government action because our government traditionally affords special protections for children. Because children cannot be held to the same standards as adults, the arguments about personal responsibility are less germane. For all these reasons, there has been relatively less debate about *whether* government should do anything to address juvenile obesity. Rather, the major question is *what* government should be doing to keep our kids from getting fat.

The most obvious target for government intervention is schools. Most American children are in public schools that are financed by taxes and governed by state legislatures and locally elected boards. What happens within their walls is a legitimate target of public concern and one can reasonably assume that our schools should be doing everything possible to promote their students' health, including encouraging physical activity, teaching proper health and nutrition, and making sure kids are eating foods high in nutritional value.

Yet, in reality, most American schools are not meeting these goals. The typical American school has vending machines selling soda, cookies, and candy and its snack bar or campus store sells highly processed and sugared foods. Few schools make time for daily physical activity and education and many students get virtually no instruction on health or nutrition. In fact, many students may often get incorrect messages about what are healthy food choices. Given the sorry state of nutrition and physical education in American schools, it is no surprise that many health advocates are blaming them for contributing to the rise in juvenile obesity.[5]

Like our general orientation toward obesity, however, these anxieties, too, are misplaced. To begin with, just because our schools are awash in junk food, it does not necessarily mean that schools are making our kids fat. Nor does it mean that schools are an appropriate place to get them to lose weight. Moreover, if you examine why our schools are selling junk food and cutting physical education, you can see the political challenges that are inherent in trying to promote better eating and more exercise.

Let us start with the issue of junk food. Many public health advocates argue that America's schools are too beholden to food and beverage companies and are too active in promoting the consumption of soda, candy, and other low-nutrition fare. In many ways, this is a valid claim. Nearly all American public high schools and three-quarters of its middle schools have vending machines, snack bars, or campus stores.[6] A recent study by the Center for Science in the Public Interest found that the overwhelming majority of school vending machines offer unhealthy drink and food options: of the drink options, 75 percent were soda, imitation juices, or sports drinks and 85 percent of snacks were candy, chips, or cookies.[7] In addition, many schools offer contracts to fast-food companies to provide lunch and breakfast. A recent survey of California schools by the Public Health Institute found that 95 percent of school districts reported selling fast-foods, the most common being Taco Bell, Domino's Pizza, and Subway.[8]

According to many critics, the problem is not simply that schools are providing such unnutritious fare; it is that they actively promoting its consumption.[9] School children get picked up in buses advertising Pepsi, carry books with covers touting sugar cereals and cookies, and learn from textbooks and lesson plans that use candy, soda, and other snack foods as examples in the materials. Sometimes students are even directly encouraged to consume junk food. A few years ago, the Colorado Springs school district received a hefty 11 million dollar exclusive contract (called a pouring contract) from Coca-Cola under the stipulation that it would sell more than seventy thousand cases of Coke a year. When it became clear that the district would not meet this sales goal, school district official John Bushey urged his principals to promote more Coke consumption. Although Bushey was lambasted as "the Coke guy" and widely criticized for pushing Coke on his students, his efforts were not isolated and school districts around the country have instituted similar, albeit more subtle ways of meeting the goals of similar pouring contracts.

Given the prevalence of soda and junk food in schools, this would seem like a ripe target for policy remediation, and many state and local governments seem to be taking action. As of 2005, twenty-five state legislatures are now considering proposals to eliminate or restrict vending machines and a handful of school districts, including in Los Angeles, New York City, and Oakland, have banned the sale of soft drinks on campus. From the headlines, one might easily get the impression that soda and junk food are on the way out of our public schools.

Yet a closer look shows that many of these restrictions are paper tigers. Most of the propositions to ban or restrict vending machines only apply to elementary and middle schools, not to high schools. In some states, such as Texas, schools ban the sale of soda and candy only during mealtimes and allow it to be sold during other parts of the school day. In Colorado, schools only require that half of the machines have nutritional items while schools in Los Angeles and Alaska ban soda but allow other high-sugar beverages such as Gatorade or Snapple. In fact, only a handful of school districts have completely eliminated soda vending machines from their campuses; in the vast majority of schools, soda vending machines are a persistent presence.

Why is there so little action on junk food in schools when the problem seems so self-evident? A big part of the resistance comes from the schools themselves. Perpetually strapped for resources, schools have found that exclusive pouring contracts with soft drink companies provide the much-needed money for extracurricular activities including band, art classes, and sports programs. With citizens often unwilling to pay more in local and state taxes, the only way many schools can fund their programs is by making deals with food and beverage companies. As Jon Peterson, deputy director of procurement for Washington, D.C., recognized, pouring contracts are "a godsend."[10]

Part of the resistance also comes from parents. Perhaps the most surprising finding in the 2001 survey I conducted on Americans' attitudes toward obesity was that only 47 percent of respondents favored banning soda and junk food from schools; nearly as many, 43 percent, were against such bans.[11] Many parents, it seems, want their kids to be able to consume whatever they want at school and believe that it is not up to the schools to regulate what their children are eating. This sentiment is backed up by the food and beverage companies themselves, who argue that they are a vital part of the public-private partnerships that sustain public education in America. The National Soft Drink Association proclaims, "Soft drink companies have had a strong and long-lasting commitment to America's education process for more than fifty years,"[12] and much of the public agrees.

Finally, many school officials argue that if students cannot buy a soda or candy bar at school, they will merely buy it elsewhere and then bring it to school. In their minds, they are only taking advantage of what is a natural market and using it to further their educational goals. Because the millions of dollars that can be had from pouring contracts and sales are so much more politically palatable than raising taxes to finance school operations, there will continue to be strong political pressure to keep fast-food and vending contracts available in many schools.

A similar problem exists with respect to physical education. A generation ago, most public schools had regular PE requirements for all students. For example, during the 1970s, when I was in elementary and junior high school in Texas, we had a state mandate of an hour of PE a day. Today, however, schools are increasingly cutting back on physical education. An Institute of Medicine report found that only 8 percent of elementary schools and 6 percent of middle and high schools provided daily PE for the whole school year and less than 30 percent of middle and high schools require PE as part of their curriculum.[13] Even though most states stipulate that their elementary and secondary schools provide a few hours of PE each week, such mandates have been undermined in recent years by school administrators both strapped for resources and facing increasing pressure to improve test scores in order to meet the standards of the No Child Left Behind provisions for funding. "Are we meeting [state physical education] requirements?" asks Wisconsin school superintendent Mark Lichte, "No. Do I care? No. Until they start allocating what they're mandating, we can't meet their mandates."[14]

Now many proponents of public education are using concerns over juvenile obesity as a way to address these problems. Their hope is that if people see obesity as a threat to their children's health, they will support extra taxes to provide better food and increase physical education funding. While these goals are undoubtedly laudable, there is a big problem with this strategy; it bases policy on weight loss.

Schools, however, are not weight-loss centers nor should they be treated as such. To begin with, it stretches their mission beyond that for which they are designed. Already, we ask our schools not only to train our children in a variety of nonacademic skills and tasks: we insist they instill good values and encourage interpersonal skills and teamwork. In many urban areas, schools are being overtaxed as social service centers and advocates of child welfare. Adding weight maintenance to the education curriculum may simply be burdening public institutions with yet another task for which they are not designed nor adequately funded.

In addition, there is no clear evidence that schools are contributing to the growth in obesity. The obesity-related complaints about school lunches, vending machines, and physical education are based largely on the assumption that these factors are causing our kids to get fat. Yet, I find little evidence to support this claim. For example, in looking at survey data on the health behavior of middle and high school students, the factor I found that best predicted whether or not a kid was obese was *tooth brushing*.[15] More important than how much junk food they ate, soda they drank, or physical education they received was whether or not they brushed their teeth. Among fourteen- to seventeen-year-olds, only 16 percent of kids who brushed their teeth more than once a day were overweight compared to 24 percent who brushed less than once a day. Of course, other factors were important as well—teenagers who play more computer games, eat more fast-food, and drink less whole milk were also more likely to be obese—but these factors were tiny in comparison with tooth brushing. Meanwhile school policies, such as whether the kid was in physical education or ate school lunches, had no predictive power for whether or not a child was obese.

Now obviously the act of brushing one's teeth plays little direct role in a child's weight, but it is a good indicator of something else—in what type of household the child lives. Children who brush their teeth more often are more likely to come from homes where health and hygiene are a priority. In households in which kids brush their teeth regularly, the children are also more likely to eat fresh fruits and vegetables, drink more milk instead of soda, and spend less time playing video games or watching television.[16] In other words, outside of genetics, the biggest factor predicting a child's weight is what type of parenting they receive.

The tremendous importance of parenting (and the relatively small impact of schools on children's weight) is also evident in the largest and most comprehensive school-based anti-obesity programs. In 1997, the Johns Hopkins School of Public Health started a five-year anti-obesity intervention they called "Pathways" in seven Native American elementary schools. Children in the targeted schools were put on special diets of high-nutrition and low-calorie foods, had increased physical education, were given extensive guidance in nutrition and exercise, and had a program of family involvement that attempted to enlist the support of parents. After three years in this program, with careful controls, researchers found that their efforts had virtually no impact on the participants' weights. Compared to a control group of students who were not in the program, students in the Pathways program did not have any significant difference in weight.[17] Although they were eating better and exercising more at school, they were not any thinner.[18] Nearly identical results also happened with a similar study, the Child and Adolescent Trial for Cardiovascular Health.[19] The results of the interventions seem pretty consistent: school programs can help somewhat to improve student nutrition and fitness but they cannot do much to influence their weight.

In sum, it is easy to argue that the soda, candy, and junk food in schools are not good for our children, but there is little evidence that schools are contributing to the growing rates of obesity. Although nutrition advocates are using juvenile obesity as a mechanism for trying to correct school lunch and food policies, we should not expect the removal of vending machines or fast-food outlets in schools to have big results. As the Pathways study revealed, even the most intensive anti-obesity programs have little impact on children's weights (although they may have health benefits). The key factor that really determines whether children are obese is the type of parenting they receive at home. Parents who emphasize good nutrition, exercise, and an absence of sugar and junk food are less likely to have children with weight problems. Of course, many parents feel powerless to monitor their children's eating and exercise behavior particularly in the face of America's fast-food culture. This leads us to the next front in the war on obesity—food advertising and nutrition information.

What We Know about Food and Nutrition

According to many public health advocates, American children are under bombardment. This year, the average American kid will see approximately ten thousand food advertisements, with the overwhelming majority being for fast-food, sugary cereals, soft drinks, candy, and high-calorie snacks.[20] Children's television is like a cartoon food bazaar: Scooby Doo and Buzz Lightyear sell Betty Crocker fruit snacks, the Rugrats promote Nabisco fruit treats, the Powerpuff Girls hawk Hunt's pudding snacks, Shrek peddles Twinkies, and so on. With so many advertisements in bright, primary colors with zany characters touting fun, happy snack foods and cereals, it is often difficult to know when the shows end and the commercials begin. When not using television, food companies are targeting children in other ways. McDonald's lures children with playgrounds, which are among the safest places to play in many urban neighborhoods. Taco Bell comes to schools, inserting their products into lesson plans and extracurricular activities. Food ads are in movies, on buses and subways, in department and toy stores, in amusement parks, and even schools. Channel One, a TV news program for middle and high schools, forces more than eight million students to watch at least two minutes of commercials each day, most of which are for fast-food, candy, and snack foods.[21] As Carol Herman, senior vice president of Grey Advertising notes, "It isn't enough to just advertise on television. . . . You've got to become part of the fabric of [children's] lives."[22] On this front, America's food companies are very successful.

Given the prevalence of food advertisements aimed at children, it is not surprising that many critics are blaming them for the rise in juvenile obesity. Even if parents are primarily responsible for their children's weights, they must compete with a multibillion-dollar advertising campaign shaping their children's preferences. Advertisers target children in the hopes of inculcating brand loyalty at an early age and by using them as leverage over their parents' spending choices. And children are quite adept lobbyists—ask any parent whose children become apoplectic whenever driving by a McDonald's about the power of the 400 million dollars that the company spends each year in its advertising campaigns directed at children. Many believe such pressure contributes to a deterioration of dietary choices over time.[23] With kids constantly pressuring parents for familiar sweet and fatty foods and many American parents harried between work and child rearing, junk food is often the de facto choice in trying to bring harmony to family time, even among parents who try to make good nutritional choices.

The case against children's food ads is but a small part of a larger battle being waged by public health advocates to improve nutrition information. Many obesity experts believe that Americans are gaining weight because they are getting too little of the right information from the government and too much of the wrong information from food makers. To correct this information gap, they have called for two policy approaches. One aims to curb the food advertisements directed at children, and the other focuses on nutritional recommendations and food labeling that are used by adults. While, in theory, both of these proposals may be important for helping Americans understand the content of what they're eating, in practice, it is unclear whether either will do much to help them lose weight or even eat healthier. Once again, this is partly because of the politics shaping how these policies get implemented and partly because these policies fail to tackle the underlying sources of Americans' food choices.

Take the fight against food advertisements. For Kelly Brownell, halting the multibillion-dollar food advertising campaigns aimed at children is a crucial part of his strategy to combat juvenile obesity. Along with groups such as the Center for Science in the Public Interest, Brownell has called for a number of policies to reduce the amount and impact of food advertising on children. Some of these are rather benign, such as asking celebrities and children's entertainment companies such as Disney to avoid endorsing unhealthy food products. Other suggestions, however, are much more drastic. One idea, which has been adopted in Sweden, would prohibit advertisements for unhealthy foods during children's television programs. Another is to apply the "fairness doctrine" to food advertisements. In the 1960s, officials from the Federal Communications Commission ruled that under a statute known as the fairness doctrine television stations would be required to run an equal amount of antismoking public service announcements for all the cigarette commercials they aired. The impact of the antismoking ads was so great that, soon afterward, the tobacco companies voluntarily withdrew all television ads and concentrated most of their advertising on the print media and billboards.[24] Even though the fairness doctrine has since been repealed, Brownell thinks a similar type of doctrine should be applied to food advertisements—for every minute of commercials promoting Coco-Puffs, Mountain Dew, or Skittles, there would be, presumably, a minute of commercials stressing the importance of eating apples, broccoli, and cottage cheese.

In terms of public opinion, such proposals actually have a lot of support. In the 2001 survey, 57 percent of respondents favored regulations on food advertisements that were directed at children, making it the most popular anti-obesity proposal on the table. Among the scores of parents I interviewed for this book, these policies were endorsed with equal fervor. Many parents feel helpless in light of the continual bombardment of food ads aimed at their children. If their kids were not constantly pressuring them for sugared cereals, fast-food, and soda, they might sustain healthier eating habits. As with junk food in schools, limiting food ads at kids would seem to be a proposal that makes a lot of sense from both a nutritional and weight standpoint.

So why then is there no significant government action to regulate food advertisements? Part of this has do to politics; the Grocery Manufacturers Association and the National Soft Drink Association are powerful lobbying groups that are sure to fight any government attempts to restrict their members' ability to sell their products. In this fight, they are joined by the television networks and entertainment companies that rely heavily on the revenue from food advertising.

But, perhaps even more important than politics are the logistical issues of trying to implement these policies, particularly in determining which foods are "junk." And this highlights the problem with government trying to encourage people to eat healthier. Food producers often argue that all foods have some nutritional content and determining which foods fail a nutritional threshold is a tricky business. Because most people's diets are varied, it is virtually impossible to attribute any one disease to a particular food product and thus difficult to know which products should not be allowed to advertise. Then there is the problem of restaurants such as McDonald's, which offer salads, chicken sandwiches, and yogurt as well as junk food. How are ads for such places to be regulated? Is the same Ronald McDonald who sells salads as villainous as the one who super sizes your trans fat laden fries? Finally, even if the government were to apply the same nutrition standards that are used for federally sponsored school lunch programs, it is not clear that this would limit advertisements for fattening foods. Kids may no longer see ads for Coco-Puffs, Mountain Dew, and Skittles, but they would still be bombarded with appeals for Frosted Raisin Bran, Capri Sun, and Fruit Roll-ups which, despite their higher nutritional contents, are still high in calories and sugars.

These same problems also confront how we handle the issue of food information for adults. Food labeling and nutritional recommendations are an important part of the FDA and USDA's mandate to promote public health. As Americans eat more processed foods and meals outside of the home, they have less and less direct control over the specific content of their diets. In response, the federal government has initiated numerous policies over the past several decades to help Americans understand what they should be consuming. These include nutritional recommendations, such as the food pyramid, as well as requirements that certain packaged foods carry information about their contents.

But, even though these programs are designed to help consumers control what they eat, many critics charge that the governments' nutritional recommendations may actually be sending the wrong message. Much of this starts with recommendations in the federal government guidelines for nutrition, particularly the authoritative food pyramid. According to such critics as Marion Nestle, the problem of the food pyramid starts with its authors, the Department of Agriculture, which has the dual missions of both protecting America's health and promoting its agricultural sector. With these competing constituencies, it is very difficult for the USDA to avoid political pressures when making its dietary recommendations. For example, the USDA originally utilized a pyramid shape rather than a circle or a bowl when making its nutritional recommendations to give hierarchical priority to fats, milk, and meat, even though it was recommending few servings of these foods. This decision was made largely in response to political pressure from the meat and dairy industries.[25]

This type of political lobbying has been clearly evident in the new USDA nutritional recommendations. Because food makers view any nutritional recommendation as having a profound impact on their markets, the major food industries spent millions lobbying Congress and the FDA to ensure that the new pyramid would not eliminate their particular product. The Dairy Council, the American Millers' Association, the U.S. Potato Board, the National Cattlemen's Beef Association, the Chocolate Manufacturers' Association, the Snack Food Association, the California Walnut Board, and the Malaysian Palm Oil Board were all very active in trying to influence the governments' updated nutrition recommendations.[26] And they succeeded. The new and highly complicated scheme of food pyramids incorporates nearly every imaginable food group. For example, there is no evidence that adults need to consume dairy products on a daily basis; nevertheless, the pyramid still recommends three servings a day of milk, cheese, or butter. Because the best way to please all these constituencies is by giving them some representation in the food recommendations, the government ends up promoting the idea of "eating more."[27]

The government's other method of informing the public about nutrition, food labels, is equally problematic. Even when food packages do have nutrition labels, they are not necessarily helpful or accurate. Consider our current listings of serving sizes. In 1990, Congress amended the Food, Drug, and Cosmetic Act to require mandatory nutrition labeling of certain packaged foods, including the amount of calories per serving, fats, carbohydrates, and sugars.[28] The regulations also required that this nutritional information be listed relative to industry standard serving sizes rather than the size of the package. This, however, can often be misleading. A twenty-ounce bottle of Coke, which is designed and sold for individual consumption contains, according to the nutritional information on the back, only twenty-seven grams of sugar and one hundred calories. But, it is only after reading the fine print that one finds the bottle actually has 2.5 servings. So in reality, the single bottle of Coke has 67 grams of sugar and 250 calories. Numerous other food products, such as chips, cookies, and candy that are packaged for individual consumption, often carry as many as three or four serving sizes. To further complicate matters, the serving sizes listed on the nutritional labels are often twice as large as the serving sizes recommended in the food pyramid. In other words, a bag of potato chips that lists two servings on its nutritional guide would correspond with nearly four servings as recommended by the food pyramid.[29]

In response to such criticisms, the FDA recently announced that it was making the accurate reporting of serving sizes a priority in its campaign against obesity. In a March 2004 letter to food manufacturers, the FDA encourages food producers to list the entire contents of packages as a single serving size if "it can reasonably be consumed at a single eating occasion."[30] The FDA warned food producers that they would correct the serving sizes listed on the packages that violated this norm but left it up to the food producers themselves to initiate changes voluntarily to their own packaging. As of February 2005, however, there does not seem to be much difference in food labeling. A survey of items in a nearby convenience store reveals that listing several serving sizes on individualized packages of soda, chips, cookies, and candy is alive and well: a King Size Baby Ruth bar had three servings (480 calories total), a "go-cup" of Nutter Butter bites had four servings (520 calories) and a ninety-nine-cent bag of Fritos contained four and a half servings (720 calories).

Once again, the failure or inability of the FDA to enforce its own nutritional recommendations demonstrates how difficult it is to formulate a policy to get people to "eat better." Part of the problem is simply political. When the FDA or USDA convenes a working group to make recommendations on labeling, it inevitably includes "stakeholder participation," which means heeding the concerns of the food and beverage industries. Or consider, once again, the FDA. The entire anti-obesity initiative of the nation's primary regulatory agency of food and diet is based on the idea, in their own words, that "calories count." The FDA claims to be tackling obesity by getting people to reduce their caloric intake. What they are not trying to do, however, is influence the types of foods people are eating, for obvious political reasons. This is tantamount to treating all calories as equal, which belies the fact that calories from certain types of fats and carbohydrates may act differently on the body and be more problematic. Nevertheless, by putting a vague emphasis on calories rather than focusing on any particular foods, the FDA avoids offending any one particular food industry.[31]

Yet, for all the understandable hand-wringing about how interest group politics are influencing food labeling and nutritional recommendations, there remains one ugly fact—all these things may have little effect on Americans' eating behaviors. When it comes to determining what people eat, considerations such as taste, convenience, and cost far outweigh concerns for nutrition. Government recommendations and food labels may play a small part in our food choices, but it is only a very small part. For example, even though most Americans are aware of the food pyramid and have a vague idea about its recommendations, only about 12 percent of the population actually follows these guidelines.[32]

Ultimately there are many reasons why nutrition recommendations have so little effect. For one, there are many competing messages regarding nutritional information and diet, particularly from fads and diet programs such as the Atkins diet. With so many different claims about the problem of carbohydrates versus fat, it is difficult to know what to believe. But more important is the simple problem of appetite. Take me. I love chocolate chip cookies. Although I know they are not good for me, I like them because they taste great and often make me feel good. When confronted with a cookie, it is far too easy to discount the future health consequences relative to the immediate gratification that it will provide. Given the power of my appetites, simply providing me more information is unlikely to make me change my behavior because I already know that it is bad. And, for some critics, this is precisely the problem—we need to help people control their impulses. From this perspective, the real target of obesity policy should not be amending nutritional labels on the foods but changing the availability of the food.

But Can You Make Them Eat It?

Nowadays, food is everywhere. Not only is there seemingly a Starbucks on every corner and a food court in every mall, but food is now turning up in new and unlikely places including drugstores, video stores, bookstores, housewares stores, and nearly every gas station. Snack food is in gyms, hair salons, record and appliance stores, and practically anywhere else that Americans shop. The problem is not simply that food is so omnipresent, but that the types of foods that are everywhere are mostly processed, packaged foods with lots of sugars and partially hydrogenated oils (or trans fats). It is the rare gas station or convenience store that offers fresh fruits or vegetables; the overwhelming majority of new places that are selling food only stock those items that have a long shelf life and have little chance of spoilage. This is particularly the case in many poor, urban areas where supermarkets are few and far between, and most food options are either fast-food restaurants or convenience stores.[33]

For many public health advocates, the biggest challenge of obesity is tackling the problem of America's food supply, particularly the inundation of processed, high-calorie meals that are so ubiquitous in American life. And this concern has some legitimacy. As we've seen, the abundance of snack foods, particularly those high in refined carbohydrates and trans fats, are probably behind much of the increase in diabetes and other metabolic disorders that are so chronic in the United States. Inevitably, if we really want to improve our health, we need to figure out what to do with all this junk food.

Regulating junk food, however, is an extremely difficult issue. Food holds a unique place in our lives and thus presents some exceptional challenges as a target for public policy. For example, compare junk food with tobacco. Although both have been labeled menaces to public health, tobacco is far easier to regulate than food—it is not necessary for our survival, its sources are easily targeted, and its elimination provides clear health benefits. None of these can be said of food in general or even junk food in particular. Nevertheless, many are calling for the same strategies that have been used against tobacco as a means of tackling junk food. As Margot Wooton of the Center for Science in the Public Interest says, "we are definitely looking to smoking as a blueprint against fast food."[34]

Perhaps the most effective antitobacco tool has been taxes, and just as cigarette taxes have had a dramatic impact on discouraging smoking, so many health experts believe that a "snack tax" might reduce snacking. The evidence, however, suggests otherwise. For not only are snack taxes ineffective (Arkansas, Virginia, and Washington already have extra taxes on soda and this has had no impact on its consumption), but they can also be harmful, particularly to the poor. The reason why snack taxes don't work is that the demand for food is relatively insensitive to price: economists generally predict that a 10 percent increase in food prices would only reduce food consumption by less than 1 percent.[35] That means if you want to reduce soda consumption by just 10 percent, you would have to impose a 100 percent tax; if you wanted to reduce soda consumption by half, you would have to make a can of coke cost about four dollars. Not only would such taxes do little to deter demand, but they would take more money out of the pockets of the poor. Ironically, this would, in turn, cause them to eat even worse. Nutritionist Adam Drewnoski has shown that when food prices rise, poorer people eat even fewer fruits and vegetables and eat more processed foods.[36] Ironically, snack taxes might actually have the opposite effect—they might encourage people to eat *more* junk.

To be fair, many anti-obesity advocates such as Kelly Brownell recognize this fact, and instead see the snack taxes as a way to subsidize public campaigns that would make healthier foods available to the poor. Yet, in an indirect way, this is already being done. This year the federal government will spend more than 31 billion dollars on food supplement programs including food stamps, school lunch programs, and supplemental support for women, infants, and children (WIC). For the 12 million food stamp recipients, fruits and vegetables are ostensibly free; yet, among these populations obesity is quite high and nutrition is quite low.[37] Other research shows that food stamp recipients tend to be more obese than equally poor women who do not participate in the program.[38] Based on this evidence, some policy experts, including Douglas Besharov at the American Enterprise Institute, argue for reducing the 31 billion dollars we spend on food supplement programs as a means of cutting obesity.[39]

Cutting off food aid to the poor may seem like a logical mechanism for lowering their weight, but it is unlikely to do much either to prevent obesity or to improve nutrition. This is because the link between food stamp usage, weight, and nutrition has less to do with the poor having too much money to spend on food and more to do with their food choices, which tend to be mostly fast-foods or processed foods with long shelf lives. The relatively high calorie-to-dollar ratio of many processed foods such as chips, candy, and cookies makes them a relative bargain for people on limited food budgets. If you are only getting $465 a month to feed your family, it makes sense to try and get the most calories you can for this money. One dollar can get you more than seven hundred calories from a grab bag of Fritos chips. It is hard to match that price-to-calorie ration with broccoli, squash, and greens (assuming one also has kitchen facilities to prepare them), particularly when you are only cooking for one or two people. For many women with children in poor areas, the most logical food options are heavily processed foods.

Now it might seem logical that if the costs of fresh fruits and vegetables are too high, then the government should simply do more to lower their prices. The problem with that logic is that just as prices are not good at discouraging food consumption they are not very good at encouraging it either. For instance, the USDA recommends that the average American needs to increase their consumption of green leafy vegetables (spinach and broccoli) and deep-yellow vegetables (squash) by 400 percent. According to their own calculations, to effect this change, the prices on these vegetables would have to drop by a negative 289 percent—in other words, we would need to pay people to eat them.[40] Thus simply subsidizing nutritious foods is unlikely to make a big impact on their consumption and would likely only benefit middle- and upper-income shoppers who buy these foods anyway.

Given this situation, others have suggested altering the food stamp program to limit what types of foods a person can buy. However, this, too, raises a thorny set of political and ethical issues. Right now the government allows food stamps to be used for any type of food "designed for human consumption." Although this list does not include tobacco, alcohol, or hot foods, it does include chips, soda, candy, and most other high-calorie foods. Recently, Minnesota petitioned the Department of Agriculture to remove certain unhealthy foods, including candy and soda, from food stamp eligibility. This proposal met with a large outcry from both activists and food makers who asked why the poor should be kept from consuming the same foods as everyone else. But the bigger problem was in determining which foods should be deemed ineligible. Under the current Minnesota provisions, a Nestle Crunch bar would be ineligible but a Nestle Kit Kat bar would be okay because the latter contains flour. Even with the ban, high-calorie items including ice cream, chips, cookies, and fruit drinks would still remain as foods. For these reasons among many others, the USDA denied Minnesota's request.

In short, America may be awash in junk food, but the current proposals either to restrain their consumption or to encourage the consumption of fruits and vegetables are unlikely to work. This does not mean that all food programs are useless. There are numerous reasons for promoting a healthy diet among American consumers. Given the billions of dollars we spend every year on subsidies to large agribusiness, it is quite reasonable to enact policies that would make produce other than corn, rice, potatoes, and wheat more readily available to American consumers, particularly those in low-income areas, where grocery stores are often inaccesible. But we should not expect these nutrition programs to alter our weights because, ultimately, such taxes and price supports are both ineffective and inappropriate mechanisms for shaping dietary behavior. It may be in the public interest to ensure that all citizens have access to healthy food, but it is not in the public interest for government to be telling certain groups of people what they can and cannot eat. Short of paying people to eat right, it is unclear what the government can do to help people eat better. This is because the problem ultimately goes beyond the particular foods we are eating.

The Government's
War on Obesity

In 2001, then surgeon general David Satcher fired the first shot in the federal government's current war on obesity when he released the *Call to Action to Prevent and Decrease Overweight and Obesity*. Citing the putative thousands of deaths and the billions in healthcare costs from obesity, the surgeon general called on the nation to take action. In turn, federal and state governments have responded over the past four years with a variety of programs designed to make the nation lose weight. Yet none of these are likely to do much to either lower our weights or improve our health because of their whole approach. Not only do they make weight the center of the policy, but they also want to address our weight with a simple "eat less, exercise more formula." The surgeon general, for instance, recommends, "reducing access to foods high in fat, calories, and added sugars, and to excessive portion sizes" and to "reduce time spent watching television and other sedentary behaviors."[41] In other words, the country needs to go on a diet.

While all these recommendations are unobjectionable as a general guide to healthy living (even if they won't do anything for our weights), they are very problematic as a matter of public policy. Consider, after all, the similar experience of millions of Americans who are trying to lose weight voluntarily. Of the millions of Americans who go on diets every year, only a tiny number are able to keep their weight off. The problem is not necessarily with the diets themselves. Nearly any popular diet program, if followed correctly, will result in some weight loss, simply because it starves the dieter. Rather, the real problem with diets is with the very idea of dieting. The term "diet" originally derived from the Greek term, *diæta*, meaning the "prescribed course of life." Adopted by ecclesiastical orders in medieval Europe, the term was meant to convey a code of conduct and set of rules by which a person would live their life. These rules would dictate how and when a person would eat, work, pray, and so forth. They were, in short, about eliminating choices and individual autonomy.

Of course, this is not how most popular diets are advertised. Almost all the best-selling diet books and commercial diet programs sell the promise of maximizing rather than limiting our choices. As Barry Sears, author of *The Zone*, says, "The beauty of the dietary system presented in this book is that . . . it doesn't call for a great deal of the kind of unrealistic self- sacrifice that causes many people to fall off the diet wagon. . . . In fact, I can even show you how to stay within these dietary guidelines while eating at fast-food restaurants."[42] Many diets even take a further step by incorporating sinful foods into the very fabric of the plan. Arthur Agatston, author of the best-selling *South Beach Diet*, sells this idea on the first page of the book: "You'll be urged to have snacks in mid-morning and mid-afternoon, *whether you need to or not*. You'll have dessert after dinner."[43] On his diet, Robert Atkins promises that "you can eat luxuriously—heavy cream, butter, mayonnaise, cheeses, meats," and so forth.[44] Like George Bush's call to consumption, the idea behind these plans is to sacrifice without sacrificing, to be disciplined without the discipline.

But, like most of the policy recommendations meant to tackle obesity, this is a false promise. By their very definition, diets are about limiting our choices. Sure, Atkins will let you eat butter, cheese, and bacon, but you must swear off bread, pasta, and bagels. Weight Watchers may allow you to choose from a wide variety of foods, but you have to scrupulously count your caloric points every day and not eat outside of your prescribed range. If these diet plans don't work over the long run it is because they are in such contradiction with every other part of our lives. Take the Atkins diet. Despite its recent popularity, the Atkins diet is by no means new or novel—low-carbohydrate diets trace back to the very first diet book written by Englishman William Banting in the mid-nineteenth century. The reason that low-carbohydrate diets continue to reappear every few decades is because they are too monotonous to maintain over a lifetime. The Atkins diet may be quite successful in helping people shed fifteen or so pounds, but keeping the weight off means adhering to a diet that allows for no bread or other carbohydrates. While a diet that allows bacon and eggs may seem appealing at first, most people find it difficult to live on bacon and eggs alone.

The failure of these popular diet plans reveals the problem in trying to induce weight loss through our public policy. Much like the hucksters who sell diet books, our political leaders are not going to ask us to lose weight by forcing us to sacrifice—such prohibitions are a sure way to political retirement. But more than being politically unpalatable, any approach to obesity that tries to make Americans "eat less and exercise more" is bound to fail because it contradicts the core principles of our liberal, democratic society. Limiting choices may work for a religiously defined community such as the Amish, who voluntarily isolate themselves from a secular, consumer-oriented society, but it is not going to have any success in a liberal democracy whose central tenet is giving its citizens as much discretion as possible. After all, getting Americans really to change their eating and exercise patterns would require a level of totalitarianism that would make even Kim Jong Il blush. The very rationale of a liberal system such as ours is that individuals are best left to decide for themselves which choices to limit, particularly as long as such decisions do not infringe on the safety or well-being of others.[45]

The problem of putting the country on a diet is also evident in the surgeon general's report. For when it comes to actual policy initiatives, the report calls for only the most vague and politically unobtrusive policy measures, including "educating" people about healthy lifestyles, creating more opportunities for physical recreation at work and in neighborhoods, and providing more food options, including fruits, vegetables, and whole grains. While such recommendations are entirely unobjectionable, they are also completely ineffective.

Not that the surgeon general is alone in making vague and contradictory recommendations—nearly every state in the union has responded to the hysteria of America's growing weight with a task force to study the issue in more detail. At least twenty-five states currently have coalitions, working groups, or impact reports to investigating the problem. If they are anything like previous commissions, they will inevitably parrot the surgeon general's *Call to Action*. They will proclaim that obesity is a major problem and that we need to fundamentally change the way people eat and exercise, but that governments should do very little beyond encouraging local community efforts or "public-private partnerships." And, of course, they all add the obligatory footnote that Americans should focus less on appearance and more on health.

Like so many other committee reports, such proposals are very politically effective ways of doing nothing. Just as the limits on school vending machines and food pyramid guidelines mentioned above ostensibly serve a political interest, so these reports are basically just political creations as well. When it comes to actual policies that try to limit food intake or create conditions that demand more exercise, there is little political will. This is even the case where political leaders are fully on board the obesity bandwagon. Take Arkansas. Despite Mike Huckabee's fervor, the "Healthy Arkansas" initiative has been slow to progress and, in some instances, ideas have been blocked. And even Huckabee himself has not resisted political pressure—siding with the soft drink industry, he has blocked efforts to remove vending machines from schools.[46]

Of course, this is not to say that the government should not do anything about obesity. There is one thing our government could do that would be more effective than anything else at combating the real problems of obesity in America—stop making weight a central policy concern. Instead of convening task forces to figure out ways to combat obesity, state and federal government should simply be telling health agencies to find better measures of health than weight. They should make rules on the conflicts of interest between obesity researchers, weight-loss doctors, and the diet and pharmaceutical industries. And they should develop programs to combat the stigma and prejudice that fat people must face and institute laws, such as those in San Francisco and Michigan, that protect people against size discrimination. In short, they should work on changing all the harmful perceptions we have about weight. This would do far more to improve the health and well-being of the American population than making us so worried about our weight.

nine

Unmaking the
Obesity Epidemic

When I was thirteen, I took my first trip to Disneyworld. Amidst all the rides and spectacles, the part I remember best is *Tomorrowland*, Disney's jet-age vision of the future. It was filled with wondrous marvels including "people-movers" that quietly whisked pedestrians across the park and rocket ships that zoomed impetuously into space. Most impressive to me was the RCA "Home of Tomorrow," which accommodated a host of then unheard of technologies: large-screen televisions with videodisc players, microwave ovens and pre-packaged foods, and computers that allowed shopping from home. Of course, being part of an amusement park, *Tomorrowland* was also brimming with candy, ice cream, soda, and savory snack foods. In my youthful eyes, the future promised a world that was free from physical chores yet filled with goodies; it was a world characterized as much by its ease as by its bounty.

Looking back a quarter of a century later, it is remarkable how much of Disney's vision has actually come into being; America is very much like the *Tomorrowland* of my youth. With all our cars and suburbs, few Americans are forced to walk or engage in any strenuous exercise. Most of us own large televisions or computers and, among cable, DVDs, and the Internet, we enjoy a near infinite range of entertainment choices. Our meals are largely precooked and, amidst the expanding panoply of restaurants, take-out, and frozen foods, Americans have an unprecedented amount of culinary options. When it came to the future, the Disney "Imagineers" of *Tomorrowland* seemed to have gotten it right.

Except for one thing—they didn't anticipate what all these innovations might actually do *to* us. *Tomorrowland* was based on the assumption that science, technology, and the free market would take care of all our problems by providing us with more of what we wanted. The nifty gadgets and labor-saving advances would only enhance the quality of our lives. No one, it seemed, stopped to wonder how these innovations might affect our health, our bodies, or even our self-perception. Looking back, none of the mannequins in the RCA "Home of Tomorrow" suffered any ill effects from spending their days being passively entertained by their wall-sized televisions or being effortlessly shuttled by their people-movers. *Tomorrowlanders* weren't taking mouthfuls of prescription drugs to keep their cholesterol low, their appetites down, or their anxiety at bay. They weren't worried about how much they weighed or if they should get their stomachs surgically bound to keep themselves from eating too much food. And, of course, no one in *Tommorowland* was fat. Ultimately, what the designers of *Tomorrowland* failed to consider was that making life easier does not necessarily make it better or that giving us more choices doesn't always give us more power. These, I would argue, are the lessons of America's obesity epidemic.

As we have seen, obesity is neither a disease nor a major cause of disease. Despite the plethora of apocalyptic warnings, there is no clear evidence that, for most Americans, their weight is putting them at any health risk. Nor is obesity an intractable public health problem. Obesity and the obesity epidemic are nothing more than medical constructs. In truth, we could end the obesity epidemic right now if we desired— all we would need to do is to redefine obesity according to the real criterion of a disease. If we simply classified obesity at a level where body fat is incontrovertibly pathological, only a fraction of Americans would qualify and this "epidemic" would vanish.

This, however, would not solve the real dilemma of obesity in America. Simply redefining what obesity means will not get at the very things that are causing us to gain weight or that are challenging our health. Our current patterns of eating and exercise are having a far greater impact than merely making us heavy; they are raising our insulin resistance, heightening our cholesterol, and making us more susceptible to a host of metabolic diseases including diabetes. Beyond this, however, they also embody a more fundamental paradox of our prosperity: all our advancement and progress no longer seems to be improving our well-being. If we want to get at the real problems that underlie the obesity epidemic, we need to look beyond the traditional scapegoats such as our willpower or even McDonald's and focus on the much larger source—the paradoxes within the American way of life.

The Progress Paradox

In the immediate aftermath of September 11, 2001, America's leaders urged their fellow citizens to engage their patriotism. America was under attack and the best way to fight terrorism, we were told, was not simply to step up our vigilance, secure our airports, or invade terrorist strongholds; rather, it was to carry on with our daily lives and consume. President Bush urged Americans to "get on airlines and get about the business of America." New York City mayor Rudolph Giuliani pleaded for the "best shoppers in the world" to get to work. Alex Penelas, the mayor of Miami-Dade County said, "Go out and contribute to the economy . . . it has never been more patriotic to go shopping."[1] The economy, already in the midst of a recession, could only withstand the fiscal aftershock of the terrorist strikes if Americans went out to dinner, took in a movie, purchased a new car, and spent as much as possible. Whereas wartime America in the 1940s was about scrap-metal drives, rationing, and self-denial, war in the twenty-first century is about consumption. We need to sacrifice precisely by not sacrificing. In short, Uncle Sam wants you to super size.

Consumerism is at the heart of the American economy. Like any nation, the United States has a vested interest in maintaining economic growth—when our economy is expanding, our wealth increases, unemployment falls, and living standards rise. But wealthy, postindustrial countries such as the United States also have a chronic problem of overcapacity. As most of our basic necessities have long ago been met and our worker productivity is so great, economic growth can only be sustained through greater consumption, that is, by convincing Americans to buy more than their essential needs.[2] Companies stimulate this demand not only by making new technologies and more innovative and labor-saving products, but by persuading consumers that happiness really can be had with white teeth, designer clothes, granite countertops, and other extraneous goods. Thus it is hardly surprising that every year, more Americans go to work in the service sector and that more of America's GNP goes toward consumable goods and services. In an economy largely based on service and convenience, affluence and consumerism are really two sides of the same coin.

Naturally, consumerism has also wormed its way into the American political ethos. Once a nation defined by economic opportunity and political freedom, American political values are now understood in terms of economic success and consumable goods. The contemporary incarnation of the rugged American individualist is the free spending American consumer. From Mexico to China, from Pakistan to Senegal, the American beacon of freedom shines in the allure of fast-food, large cars, and grand homes. American liberty is not simply the freedom to speak one's mind or carry a gun, rights enjoyed in many other places; rather, it is the access to whatever goods you want, when you want them. It is the drive-thru window, the twenty-four-hour mini-mart, and the mall.

But if America's political values are understood through its consumer goods (by both Americans themselves and the rest of the world), it is because our affluence and political principles are inexorably linked. America is living testament that Adam Smith, the great prophet of free-market liberalism, was right—a political system that emphasizes individual rights and an economy with limited state intervention will yield great wealth.[3] For Smith, the fundamental problem of society was scarcity—the lack of basic goods such as clothing, food, and shelter is the primary impediment to human freedom and happiness. If privation keeps us enslaved and miserable, then wealth will do the opposite. All that is required, in Smith's view, is expanding a society's political liberties, particularly with regard to the mode of commerce.[4] Smith reasoned that if you give people the maximum amount of freedom to conduct business as they see fit (with a small number of correctives), they would end up creating more goods and services that would, in turn, maximize their freedom in the material realm and generally elevate their condition. In short, liberty will beget prosperity, which will beget health, happiness, and freedom—the more wealth and prosperity you can get, the more health, happiness, and freedom you can enjoy.

Yet, in America, this no longer seems to be the case. Instead, we seem to be suffering from what Greg Easterbrook calls the "progress paradox": despite the fact that materially we are doing much better, we do not seem to be any happier.[5] Although income, wealth, leisure time, and mobility have all risen dramatically in the past half century, Americans are less contented than their grandparents were—by all indicators Americans are less happy, more stressed, and more depressed than at any time since World War II.[6] In fact, a majority of Americans regularly report that things are actually getting worse and fear some eminent catastrophe is lurking around the corner.[7] And this is not merely an American phenomenon—across all industrialized nations, subjective levels of happiness have remained relatively constant since 1950 even though incomes and material standards have risen considerably during this time.[8] Rather than making us steadily happier, our increasing affluence and consumerism seem to have trapped us.

America's growing weight is emblematic of this progress paradox. Few Americans want to be fat, yet we continue to gain weight, largely because the minute benefits of tasty snack foods and refreshing sodas are simply too difficult to resist. This, however, was not the promise of Adam Smith's free-market or the vision of *Tomorrowland*. By not having to cook all our meals, walk to our jobs, or exhaust ourselves in daily chores, we were supposed to have more time and energy to do and be what we want.[9] We are supposed to be *empowered* by all these conveniences. That we continue to gain weight, despite our desire to be thin, belies just how little control we may actually have.

The underlying dilemma behind this paradox is choice, which makes this problem a particularly American one. After all, the freedom to choose is the basis of America's political ethos. We are free to choose our leaders and laws, where we live and work, and how and when we eat, exercise, or entertain ourselves. Maximizing our individual choice is the core principle upon which our society, laws, and the free market are based. But, as the obesity epidemic shows, maximizing our choices does not necessarily maximize our freedom or power. In the previous chapters, we have seen how increased choices in food and exercise have left us vulnerable to weight gain, how increased social mobility and sexual liberation have created a punitive standard of thinness, and how expanding healthcare options have generated ever more "diseases" to preoccupy us. The expansion of choices is no longer making our lives any easier; in fact it may be making them harder.[10]

Nowhere is the dilemma of choice more pronounced than with regard to our health. Irrespective of whether or not one believes that obesity is a disease, nearly everyone would agree that maintaining good nutrition and fitness is a challenge in our consumer-oriented society. Indeed, some of the biggest challenges come from the very same innovations that give us such pleasure: snacking, driving, and television. By themselves and in small doses, each of these is not necessarily bad, yet each makes it harder to eat well and be fit. Cars increase our mobility but they eliminate the need for the necessary exercise that keeps our bodies optimally functioning. Snack foods are tasty, but they flood our bodies with glucose and lipids that wreak havoc on our metabolic and cardio-vascular systems. By making the central elements of our existence (ex-ercise and food) subject to our own discretion, they also make them subject to our own natural impulses, which are to relax and eat.

For me, this dilemma is epitomized by the package of cookie dough that lurks in my refrigerator. I love the cookie dough even though I know that it is bad for me, but one little bite is unlikely to cause me much harm. Besides, when I'm bored or anxious, that little bite gives a bit of comfort (plus a healthy shot of sugar). Of course, after that bite is gone, I soon face the same choice again and, in no time, the entire pack-age has vanished and my body is filled with polyunsaturated fats and sugars. The same goes with getting some exercise—after a long and stressful day, it is far easier to unwind in front my television and be passively entertained than to do something healthy like take a walk, much less go to the gym. While not bad on any particular day, over time such behavior makes me slothful, irritable, and fatigued.

Which brings up the paradox of progress. What Adam Smith or the Disney Imagineers did not take into account was human biology. The scarcity and privation they sought to correct were the very circumstances that shaped us. We are designed to have strong appetites, to save our energy in fat cells, and to expect few sugars and fats from our food supply. Consequently, the price of our progress and innovations is that we must now be much more purposeful and conscientious about main-taining our health. With so many decisions to make about what to eat or how to exert ourselves, we must summon the will to make healthy choices at every moment of every day. This is particularly challenging considering that any one transgression is unlikely to be all that bad, but a series of transgressions can be disastrous over the long haul.

Now in some ways this is a timeless dilemma—humans have been faced with the challenge of impulse control since the dawn of civiliza-tion. But with obesity this dilemma has taken a new form. Unlike most other impulses, eating and exercise are indispensable to our existence. When comes to eating and exercise, we are hard-wired to consume and relax as much as we can. Thus, trying to rein in our appetites or change our physical habits presents a host of unique challenges that do not occur with other behaviors. Not only must we contend with an array of goodies that stoke our desire, but we must also deal with those desires themselves which, in the case of our appetite and metabolism, are the product of eons of evolution. This struggle is exacerbated by our very liberal, individualistic ethos, by which each of us has to make these choices in relative isolation. With often contradictory information and little social support, each of us must continually draw on own our wherewithal just to get by.

Now many hope that the consumer economy will provide a way out of this dilemma. Instead of trying to eradicate the source of our ills (that is, the free market), we can try to alleviate its unwanted by-products. Nowhere is this symptom-oriented approach more evident than with drugs and our health. Fatness is not the only by-product of our consumer-oriented lifestyle—chronic stress, anxiety, hypertension, and depression are other side effects arising from the way we live. Yet, rather than trying to address these problems by altering our eating and exercise patterns, increasingly we are coming to rely on a rainbow of pharmaceutical remedies for everything from anxiety to hypertension. And there is a certain logic to this—it is much easier to pop a pill than to continually rein in our natural impulses or to fight a consumer economy constantly beseeching us to take in more.

However, this strategy, too, is not without its own set of problems. Most of the medicines we take for our ills themselves carry hefty side effects that require still further money and medication to counteract. Then, there is the other problem that our weight isn't one of those conditions that easily yields to treatment. Consider the long history of dieting. From the obsessive masticating diets of Horace Fletcher to the gastric-bypass surgeries of today, Americans have been trying to make themselves thin for more than a century. Not only have most of these efforts been failures, but many have had severely negative consequences, often resulting in death, disease, and disfigurement. For example, nearly every pharmaceutical cure for fatness (Redux, Meridia, Xenical, and so on) has been both ineffective at keeping weight loss off and comes with debilitating side effects. It is quite telling that right now the most reliable method of sustained weight loss involve either smoking or gastric-bypass surgery, treatments that both involve ostensible diseasing the user. In many respects, this is the only real "crisis" with regard to obesity—unlike most other metabolic conditions, our increasing weight is not something that we can treat with a simple pill.

Real Solutions

So, if we can't solve all our problems with a pill, what options are left for us? If we want to improve our eating and exercise patterns, there aren't many. Some have offered imaginative approaches such as community gardens in the poor neighborhoods, the "slow food" movement that emphasizes seasonal and locally grown foods, or the Rails-to-Trails conservancy that converts abandoned rail lines into bike paths. While such approaches are undoubtedly laudable, they are unlikely to make a big difference given the magnitude of the forces behind America's sugary, fatty diet and sedentary lifestyle. Perhaps the best we can hope for over the long run is that a market will emerge for more healthy, tasty foods and exercise opportunities. For many of our ills, market-based solutions have often provided the most optimal and efficient remedies. When more people come to demand organic foods, bike paths, sidewalks, and the like, they will become more available.

Although solving the problems with how we eat and exercise may take generations, there is a very simple solution for the problem of obesity in America; and it comes, ironically, from some of the very people who are supposed to be "diseased," the obese. Among the scores of doctors, health researchers, and government officials whom I interviewed for this book, the people who had the most clear-eyed understanding of obesity were not the "experts" but the activists who were challenging the very system that seeks to profit from their weight. Unlike the mostly thin doctors and academic health researchers, these were the people who face the daily burdens of living in a society that constantly judges them for their size. They are the ones who must cope with the numerous health warnings, the vicious fat prejudices, and the false and dangerous promises of most diet programs. They are the ones who are told that they are sick and diseased, that they need to lose weight in order to be healthy and normal, and that anyone can lose weight if they only have the discipline and willpower. For them, the obesity epidemic is not simply a remote headline but a pernicious fiction that constantly bombards their lives.

When I ask fat activists Marilynn Wann or Lynn McAfee what they would do about the obesity epidemic, they give a relatively simple and straightforward answer. Rather than continuing this mad and pointless effort to either fight our biology or stifle the free market, the best way to get over our weight problem is to stop worrying so much about our weight. In their experience, it is fat biases and prejudices that are causing more harm than any of the health problems that come from being fat. Not only do these prejudices distort our understanding of body weight and health, but they are also fueling a public hysteria over our recent weight gains and how we should respond. Until we let go of our hostility toward fatness, our government will continue to waste billions on ineffective and misguided weight-loss policies and millions of Americans will continue to suffer from the stigma and frustration of simply living naturally.

Of course, like trying to eradicate any type of discrimination, ending fatism is a Herculean task. Part of the problem is that fatness is still widely believed to be a reflection of someone's character. As long as we continue to harbor the myth that our weight is something that we can easily control, fatness will continue to be equated with individual moral failure and will remain an all-too-convenient mechanism for social denigration, particularly of minorities and the poor. This also holds for the fat prejudice aimed at white women. As we've seen, a curious by-product of our large sexual marketplace is a cultural demand that women of status embody a thin and nubile vision of youthful fertility. Size prejudice against women, particularly in the upper echelons of society, may be an unavoidable consequence of our biology and social mobility.

But while the fat prejudice that pervades American culture may be difficult to change, there is one place where our negative attitudes about obesity can be more easily corrected—America's public health establishment. It is the very medical researchers and health experts who have stoked the fears of an epidemic who should be most ready to reconsider their positions. After all, the science is not on their side. As we've seen, we have no clear evidence that excess fat is, by itself, harmful for most Americans. Indeed, about the worst thing that comes from being heavy is that it puts great pressure on people's joints and inhibits their ability to exercise.[11] Beyond that, we have little proof that, by itself, obesity is causing heart disease, hypertension, or most other ailments. It is time that the medical and health establishment acknowledges this fact and stops making weight a barometer of health. The best way we can begin to solve the obesity epidemic is not by trying to get everyone to lose weight, but by no longer making weight a subject of official concern.

Notes

Introduction

1. Olshansky, J., et al. 2005. "A Potential Decline in Life Expectancy in the United States in the 21st Century," *New England Journal of Medicine* 352 (March 17):1138–1146.
2. I didn't know it at the time, but independently, Paul Campos, author of *The Obesity Myth*, was coming to a similar conclusion; his argument was influenced largely by Glen Gaesser's pioneering book *Big, Fat Lies*.
3. Mokdad, A. H., J. S. Marks, D. F. Stroup, and J. L. Gerberding. 2004. "Actual Causes of Death in the United States, 2000," *Journal of the American Medical Association* 291: 1238–1245.
4. A full description of this will be provided in chapter 1.
5. The CDC researchers estimated the number of deaths at numerous weight ranges using the latest NHANES (National Health and Nutrition Examination Survey) data from 1999. Compared to people with a "normal weight" (i.e., a BMI of 18.5–24.9), overweight people (a BMI of 25–29.9) had 86,094 fewer deaths, while those who are "obese" (a BMI of 30–34.9) had only 29,843 deaths; "extremely obese" people (a BMI of 35 or above) accounted for 82,066 deaths. If you subtract the number of overweight people who are living longer from the number of obese people who are living shorter, you only get 25,814 deaths, fewer than the number of deaths from underweight people (i.e., a BMI of under 18.5), which is 33,746 (Flegal, K., et al. 2005. "Excess Deaths Associated with Underweight, Overweight, and Obesity," *Journal of the American Medical Association* 293 (April 20, 2005):1861–1867. The editors of the prestigious *New England Journal of Medicine*, after evaluating the numerous studies on obesity and mortality, came to the following conclusion:

> The data linking overweight and death, as well as the data showing the beneficial effects of weight loss, are limited, fragmentary, and often ambiguous. Most of the evidence is either indirect or derived from observational epidemiologic studies, many of which have serious methodologic flaws. . . . Although some claim that every year 300,000 deaths in the United States are caused by obesity, that figure

is by no means well established. Not only is it derived from weak or incomplete data, but it is also called into question by the methodologic difficulties of determining which of many factors contribute to premature death. (Kassirer, J., and M. Angell. 1998. "Losing Weight—An Ill-Fated New Year's Resolution," *New England Journal of Medicine* 338: 52–54.).

6. Bjerklie, D., et al. 2004. "The Year in Medicine from A to Z," *Time* (December 6), pp. 56–62.
7. Wolf, A., and G. Colditz. 1998. "Current Estimates of the Economic Cost of Obesity in the United States," *Obesity Research* 6: 97–106.
8. For a nice description of this, particularly as it is evident in Greg Critser's 2004 book, *Fat Land: How Americans Became the Fattest People in the World* (New York: Mariner), see: Campos, P. 2004. "Fear and Loathing in Los Angeles: Fat Hatred Masquerades as Concern," *NAAFA Newsletter* (Winter).

Chapter One

1. Similarly, if obesity is termed a "disease," then some may be entitled to government tax benefits.
2. Medical definitions of obesity are no less problematic. Webster's *New World/Stedman's Concise Medical Dictionary* defines obesity as "an abnormal increase of fat in the subcutaneous connective tissues" but subcutaneous fat is far less dangerous than intra-abdominal visceral fat, and some types of subcutaneous fat inhibit cardiovascular disease.
3. Shell, E. 2002. *The Hungry Gene: The Science of Fat and the Future of Thin.* Boston: Atlantic Monthly Press.
4. In many ways, this made Quetelet the father of modern, quantitative social science.
5. Hacking, I. 1990. *The Taming of Chance.* New York: Cambridge University Press.
6. Gould, S. 1981. *The Mismeasure of Man.* New York: W.W. Norton.
7. Ibid.
8. Murray, C., and R. Herrnstein. 1995. *The Bell Curve.* New York: Free Press.
9. Gaesser, G. 2002. *Big Fat Lies: The Truth about Your Weight and Your Health.* 2nd ed. Carlsbad, CA: Gurze.
10. Troiano, R., et al. 1996. "The Relationship between Body Weight and Mortality: A Quantitative Analysis of Combined Information from Existing Studies," *International Journal of Obesity* 20: 63–75.
11. Fontaine, K., D. Redden, C. Wang, A. Westfall, and D. Allison. 2003. "Years of Life Lost Due to Obesity," *Journal of the American Medical Association* 289: 187–193.
12. For example, much of the standard for defining overweight comes from the mortality data from Metropolitan Life. But from a scientific perspective, the predictions from the Met Life tables are untenable because they were derived from Met Life's insurance pool, which was overly white, male, and middle-class, and not a representative sample of the general population. In addition, the methods Met Life used to calculate mortality

rates relative to the weight ranges are themselves problematic. According to one statistician, the methods used to calculate the mortality rates are largely incomprehensible. See Jarrett, R. 1986. "Is There an Ideal Body Weight?" *British Medical Journal* 293: 493–495.

13. Prentice, A., and S. Jebb. 2001. "Beyond Body Mass Index," *Obesity Reviews* 2: 141–147.

14. Janssen, I., et al. 2004. "Waist Circumference and Not Body Mass Index Explains Obesity Related Health Risk," *American Journal of Clinical Nutrition* 79: 379–384.

15. Flegal, K., et al. 2001. "Aim for a Healthy Weight: What Is the Target?" *Journal of Nutrition* 131: 440S–450S.

16. These numbers were not based on mortality figures but on the distribution of weight among the twenty- to twenty-nine-year-old population. Like Quetelet, the U.S. health agencies simply defined overweight relative to the weight distribution in the general population (albeit the young population). Of course, this type of scheme also meant that if the population started getting heavier, then the definition of overweight would necessarily have to rise. And, indeed, this is what began to happen.

17. World Health Organization. 1997. *Obesity: Preventing and Managing the Global Epidemic: Report of a WHO Consultation* (WHO Technical Series).

18. Kuczmarski R., et al. 1994. "Increasing Prevalence of Overweight among U.S. Adults: The National Health and Nutrition Examination Surveys, 1960 to 1991," *Journal of the American Medical Association* 272 (1994): 205–211.

19. National Institutes of Health. 1998. *Clinical Guidelines on the Identification, Evaluation, and Treatment of Overweight and Obesity in Adults: The Evidence Report*. NIH Publication No. 98-4083.

20. Andres, R. 1999. "Beautiful Hypotheses and Ugly Facts: The BMI-Mortality Association," *Obesity Research* 7: 417–419.

21. My italics. The only publicly available and refereed article cited by the NIH board was Troiano et al. 1996. This study is a review of all of studies linking BMI and mortality and not even a direct study of any data on this issue. Not only did they find that the insurance data differed dramatically from the population at large, but they also found a U-shaped relationship between BMI and mortality. Moreover, the increased mortality was typically not evident until well beyond a BMI level of 30

22. Allison, D., et al. 1999. "Annual Deaths Attributable to Obesity in the United States," *Journal of the American Medical Association* 282: 1530–1538. Mokdad, A., et al. 2004. "Actual Causes of Death in the United States, 2000," *Journal of the American Medical Association* 291: 1238–1245.

23. Allison et al. 1999.

24. Fontaine, K., et al. 2003. "Years of Life Lost Due to Obesity," *Journal of the American Medical Association* 289: 187–193. This research finds virtually no effect of body weight on expected mortality among the elderly, except among African Americans, where it has a positive effect (i.e., obese African Americans actually live longer than those with lower BMIs). The only measurable impact is among white women with a BMI over 40—elderly women with this much weight make up only a tiny fraction of the population.

25. Another factor with these studies is that these estimates inevitably are rounded to very high levels, generally to the 100,000 level. With such large rounding, it is quite difficult to know the magnitude of the trend. Moreover the increasing deaths seem to fly in the face of other trends. In 1980, an article by the Carter Center gave an estimate of 290,000 deaths per year due to over-nutrition, a decade later research by McGinnis estimated only 300,000 deaths. After twenty years of population growth and increased obesity, Mokdad's estimate is up to 400,000. Yet, with a slight reinterpretation of the number (which was within the confidence interval), Mokdad might have reported 300,000 deaths, which would have been a decrease in the rate of obesity-related mortality relative to the population. In other words, despite the massive increase in obesity in the American population, one could easily estimate that the number of deaths attributable to obesity have either remained constant or even declined during the past twenty years!

26. As of January 2005, the CDC reports that the problems with the earlier estimates were due to a "computer error" or a "software error," which seems highly implausible given the state of most statistical software at this point in time.

27. Flegal, K., et al. 2005. This number is calculated by considering the estimated number of deaths from obesity at around 110,000 a year and the deaths attributable to overweight, which is a minus 86,094.

28. Gaesser, 2002.

29. Ibid.

30. National Institutes of Health. 1998, p. 30.

31. For example, see Wei, M., et al. 1999. "Relationship between Low Cardio-Respiratory Fitness and Mortality in Normal-Weight, Overweight, and Obese Men," *JAMA* 282: 1547–1553.

32. MacMahon, B., and D. Trichopoulos. 1996. *Epidemiology: Principles and Methods.* 2nd ed. Boston: Little, Brown.

33. Most of the studies rely on self-reported measures among the respondents particularly regarding their diet and exercise patterns, if they are asked at all. Other problems include the failure to measure weight over time (or diet and exercise over time), a failure to take smoking into account, and most important a failure to elucidate a causal pathway between the fat and disease that can be directly measured. Campos, P. 2004. *The Obesity Myth: Why America's Obesession with Weight Is Hazardous to Your Health.* New York: Gotham. Gaesser. 2002.

34. Gaesser. 2002, pp. 65–70.

35. Scwarzc, S. 2003. "Where's the Epidemic?" www.techcentralstation.com.

36. Grady, D. 2004. "Fat: The Secret Life of a Potent Cell," *New York Times* (July 6).

37. As quoted in "How Does Fat Kill Thee? Many Ways," Associated Press, May 11, 2004.

38. William Dietz, from personal interview.

39. In order to gain status as a nongovernmental (i.e., nonprofit) organization and thus claim official links with the WHO, the IOTF was forced to link itself with the IASO as an "ad hoc committee."

40. Although the IOTF resists full disclosure of their funding sources, according the London *Daily Mail*, 75 percent of its million-dollar-plus budget comes from Hoffman-La Roche and Abbott. The IOTF has also been supported by Servier, the maker of the weight-loss drug Redux. The *Mail on Sunday* (March 6, 2005). As quoted by www.consumerfreedom.com/news_detail.cfm?headline=2763.

41. According to the website of the International Union of Nutritional Sciences, "In June 1997 the WHO, together with the IOTF, held an expert consultation on obesity to review the extent of the obesity problem and examine the need to develop public health policies and programmes [sic] to tackle the global problem of obesity. The consultation resulted in the publication of an interim report: 'Obesity—preventing and managing the global epidemic' (WHO 1998) and the subsequent WHO Technical Report Series 894." This puts a nice spin on what the North American Association for the Study of Obesity calls "the first major initiative of the IOTF."

42. Marsh, P., and S. Bradley. 2004. "Sponsoring the Obesity Crisis," Social Issues Research Center, www.sirc.org/articles/sponsoring_obesity.shtml.

43. Information from the Center for Science in the Public Interest website.

44. Birmingham, K. 1999. "Lawsuit Reveals Academic Conflict-of-Interest," *Nature Medicine* 5: 717. Although Pi-Sunyer did not take a fee for the articles he did not write but put his name on, he has been paid numerous consulting fees by other pharmaceutical companies.

45. Another indication of the power of these recommendations can be seen on the website of Roche Labs. It cites both the WHO report (which they are responsible for authoring) and the low BMI standards for overweight and obese.

46. Moore, T. 1993. *Lifespan: New Perspectives on Extending Human Longevity.* New York: Touchstone.

47. Hart, D. 1999. *Funding Science in America: Congress, Universities, and the Politics of the Academic Pork Barrel.* New York: Cambridge University Press.

48. For example, Pi-Sunyer, wrote an article in the *Journal of the American Medical Association* that accompanied the 1994 report on rising obesity rates. Locating the sources of obesity primarily in the body he said: "No permanent resolution to this [obesity] problem is likely until we better understand the underlying biological determinants of obesity. . . .To gain this much needed knowledge, *greater support of obesity research* is vitally important" (my italics). As with much of his writing, the paper ends with a call for greater research funding. These scientists and agencies employ a variety of practices to ensure and expand their appropriations, including linking with the private sector (especially the diet and drug industries), direct public information campaigns, and with claims to their own expertise. This is particularly the case with the federal bureaucracy. Government agencies justify their budgets and missions relative to their professional expertise: the military assesses threats and specifies how much money and men it needs to defend the country; the Department of Transportation evaluates how much is needed for highways, and so on. In the case of obesity this expertise has been used to make claims about the

severity of America's weight problem as well as the funding needed, primarily for more research, about its solution.

49. Statement by Department of Health and Human Services secretary Tommy G. Thompson on "Preventing Chronic Disease through Healthy Lifestyle" before the United States Senate Committee on Appropriations Subcommittee on Labor, Health, and Human Services, Education, July 15, 2004. www.hhs.gov/asl/testify/t040715.html.

50. Kuczmarski, R., et al. 1994.

51. Some of the first common usages of the idea of an obesity epidemic occurred in *JAMA* in 1999 in a special edition on obesity.

52. Mokdad, A., et al. 2004.

53. Marshall, E. 2004. "Public Enemy Number One: Tobacco or Obesity?" *Science* 304 (May 7): 5672–5804. The studies referred to are Allison et al. 1999 and Mokdad 2004, which use identical methods. Once again, these were hazard ratios that had enormous error terms and provided very small confidence intervals.

54. Ibid.

55. Gaesser. 2002.

56. See for example Ernsberger, P., and P. Haskew. 1987. *Rethinking Obesity: An Alternative View of Its Health Implications.* New York: Human Sciences Press.

57. In chapter 3, I will review all the research on discrimination against the obese.

58. The data from the 1994–1996 Continuing Survey of Food Intakes by Individuals and the Diet and Health Knowledge Survey, a follow-up survey of more than five thousand Americans conducted by the U.S. Department of Agriculture. The survey question asked, "Do you consider yourself to be overweight, underweight, or about right?" I excluded women who were pregnant and used sampling weights to make the estimates representative of the whole population. For the simplicity of analysis, I also did not include Latinos although their weight perceptions do not differ markedly from those of black women or men.

59. Cassidy, C. 1991. "The Good Body: When Big Is Better," *Medical Anthropology* 13: 181–213.

Chapter Two

1. "Scientists Still Seeking Cure for Obesity," *The Onion* (July 14, 2004).

2. These numbers were calculated from doing a LexisNexis search on newspaper and magazine articles featuring the terms obesity, disease, and epidemic in their headlines or lead paragraphs. I am indebted to my student Kathryn McLellan who first brought these numbers to my attention.

3. *Stedman's Medical Dictionary*, 27th ed. 2000. New York: Lippincott, Williams, and Wilkins.

4. Gaesser, 2002.

5. Ibid.

6. The classic work on diffusion theory is Rogers, E. 1962. *Diffusion of Innovations.* New York: Free Press.

7. For an engaging summary of this see Gladwell, M. 2000. *The Tipping Point.* Boston: Back Bay.
8. Shilts, R. 1987. *And the Band Played On.* New York: St. Martin's. Dugas's responsibility for the spread of the HIV virus is a highly contested matter, although it is clear that a large percentage of the first documented cases of HIV reported sexual contact with either Dugas or one of his partners.
9. Around fifteen years ago, the CDC started the Center for Chronic Disease Prevention, in which health conditions such as obesity, high cholesterol, and hypertension became foci of concern, although various scientists had been working on related issues before this.
10. In a historical review of medical textbooks, Chang and Christakis found that the entries for obesity developed from a model that stresses personal behavior to one that focuses on environmental sources and that puts the individual in a position of far less accountability. Chang, V., and N. Christakis. 2002. "Medical Modeling of Obesity: A Transition from Action to Experience in a 20th-Century American Medical Textbook," *Sociology of Health and Illness* 24: 151–177.
11. The current CDC maps use yellow for the stages between blue and red.
12. Personal interview, December 23, 2004.
13. Mokdad, A. H., M. K. Serdula, W. H. Dietz, et al. "The Spread of the Obesity Epidemic in the United States, 1991–1998," *JAMA* 282 (1999): 1519–1522.
14. From personal interview.
15. For a classic commentary on this see, Wilson, J. 1989. *Bureaucracy: What Government Agencies Do and Why They Do It.* New York: Basic.
16. A good example of this was a recent cover story in *Time* magazine (December 6, 2004) proclaiming in an article titled "The Stealth Killer" that "America's high blood pressure crisis is spinning out of control. Learn about it, treat it and maybe save your own life."
17. Figures on mortality from U.S. National Center for Health Statistics, *Vital Statistics of the United States.* Washington, DC (http://purl.access.gpo.gov/GPO/LPS25040). Figures on estimated percentage of GDP on health services spending from Hilsenrath, P., et al. 2003. "An Institutional Retrospective on South African and American Health Sectors," *Journal of the Academy of Business and Economics* (April).
18. www.obesity.org/subs/advocacy/advocacy.shtml.
19. Stein, R., and C. Connolly. 2004. "Medicare Changes Policy on Obesity," *Washington Post* (July 16).
20. The AOA's board is a veritable who's who of the leading obesity researchers with significant conflicts of interest with the diet and pharmaceutical industry including Richard Atkinson, George Blackburn, and George Bray.
21. See for example Nestle, M., and M. Jacobson. 2001. "Halting the Obesity Epidemic: A Public Health Policy Approach," *Public Health Reports* (January/February) 115: 12–25, or Young, L., and M. Nestle. 2002. "The Contribution of Expanding Portion Sizes to the U.S. Obesity Epidemic," *American Journal of Public Health* 92: 246–249.
22. Nestle, M. 2001. *Food Politics: How the Food Industry Influences Nutrition and Health.* Berkeley: University of California Press. P. 174.

23. Starr, P. 1984. *The Social Transformation of Medicine*. New York: Basic.
24. See comments in Gaesser 2002 or in Campos 2004.
25. Harvard School of Public Health. 2005. "Obesity Controversy," *Nutrition Source* (May 9).
26. Conrad, P. 1992. "Medicalization and Social Control," *Annual Review of Sociology* 18: 209–232.
27. Friedson, E. 1988. *Profession of Medicine: A Study of the Sociology of Applied Knowledge*. Chicago: University of Chicago Press.
28. The announcement of the recent World Obesity Congress and Exposition conference promotion can be seen at www.global8.com/BA801/BA801intro.html.
29. The lion's share of this estimate is in the consumption of diet sodas, health club memberships, fat-free or low-carb foods, and diet books and programs such as Weight Watchers.
30. Gura, T. 2003. "Obesity Drug Pipeline Not So Fat," *Science* 299: 849–852.
31. In a recent Roper poll commissioned by Bankrate.com, the average American woman said she wanted to lose about twenty-three pounds. Results posted on www.bankrate.com/brm/about/pr/01132003.asp.
32. Gura. 2003, p. 850. Not surprisingly, Xenical is declining in popularity nor was it ever very effective. Endocrinologist Stephen Bloom estimates that the amount of weight the typical user of Xenical loses from taking the drug is about "equal to the weight of the number of Xenical tablets you have taken."
33. Johannes, L., and S. Stecklow. 1998. "Dire Warnings about Obesity Based on a Slippery Statistic," *Wall Street Journal* (February 9).
34. This link was based on a paper written by obesity researcher and drug company consultant Theodore VanItallie. His paper was filled with numerous problems and questionable statistical procedures. According to Johannes and Stecklow (1998), "Dr. VanItallie's figures may be exaggerated. In calculating the [mortality] figure, he drew on previously published reports on obesity and death. But without correcting for age differences of the effects of smoking in these studies, he concluded that obesity is to blame for 20% of all U.S. deaths. The problem is that many deaths occur among heavy smokers, or in people in their 70s and 80s [a group not in his data set]. Dr. VanItallie concedes his analysis is 'very rough.'"
35. Other types of surgery, such as cosmetic or plastic surgery, are not considered general surgery. I thank Dr. Heena Patel for bringing this to my attention.
36. This figure is a conservative estimate based on the predicted mortality and postsurgical complications rates as reported in the *Journal of the American Medical Association*. The mortality rates vary considerably by procedure but average about 1 percent across all procedures. See. Buchwald, H., et al. 2004. "Bariatric Surgery: A Systematic Review and Meta-Analysis," *Journal of the American Medical Association* 292: 1724–1737.
37. National Institutes of Health. 2001. *Gastrointestinal Surgery for Severe Obesity*. NIH Publication No. 01-4006.
38. Kolata, G. 2004. "Health and Money Issues Arise over Who Pays for Weight Loss," *New York Times* (September 30). Togerson, J., and L. Sjostrom. 2001.

"The Swedish Obese Subjects (SOS) Study: Rationale and Results," *International Journal of Obesity and Related Metabolic Disorders* 25: S2-4.
39. Sontag, S. 1978. *Illness as Metaphor*. New York: Farrar, Straus and Giroux.
40. *Stedman's* defines disease as "an interruption, cessation, or disorder of body function, system, or organ," yet there is no clear evidence that having a BMI of 30 or above automatically qualifies a person as having a disorder, cessation, or interruption of any bodily function.

Chapter Three

1. In 2002, Jazzercise, under mediation from the San Francisco Human Rights Commission, dropped its requirement that its employees retain a thin look.
2. Mayer, J. 1968. *Overweight: Causes, Cost, and Control*. Englewood Cliffs, NJ: Prentice-Hall. Neumark-Sztainer, D., M. Story, and L. Faibisch. 1998. "Perceived Stigmatization among Overweight African American and Causcasian Adolescent Girls," *Journal of Adolescent Health* 23: 264–270. Weiler, K., and L. Helms. 1993. "Responsibilities of Nursing Education: The Lessons of *Russell v. Salve Regina*," *Journal of Professional Nursing* 9: 131–138.
3. Klassen, M., C. Jasper, and R. Harris. 1993. "The Role of Physical Appearance in Managerial Decisions," *Journal of Business Psychology* 8: 181–198. Pingitore, R., B. Dugoni, R. Tindale, and B. Spring. 1994. "Bias against Overweight Job Applicants in a Simulated Employment Interview," *Journal of Applied Psychology* 77: 143–168. Cawley, J. 2004. "The Impact of Obesity on Wages," *Journal of Human Resources* 39: 451–474.
4. Maiman, L., V. Wang, M. Becker, J. Finlay, and M. Simonson. 1979. "Attitudes toward Obesity and the Obese by Professionals," *Journal of the American Dietetic Association* 74: 331–336. Nordholm, L. 1980. "Beautiful Patients Are Good Patients: Evidence for the Physical Attractiveness Stereotypes in First Impression of Patients," *Social Science Medicine* 14: 81–83.
5. Karris, L. 1977. "Prejudice against Obese Renters," *Journal of Social Psychology* 101: 159–160.
6. Greenberg, B., E. Eastin, L. Hofschire, K. Lachlan, and K. Brownell. 2003. "Portrayals of Overweight and Obese Individuals on Commercial Television," *American Journal of Public Health* 93: 1342–1348.
7. For a classic summary of this research see Allon, N. 1982. "The Stigma of Overweight in Everyday Life," in B. Wolman, ed., *Psychological Aspects of Obesity: A Handbook*. New York: Van Nostrand Reinhold.
8. Puhl, R., and K. Brownell. 2001. "Bias, Discrimination, and Obesity," *Obesity Research* 9: 788–805.
9. Oliver, J., and T. Lee. 2005. "Public Opinion and the Politics of Obesity." *Journal of Health Politics, Policy, and Law* (forthcoming).
10. Price, J., S. Desmond, R. Krol, F. Snyder, and J. O'Connell. 1987. "Family Practice Physicians' Beliefs, Attitudes, and Practices Regarding Obesity." *American Journal of Preventative Medicine* 3: 339–345. Bagley, C., D. Conklin, R. Isherwood, D. Pechiulis, and L. Watson. 1989. "Attitudes of Nurses toward Obese Patients," *Perception and Motor Skills* 68: 954.

11. As quoted on their website: www.obesity.org.
12. Brown, P. J., and M. Konner. 1987. "An Anthropological Perspective on Obesity," *Annals of the New York Academy of Sciences* 499: 29–46.
13. De Garine, I. 1995. "Sociocultural Aspects of the Male Fattening Sessions among the Massa of Northern Cameroon," in I. de Garine and N. Pollock, eds., *Social Aspects of Obesity*. Amsterdam: Gordon and Breach.
14. Pollock, N. 1995. "Social Fattening Patterns in the Pacific: The Positive Side of Obesity—A Nauru Case Study," in de Garine and Pollock, *Social Aspects of Obesity*.
15. Sobal, J., and A. Stunkard. 1989. "Socioeconomic Status and Obesity: A Review of the Literature," *Psychological Bulletin* 105: 260–275.
16. Beller, A. S. 1977. *Fat and Thin: A Natural History of Obesity*. New York: McGraw-Hill.
17. For more on this, see Sobal and Stunkard. 1989.
18. Diamond, J. 1999. *Guns, Germs, and Steel: The Fates of Human Societies*. New York: W.W. Norton.
19. The value of fatness is evident in the earliest known depiction of the human form, the "Venus of Willendorf." This twenty-five-thousand-year-old limestone statuette is notable not only for its age but for its conception of an idealized human as enormously fat with large breasts hanging over a tremendous belly. Although the meaning of the figurine is subject to considerable speculation (some think she was a fertility goddess; others consider her an erotic image), it is clear she is an emblem of political reverence. Like the Polynesian queens who were fattened and paraded to demonstrate the affluence and clout of a tribe, the corpulent Venus is an emblem of a political ideal.
20. For other examples see Klein, R. 1995. *Eat Fat*. New York: Vintage.
21. Gilman, S. 2004. *Fat Boys*. Lincoln: University of Nebraska Press.
22. In classical Greek thought, the ideal of stoicism emphasized liberation from the body, which was viewed as a restraint on true freedom and divine reality. Aristotle and Plato all counseled against a high proportion of fat not just as unhealthy to the body but as part of a larger concern with how uncontrolled appetites could undermine the rational, moral life. Homer depicted Odysseus's gluttonous sailors as being transformed into pigs and devoured by the sea with Circe. While these may seem like moral tales, the classical condemnation of gluttony also represented a radical political ideology. To withstand the desires of the body is to withstand a primary mechanism of political control—food. The best way to subvert the rule of those tyrannical forces that control the food supply is to overcome the influence of appetite.
23. Thomas Aquinas thought overeating violated "the reasonable order of life in which the moral good is found." See Schimmel, S., 1997. *The Seven Deadly Sins*. New York: Oxford University Press.
24. Prose, F. 2003. *Gluttony*. New York: Oxford University Press.
25. Manchester, W. 1992. *A World Lit Only by Fire*. New York: Little, Brown.
26. Interestingly, according to the *Oxford English Dictionary*, most of the earliest usages of the term "obese" make reference to religious figures.

27. Gonzalez, J. 1984. *The Story of Christianity.* San Francisco: Harper.
28. Large-scale commercial farming, such as American and Caribbean plantations, were primarily concerned with nonfood staples such as tobacco, cotton, sugar for rum, and coffee.
29. Levenstein, H. 1988. *Revolution at the Table: The Transformation of the American Diet.* New York: Oxford University Press.
30. Ibid. It is also important to note that this transformation in attitudes was not linear, nor did it occur uniformly across the population. Well into the 1920s, plenty of middle-class Americans and Europeans still valued corpulent bodies. Food, while becoming more plentiful, was still relatively scarce and diseases relating to malnutrition were still quite common. In fact, well into the 1970s, the U.S. government continued to encourage Americans to eat more of all types of food (see Nestle, M. 2001. *Food Politics.* Berkeley: University of California Press). Yet, starting in the 1980s, attitudes about body fat underwent a seismic change. This change was driven by a complicated set of factors and the greatest of these was social class.
31. Schwartz, H. 1983. *Never Satisfied: A Cultural History of Diets, Fantasies, and Fat.* New York: Free Press.
32. Weber, M. 2001 (1904). *The Protestant Ethic and the Spirit of Capitalism,* trans. T. Parsons. New York: Routledge.
33. Morone, J. 2003. *Hellfire Nation: The Politics of Sin in American History.* New Haven, CT: Yale University Press.
34. Schwartz. 1986.
35. Seid, R. 1989. *Never Too Thin.* New York: Prentice Hall. Stearns, P. 1997. *Fat History: Bodies and Beauty in the Modern West.* New York: New York University Press.
36. Bordo, S. 1993. *Unbearable Weight: Feminism, Western Culture, and the Body.* Berkeley: University of California Press.
37. Advances in offset lithography now made it possible to transfer illustrations and photographic images more cheaply and easily than before.
38. Schwartz. 1986, p. 356.
39. Ibid., p. 357.
40. Schorman, R. 2003. *Selling Style: Clothing and Social Change at the Turn of the Century.* Philadelphia: University of Pennsylvania Press.
41. Schwartz. 1986.
42. For an excellent summary of this development, see Seid. 1989, pp. 120–121.
43. Ibid.
44. Hofstadter, R. 1998 (1956). *The American Political Tradition: And the Men Who Made It.* New York: Vintage.
45. For a timely and classic statement of this perspective see Alexis de Tocqueville's *Democracy in America.* Although written more than 150 years ago, many of his observations about American political culture still ring true today. See also McClosky, H., and J. Zaller. 1984. *The American Ethos.* Cambridge, MA: Harvard University Press.
46. This individualism must also be understood, however, in relation to American class politics. Unlike the rest of the industrial world, the United States never had a large socialist party nor a significant self-identified

working class, largely because working-class consciousness was stymied by the nation's exceptionally individualistic political culture. This included the widespread belief that society is comprised of individuals, that individuals can best pursue their own interest in isolation, and that moral worth is largely the consequence of one's individual behavior. Lipset, S., and G. Marks. 2001. *It Didn't Happen Here: Why Socialism Failed in the United States.* New York: W. W. Norton.

47. Gilens, M. 1999. *Why Americans Hate Welfare.* Chicago: University of Chicago Press. Gilens also argues that this is directly tied to misperceptions that welfare recipients are largely black.

48. Kinder, D., and D. Sears. 1981. "Prejudice and Politics: Symbolic Racism versus Racial Threats to the Good Life," *Journal of Personality and Social Psychology* 40: 414–431.

49. Schuman, H., C. Steeh, L. Bobo, and M. Krysan. 1998. *Racial Attitudes in America: Trends and Interpretations.* Cambridge, MA: Harvard University Press.

50. Kinder, D., and L. Sanders. 1996. *Divided by Color.* Chicago: University of Chicago Press. Not surprisingly, Americans' attitudes toward blacks and the poor are closely related. Gilens (1999) finds that most Americans oppose welfare not because the poor are undeserving, but because they think blacks are the primary recipients of welfare and that blacks are morally undeserving of public support. The cultural norm of individualism is an important mechanism for sustaining both income and racial inequality in the United States.

51. In 2001, the Princeton University Survey Research Center conducted a national random survey. In a 2004 survey of a random sample of 895 American adults conducted by Knowledge Networks, the following question was asked; "These days we hear a lot of reasons for why Americans are overweight. Below are several explanations that are commonly heard. Select the one you believe is the most important reason why Americans are overweight: People are too lazy to exercise and eat properly; There is too much unhealthy food in restaurants and supermarkets; Weight is an inherited, genetic trait and most people are overweight because they are born that way." Seventy-one percent thought individual laziness was the most important reason, 20 percent thought unhealthy foods was the most important, and only 9 percent thought genetics was the most important cause.

52. Crandall, C., and M. Biernat. 1990. "The Ideology of Anti-Fat Attitudes," *Journal of Applied Social Psychology* 20: 227–243.

53. Crandall, C. 1994. "Prejudice against Fat People: Ideology and Self-Interest," *Journal of Personality and Social Psychology* 66: 882–894. Also see DeJong, W. 1980. "The Stigma of Obesity: The Consequences of Naïve Assumptions Concerning the Causes of Physical Deviance," *Journal of Health and Social Behavior* 21: 75–87.

54. Crandall. 1994.

55. Oliver, J. E. 2001. *Survey of American Attitudes toward Obesity.* Princeton, NJ: Princeton University Survey Research Center. In this survey, I asked respondents how much they agreed with a number of stereotypical state-

ments about blacks including one that said, "On the whole, blacks would rather rely on welfare benefits than work." Their scores were ranked on a ten-point scale.

56. Ibid.

57. Crandall, C., and R. Martinez. 1993. "Culture, Belief, and Anti-Fat Attitudes," *Personality and Social Psychology Bulletin* 22: 1165–1176.

58. And a similar argument is made to condemn the poor. Poor people are judged to be deserving of their poverty because of their failure to control their own behavior. The fat, like African Americans and the poor, are seen by many Americans as simply being morally inferior and worthy of whatever judgment is passed upon them.

59. Mokdad, A. H., B. A. Bowman, E. S. Ford, et al. 2003. "Prevalence of Obesity, Diabetes, and Obesity-Related Health Risk Factors, 2001," *Journal of the American Medical Association* 289: 76–79.

60. Ibid.

61. For an excellent depiction of this, see Glassner, B. 2000. *The Culture of Fear.* New York: Basic.

62. Levitt, S., and S. Dubner. 2005. *Freakonomics: A Rogue Economist Explores the Hidden Side of Everything.* New York: William Morrow.

63. Sociologist Abigail Saguy, in reviewing the press coverage of obesity, has found that a majority use incendiary metaphors such as "time bomb." Saguy, A. C., and K. Riley. 2005. "Mortality, Morality, Science, and Social Inequality: Framing Contests and Credibility Struggles over Obesity," *Journal of Health Politics, Policy and Law* 30[5] (forthcoming).

64. For an excellent description of this see, Easterbrook, G. 2003. *The Progress Paradox: How Life Gets Better While People Feel Worse.* New York: Random House.

Chapter Four

1. Gilman, S. 2004. *Fat Boys.* Lincoln: University of Nebraska Press.

2. Greenberg, B., et al. 2003. "Portrayals of Overweight and Obese Individuals on Commercial Television," *American Journal of Public Health* 93: 1342–1348.

3. Ibid.

4. Cawley, J. 2004. "The Impact of Obesity on Wages," *Journal of Human Resources* 39: 451–474. He uses a variety of sophisticated econometric models to calculate the impact of body weight on income after all other explanatory factors, such as age, race, and education, are taken into account.

5. Goldbatt, P., M. Moore, and A. Stunkard. 1965. "Social Factors in Obesity," *JAMA* 192: 1039–1044.

6. Author's analysis of U.S. Department of Agriculture Health Knowledge Surveys 1994–1996.

7. Oliver, J. E. 2001. *Survey of American Attitudes toward Obesity.* Princeton, NJ: Princeton University Survey Research Center. Overweight as defined by a BMI between 25 and 29.

8. Author's analysis of USDA Health Knowledge Survey 1994–1996.

9. Carpenter, K., D. Hasin, D. Allison, and M. Faith. 2000. "Relationships between Obesity and DSM-IV Major Depressive Disorder, Suicide Ideation, and Suicide Attempts: Results from a General Population Study," *American Journal of Public Health* 90: 251–257. Interestingly, the study also found that large men were actually less likely to be depressed the heavier their reported weight. This important distinction is discussed below.

10. Cawley. 2003. Sobal, J. 1984. "Marriage, Obesity, and Dieting," *Marriage and Family Review* 7: 115–140.

11. Estimates of eating disorders among the female population vary. See Fairburn, C., and K. Brownell. 2002. *Eating Disorders and Obesity: A Comprehensive Handbook*, 2nd ed. New York: Guilford.

12. I am hesitant to use the term "feminist" largely because I am not covering the wide variety of perspectives that encompass the vast "feminist" literature on the female body. Although there is significant disagreement on the function and role of patriarchal power in subjugating women through body standards, I believe, to whatever extent it is possible, that I am summarizing the most widely held view within the extensive writings on this topic.

13. Goodman, C. 1995. *The Invisible Woman: Confronting Weight Prejudice in America*. Carlsbad, CA: Gurze.

14. Anna Vosburgh is one of many women I interviewed who had similar experiences regarding their weight.

15. Weitz, R. 2003. "A History of Women's Bodies," in R. Weitz, ed., *The Politics of Women's Bodies: Sexuality, Appearance and Behavior*. New York: Oxford University Press.

16. For popular accounts of this see Chernin, K. 1981. *The Obsession: Reflections on the Tyranny of Slenderness*. New York: HarperCollins; Orbach, S. 1978. *Fat Is a Feminist Issue*. New York: Paddington; Wolf, N. 1991. *The Beauty Myth: How Images of Beauty Are Used against Women*. New York: Morrow.

17. Bartky, S. 1988. "Foucault, Femininity, and the Modernization of Patriarchal Power," reprinted in Weitz. 2003.

18. Chernin. 1981.

19. In a now famous study, Dr. Ancel Keys (inventor of the army K-ration) demonstrated that a prolonged period on a low-calorie diet will have negative physiological and psychological consequences. People on reduced-calorie diets become increasingly preoccupied with food, become depressed and emotionally volatile, and lose the ability to concentrate and perform basic motor functions. Keys, A., et al. 1950. *Biology of Human Starvation*. Minneapolis: University of Minnesota Press.

20. Among academic feminists, who have considered these issues in more depth than I, there is considerable debate over what drives the thin beauty standard and some even question the very line of inquiry. Some feminists see the thin beauty standard through the lens of class or race politics, with thinness being a mechanism of class differentiation, similar to the argument I make in chapter 2. Others see thinness as empowering to women, a rejection of the traditional feminine body (see Striegel-Moore, R. 1995. "A Feminist Perspective on the Etiology of Eating Disorders" in

Fairburn and Brownell. 2002). Still others have argued that theories of women's subjugation are "reductionist, totalizing, inadequately nuanced, valorizing of gender difference, unconsciously racist, and elitist" (see Bordo, S. 1993. *Unbearable Weight: Feminism, Western Culture, and the Body*. Berkeley: University of California Press. P. 216).

Other feminists argue that the idea of gender itself is too much of an "essentialist" or "binary" concept. Postmodern theorists such as Judith Butler assert that any attempt to frame the discussion of power and social organization along sex lines is simply to frame the debate in preexisting patriarchal terms. Instead, Butler suggests, in classic postmodern prose, that "the rules governing signification not only restrict but enable the assertion of alternative cultural intelligibility." The question of what "alternative cultural intelligibility" is, however, remains something of a point of contention. Of course, once one starts down this path of questioning the basic terms of this analysis, one quickly devolves into a quagmire of relativism. If the very idea of gender is rejected, then one has no basis for arguing in support of a gendered difference in beauty standards. Such postmodern feminist theorizing may animate the esoteric discussions within university seminars, but its often impenetrable jargon and relentless deconstructionism offer little explanatory utility for those outside of the academy. Butler, J. 1990. *Gender Trouble: Feminism and the Subversion of Identity*. New York: Routledge.

21. Wolf. 1991, p. 187.
22. See also Stearns, P. 1997. *Fat History: Bodies and Beauty in the Modern West*. New York: New York University Press.
23. Chernin. 1981.
24. For example, Cawley (2003) finds that weight-related wage discrimination occurs more frequently among white, educated women than minority women.
25. This is particularly the case in the writings of Wolf and Chernin who are offering mostly cultural criticism.
26. Personal interview with Anna Vosburgh.
27. This generalization relates to heterosexual relationships. I did not interview enough lesbians to know whether thin beauty standards affect their relationship dynamics.
28. Sobal. 1984. Again, these findings refer solely to heterosexual relationships. I am unaware of any systematic research on the relationship between body weight and the romantic and social lives of lesbians.
29. Elder, G. 1969. "Appearance and Education in Marriage Mobility," *American Sociological Review* 34: 519–533.
30. For example see, Blum, D. 1997. *Sex on the Brain: The Biological Differences between Men and Women*. New York: Penguin; Etcoff, N. 1999. *Survival of the Prettiest*. New York: Anchor; Ridley, M. 1993. *The Red Queen: Sex and the Evolution of Human Nature*. New York: Penguin.
31. Indeed, what body weight is for women, height is for men; men who are taller tend to earn significantly more when all other factors are equal. Etcoff (1999) cites numerous studies demonstrating how tall men are more likely to be seen as desirable and to earn more than short men.

32. Buss, D. 1989. "Sex Differences in Human Mate Preferences: Evolutionary Hypothesis Tested in 37 Cultures," *Behavioral and Brain Science* 12: 1–14.
33. Wiederman, M., and E. Allgeier. 1992. "Gender Differences in Mate Selection Criteria: Sociobiological or Socioeconomic Explanation?" *Ethology and Sociobiology* 13: 115–124.
34. Etcoff. 1999.
35. For a summary see Ridley. 1993.
36. Singh, D. 1993. "Adaptive Significance of Female Attractiveness: Role of Waist-to-Hip Ratio," *Journal of Personality and Social Psychology* 65: 293–307.
37. Singh, D. 1995. "Ethnic and Gender Consensus for the Effect of Waist-to-Hip Ratio on Judgment of Women's Attractiveness," *Human Nature* 6 : 51–65.
38. Ridley. 1993.
39. Johannes, L., and S. Stecklow. 1998. "Dire Warnings about Obesity Based on a Slippery Statistic," *Wall Street Journal* (February 9).
40. Etcoff. 1999, p. 24.
41. As quoted in Etcoff (1999). Interestingly, men who are seen with attractive women are generally rated as more intelligent and likeable but the reverse does not hold for women—being seen with attractive men does nothing for their status.
42. Etcoff (1999) summarizes this research.
43. Seid. 1989.
44. Roper poll commissioned by Bankrate.com. Results posted on www.bankrate.com/brm/about/pr/01132003.asp.
45. In the 2001 *Survey of American Attitudes toward Obesity*, 25 percent of women said their weight was a "very serious" or "serious" problem compared to only 8 percent of men. Thirty percent of women in the sample said they had gone on a diet in the past year compared to only 15 percent of men.
46. Interestingly, among the "obese" (a BMI of 30 or more) surveyed in the 2001 *Survey of American Attitudes toward Obesity* there were no such sex differences.
47. As quoted in an interview on www.ivillage.com/books/intervu/spirit/articles/0,,261075_87891-3,00.html.
48. According to Alan Wolfe, many of the churches where Shamblin's seminars are held "rarely allow women to assume positions of religious authority, and insist on the Biblically inspired notion that men should rule over women just as Jesus rules over humanity." Wolfe, A. 2003. *The Transformation of American Religion.* New York: Free Press.
49. Comments made at the North American Association for the Study of Obesity, Annual Meeting (November 15, 2004), Las Vegas, Nevada.

Chapter Five

1. Copeland, L. 2002. "Snack Attack," *Washington Post* (November 3), p. F1. Initially, the courts dismissed these cases. The judges basically said that the law does not protect consumers from their own excesses if the consequences are known, but since then the cases have been reinstated on appeal.

2. As the Republican study committee concludes, "the responsibility for watching the waistlines of Americans lies with each individual consumer of food." Pence, M. 2004. "The Government Should Watch Its Waste, Not Your Waistline," The Conservative Viewpoint, Republican Study Committee (March 10).

3. As quoted in Hulse, C. 2004. "Vote in House Offers a Shield in Obesity Suits," New York Times (March 11).

4. Nestle, M. 2003. "The Ironic Politics of Obesity," Science 299: 781.

5. Oliver, J., and T. Lee. 2005. "Public Opinion and the Politics of Obesity," Journal of Health Politics, Policy, and Law (forthcoming).

6. Hill, J., et al. 2003. "Obesity and the Environment: Where Do We Go from Here?" Science 299: 853–855. Interestingly, the experts cited are the authors themselves.

7. Ibid.

8. Friedman, J. 2003. "A War on Obesity, Not the Obese," Science 299: 856–858.

9. Between the NHANES (National Health and Nutrition Examination Survey) II and NHANES III surveys, the number of obese Americans rose from 14 to 22 percent of the total population.

10. Pool, R. 2001. Fat: Fighting the Obesity Epidemic. New York: Oxford University Press.

11. Ibid.

12. Ibid.

13. Barsh, G., I. Farooqi, and S. O'Rahilly. 2000. "Genetics of Body-Weight Regulation," Nature 404: 644–651.

14. Ibid.

15. Kagan, J., et al. 1995. Galen's Prophecy: Temperament and Human Nature. Boulder, CO: Westview.

16. For a terrific description of this research, see Pool (2001) and Shell, E. 2002. The Hungry Gene: The Science of Fat and the Future of Thin. New York: Atlantic Monthly Press.

17. Leibel, R, M. Rosenbaum, and J. Hirsch. 1995. "Changes in Energy Expenditure Resulting from Altered Body Weight," New England Journal of Medicine 332: 621–628.

18. "Mayo Clinic Discovers a Key to Low Metabolism—Major Factor in Obesity," Science Daily (January 27, 2005). www.sciencedaily.com.

19. Shell. 2002.

20. Bouchard, C. 2002. "Genetic Influences on Body Weight and Shape," in C. Fairburn and K. Brownell, eds., Eating Disorders and Obesity: A Comprehensive Handbook, 2nd ed. New York: Guilford.

21. Ravussin et al. 1988. "Reduced Rate of Energy Expenditure as a Risk Factor for Body Weight Gain," New England Journal of Medicine 318: 467–472. As cited in Pool. 2001.

22. Fraser, L. 1997. Losing It: False Hopes and Fat Promises in the Diet Industry. New York: Penguin.

23. For an excellent description of the study see Pool. 2001.

24. www.uscensus.gov.

25. Willet, W. 2001. Eat, Drink, and Be Healthy. New York: Simon and Schuster. P. 51.

26. Pool. 2001, p. 159.
27. While our aging may explain part of the reason why we're getting heavier as a society, it does not explain the overall increase. Kathryn Flegal at the National Center for Health Statistics has tracked the changing body weights of the American population for different age groups since the early 1970s. She notes that even though Americans are getting older, each age group has also gotten heavier over the past two decades. In other words, a forty-five-year-old today is, on average, heavier than a forty-five-year-old in 1970. Flegal, K., and R. Troiano. 2000. "Changes in the Distribution of Body Mass Index of Adults and Children in the U.S. Population," *International Journal of Obesity* 24: 807–818.
28. Hill, J. O., M. Paliassotti, and J. Peters. 1994. "Nongenetic Determinants of Obesity," in Bouchard, C., ed. *Genetic Determinants of Obesity.* Boca Raton, FL: CRC Press.
29. Booth, F., et al. 2002. "Waging War on Physical Inactivity: Using Modern Molecular Ammunition against an Ancient Enemy," *Journal of Applied Physiology* 88: 774–787.
30. Sturm, R. 2003. "Prevalence of Severe Obesity Increasing Faster Than Obesity in the United States," *Archive of Internal Medicine* 163: 2146–2148.
31. Leptin and insulin are mechanisms for long-term weight maintenance; ghrelin and other peptides are signals about short-term satiety that come from the stomach.
32. See Pool (2001) for a great description of this.
33. Friedman, J., and J. Halaas. 1998. "Leptin and the Regulation of Body Weight in Mammals," *Nature* 395: 763–770.
34. This, however, is mere speculation and there is no evidence to back up the idea that changes in leptin or leptin sensitivity are behind the increase in Americans' weights.
35. Weigle, D. 2002. "Pharmacological Therapy of Obesity," *Science* 88: 2462.
36. Ritter, M. 2004. "Anti-Obesity Pill Might Fight Drug Abuse," Associated Press Online (November 15).
37. Friedman has not given up hope on leptin. He now suggests that the problem may be one of leptin sensitivity in the brain rather than leptin deficiencies in the bloodstream, but how this will be translated into a treatment remains unclear.
38. Gura, T. "Obesity Drug Pipeline Not So Fat," *Science* 299: 849–852.
39. Ibid.
40. Hill. 2003.
41. Miller, J., et al. 1996. *The New Glucose Revolution.* New York: Marlowe.
42. Reavan, G., T. Strom, and B. Fox. 2000. *Syndrome X the Silent Killer.* New York: Fireside.
43. Ibid.
44. Ibid., p. 58.
45. See Reaven et al. 2000.
46. Although there are theories that adiposity may reduce insulin receptivity by elevating free fatty acids in the blood or by inflaming cell walls, there is no conclusive evidence that this is the case.

47. De Boer, H., et al. 2004. "Prevention of Weight Gain in Type 2 Diabetes Requiring Insulin Treatment," *Diabetes, Obesity, and Metabolism* 6: 114–119. High levels of insulin may also increase people's appetites. Although the traditional view is that insulin in an appetite suppressant, it may, in fact, act as the opposite. This point is still speculative but people who are insulin resistant may not get proper signals in the brain regarding their satiety.

48. Neel, J. 1962. "Diabetes Mellitus: A 'Thrifty' Genotype Rendered Detrimental by 'Progress'?" *American Journal of Human Genetics* 14: 353–362.

49. Gaesser, G. 2002. *Big, Fat Lies: The Truth about Your Weight and Your Health.* Carlsbad, CA: Gurze. P. 75.

50. Reaven et al. 2000.

51. Ibid.

Chapter Six

1. Critser, G. 2003. *Fat Land: How Americans Became the Fattest People in the World.* New York: Houghton-Mifflin; Pollan, 2002.

2. Tillotson, J. 2003. "Pandemic Obesity: Agriculture's Cheap Food Policy Is a Bad Bargain," *Nutrition Today* 38: 186–190. Taubes, G. 2001. "The Soft Science of Dietary Fat," *Science* 5513.

3. For classic examples of this see Nestle, M. 2002. *Food Politics: How the Food Industry Influences Nutrition and Health.* Berkeley, CA: University of California Press; and Brownell, K., and K. Horgen. 2003. *Food Fight: The Inside Story of the Food Industry, America's Obesity Crisis, and What We Can Do About It.* Chicago: Contemporary.

4. Taubes, G. 2002. "What If It's All Been a Big Fat Lie?" *New York Times Magazine* (July 7).

5. Taubes, G. 2001, p. 2,536.

6. Nestle. 2002.

7. Taubes. 2001. The problem, according to Taubes, was that these recommendations were not necessarily supported by the scientific data. The traditional view was that dietary fat was a threat because of its link to heart disease, but scientists have never found any direct data linking the two. While there is evidence that dietary fat increases cholesterol levels and that higher levels of LDL cholesterol are responsible for heart disease and clogged arteries, there has been no direct link between dietary fat and heart disease. For example, after spending two decades and 100 million dollars in the most comprehensive study of diet and heart disease, researchers at Harvard's School of Public Health were unable to find any connection between fat consumption and heart disease risk. After all this work, an expert committee that came together to study this issue concluded that saturated fats were no worse for your heart than carbohydrates. And then there was the whole problem of the "French paradox" regarding dietary fats: if dietary fat was so evil, how was it that the French manage to have a diet high in saturated fats yet still have much lower heart disease and obesity rates than Americans? Nevertheless,

despite the absence of any scientific evidence, millions of Americans continue to cut their fat consumption.

8. Putnam, J., J. Allshouse, and L. Kantor. 2002. "U.S. Per Capita Food Supply Trends: More Calories, Refined Carbohydrates, and Fats," *Food Review*, pp. 31–38. United States Department of Agriculture, Economic Research Service.

9. This comes from the U.S. Department of Agriculture's (USDA) Continuing Survey of Food Intake of Individuals (CSFII). This survey is based on food diaries, however, and its reliability is questionable. Nevertheless, it corresponds with changes in food produced, particularly in whole milk and beef.

10. Center for Disease Control and Prevention. 2004. "Trends in Intake of Energy and Macronutrients—United States, 1971–2000," *Morbidity and Mortality Weekly Report* (February 6).

11. Kantor, L. 1999. "A Comparison of the U.S. Food Supply with the Food Guide Pyramid Recommendations," in E. Frazão, ed., *American Eating Habits: Changes and Consequences*. Washington, DC: USDA/Economic Research Service.

12. Putnam et al. 2002.

13. Center for Disease Control and Prevention. 2004.

14. U.S. Department of Agriculture's Continuing Study of Food Intake of Individuals (CSFII).

15. Putnam et al. 2002.

16. Winter, G. 2002. "Primal Urge May Make You Fat," *Seattle Times* (July 7), quoting a USDA report.

17. Dyson, L. 2000. "American Cuisine in the Twentieth Century," *Food Review* 23: 2–7.

18. Nestle, M. 2003. *Food Politics: How the Food Industry Influences Nutrition and Health*. Berkeley, CA: University of California Press. P.18.

19. Gardner, B. 2003. *American Agriculture in the Twentieth Century—How It Flourished and What It Cost*. Cambridge, MA: Harvard University Press. Agriculture is a difficult business—it requires intensive capital investments for a highly unpredictable output. Collectively, farmers must balance between producing enough individually to survive but not producing so much collectively that commodity prices fall. When farms were mostly small, family-run enterprises, farmers were subjected to tremendous economic hardships from various economic upheavals and price swings. After the collapse of food prices in the Great Depression, the U.S. federal government instituted a series of complicated programs to protect farmers from market fluctuations. These included subsidies for idling land, crop insurance, tariffs, import quotas, and, most important, loan guarantees. Under this latter program, the government gave the farmers loans against their crops. If commodity prices rose above a government target price, farmers could sell their crops on the open market and make more money; if prices were below the target price, farmers could keep the loans and the government would take their farm yield as collateral.

20. Putnam et al. 2002.

21. National Corn Growers Association. www.ncga.com. The vast majority of the corn produced goes to animal feed, export, seed, and ethanol.

Only about 1.1 of the 9 billion bushels goes directly for American food consumption.

22. Pollan. 2002.
23. Smith, S. 1998. "High Fructose Corn Syrup Replaces Sugar in Processed Food," *Environment Nutrition* 11: 7–8.
24. Putnam, J., and J. Allshouse. 1999. "Food Consumption, Prices, and Expenditures, 1970–97" in *U.S. Department of Agriculture Statistical Bulletin, no. 965* (April). Washington, DC: Government Printing Office.
25. Putnam et al. 2002.
26. Higley, N., and J. White. 1991. "Trends in Fructose Availability and Consumption in the United States," *Food Technology* 45: 118–122.
27. Pollan. 2002.
28. Critser. 2003, p. 18.
29. U.S. Department of Agriculture, Economic Research Service. "Food CPI, Prices, and Expenditures at Constant Prices."
30. Dunham, D. 1994. *Food Costs ... From Farm to Retail in 1993*. Washington, DC: USDA Economic Research Service, No. 696. For estimate on HFCS see United States Department of Agriculture. 2001. *Sugar and Sweetener Outlook*. Economic Research Service Report (January 25).
31. It also ignores the fact that most of the corn produced goes to animal feed (55 percent), export (18 percent), or is kept in reserve (15 percent). In fact, only 10 percent of the American corn produced actually goes for sweeteners or starches. Similarly, the cheap cost of corn is not solely responsible for falling beef prices; rather, falling demand for beef is a much more likely source as well as the low cost of transportation during most the 1980s and 1990s.
32. U.S. Department of Labor. www.dol.gov/esa/whd/flsa/.
33. Both Brownell and Nestle were featured in the June 7, 2004, edition of *Time* magazine as the leading "obesity warriors" and "fat fighters" in America. Brownell has written scores of editorials and commentaries on the food industry and obesity. His most recent book, co-authored with Katherine Horgen, is *Food Fight* (2003). Nestle has also been an outspoken critic of the food industry particularly with regard to the politics surrounding nutrition policy. Her most recent book is *Food Politics* (2002).
34. Brownell and Horgen. 2003, p. 197.
35. Gutherie, J., et al. 1999. "What People Know and Do Not Know about Nutrition," in Frazão, ed., *American Eating Habits*.
36. Young, L., and M. Nestle. 1995. "Portion Sizes in Dietary Assessment: Issues and Policy Implications," *Nutrition Review* 53:149–158.
37. Nestle. 2002, p. 26.
38. French et al. 2001. "Environmental Influences on Eating and Physical Activity," *Annual Review of Public Health* 22: 309–335.
39. Biing-Hwan, L., J. Guthrie, and E. Frazão. 1999. "Nutrient Contribution of Food away from Home," in Frazão, ed., *American Eating Habits*.
40. Young, L., and M. Nestle. 2002. "The Contribution of Expanding Portion Sizes to the U.S. Obesity Epidemic," *American Journal of Public Health* 92: 246–249.

41. Cutler, D., E. Glaeser, and J. Shapiro. 2003. "Why Have Americans Become More Obese?" *National Bureau of Economic Research*, Working Paper 9446.
42. Levenstein, H. 2003. *Revolution at the Table: The Transformation of the American Diet*. Berkeley, CA: University of California Press.
43. Spake, A. 2002. "America's Supersize Diet Is Fattier and Sweeter—and Deadlier," *U.S. News and World Report* (August 19).
44. These statistics were provided by Cutler et al. (2003) using data from the U.S. Department of Agriculture.
45. According to Cutler's calculations, by the mid-1990s, breakfast and lunch calories increased slightly and dinner decreased slightly, but snacking had increased dramatically.
46. According to Horizon Milling, Americans spent 18.8 billion dollars on salted snacks and 20 billion dollars on fortified foods and beverages. Americans spent roughly 16 billion dollars on higher education in 2002.
47. Tippett, K., and L. Cleveland. 1999. "How Current Diets Stack Up: Comparison with Dietary Guidelines," in Frazão, ed., *American Eating Habits*.
48. Ibid.
49. Putnam, J., and S. Gerrior. 1999.
50. Harnack, L., J. Stang, and M. Story. 1999. "Soft Drink Consumption among U.S. Children and Adolescents: Nutritional Consequences," *Journal of the American Dietary Association* 99: 436–441.
51. Levenstein. 2003, p. 7.
52. Levenstein. 2003.
53. The exception may be fruits in the tropics but here, too, there are seasonal cycles that determine when certain types are ripe.
54. While only 30 percent of American women were employed outside the home in 1950, today more than 60 percent of women are. Bowers, D. 2000. "Cooking Trends Echo Changing Roles of Women," *Food Review* 23: 23–29. In 1950, the typical American housewife spent forty hours a week in food preparation and household work; today that number is about twenty hours a week. When women worked outside of the home in the past, it was largely in unpaid agricultural labor.
55. Cutler et al. 2003.
56. Levenstein, H. 1993. *Paradox of Plenty: A Social History of Eating in Modern America*. New York: Oxford University Press.
57. United States Department of Agriculture. 2002. *Agriculture Fact Book 2001–2002*. Washington, DC: Government Printing Office.
58. U.S. Department of Agriculture Economic Research Service. 2002. *U.S. Food Marketing System*. AER-811.
59. Ibid. In 1998, the top ten food makers were Philip Morris, PepsiCo, Coca-Cola, ConAgra, IBP, Sara Lee, Anheuser-Busch, H.J. Heinz, Nabisco, and Bestfoods.
60. Nelson, E. 2002. "Marketers Push Single Servings and Families Hungrily Dig In," *Wall Street Journal* (July 23).
61. Duffy, V., and L. Bartoshuk. 1996. "Sensory Factors in Feeding," in E. Capaldi, ed., *Why We Eat What We Eat*. Washington, DC: American Psychological Association.

62. Levenstein. 2003.
63. Weil, A., and W. Rosen. 1998. *From Chocolate to Morphine: Everything You Need to Know about Mind Altering Drugs*. New York: Mariner.
64. Proceedings of the National Academy of Sciences (September 2003).

Chapter Seven

1. Stein, J. 2004. "The Amish Paradox," *Los Angeles Times* (January 12).
2. Blair, S., and M. Nichaman. 2002. "The Public Health Problem of Increasing Rates of Obesity and What Should Be Done about It," *The Mayo Clinic Proceedings* 77: 109–113.
3. Lakdawalla, D., and T. Philipson. 2002. "The Growth of Obesity and Technological Change: A Theoretical and Empirical Examination," National Bureau of Economic Research Working Paper No. 8946.
4. Martinez-Gonzalez, M. 1999. "Physical Inactivity, Sedentary Lifestyle, and Obesity in the European Union," *International Journal of Obesity and Related Metabolic Disorders* 23: 1192–1201.
5. The report, at www.fitness.gov/activity/activity7/obesity/obesity.html, quotes Wilmore, J., and D. Costill. 1994. *Physiology of Sports and Exercise*. Champaign, IL: Human Kinetics.
6. www.corn.org/web/CRAObesity Position.html.
7. Pressler, M. 2003. "Survey Links Obesity with Food Portions," *Washington Post* (July 18), A03.
8. Tanson, W. 2003. "Adolescent Obesity Largely Caused by Lack of Physical Exercise," University of North Carolina School of Public Health Press Release (April 14). This commented on an unpublished study by Dr. Lisa Sutherland of obesity in adolescents.
9. Centers for Disease Control and Prevention. 2004. "Prevalence of No Leisure-Time Physical Activity," *Morbidity and Mortality Weekly Report* (February 6).
10. Brown, D. 2002. "Study Says 38 Percent of Adults Are Sedentary in Leisure Time," *The Washington Post* (April 8).
11. Huggins, C. 2001. "Couch Potatoes May Overestimate Their Activity," *Preventive Medicine* 33: 18–26.
12. Ward, A. 1990. "Americans Step into a New Fitness Market," *Advertising Age* 61: 33–39.
13. Robinson, J., and G. Godbey. 1997. *Time for Life: The Surprising Ways Americans Use Their Time*. University Park: Pennsylvania State University Press; and Cutler, D., E. Glaeser, and J. Shapiro. 2003. "Why Have Americans Become More Obese?" *National Bureau of Economic Research*, Working Paper 9446.
14. U.S. Bureau of the Census. Website database http://factfinder.census.gov.
15. Ibid.
16. Jackson, R. 2003. "The Impact of the Built Environment on Health," *American Journal of Public Health* 93: 1382–1383.
17. Flint, A. 2001. "Suburban Sprawl Seen as Health Hazard," *The Boston Globe* (October 8).

18. "Caught in the Crosswalk." Report by Surface Transportation Policy Project (www.transact.org).
19. French et al. 2001. "Environmental Influences on Eating and Physical Activity," *Annual Review of Public Health* 22: 319.
20. Nielsen Media Research. 2000. *2000 Report on Television: The First Fifty Years.* New York: AC Nielsen.
21. Nei, N., et al. 2004. *Ten Years after the Birth of the Internet: How Do Americans Use the Internet in Their Daily Lives?* Report for the Stanford Center for the Quantitative Study of Society.
22. Walsh, D., et al. 2003. *Eighth Annual MediaWise Video Game Report Card.* Report from the National Institute on Media and the Family.
23. Frank, L., M. Andresen, and T. Schmid. 2004. "Obesity Relationships with Community Design, Physical Activity, and Time Spent in Cars," *American Journal of Preventative Medicine* 27: 87–95.
24. Centers for Disease Control and Prevention. 2001. "Creating a Healthy Environment: The Impact of the Built Environment on Public Health," *Centers for Disease Control Report* (November 1).
25. Ahrens, F. 2002. "Letter from Texas—The City That Always Eats," *The Washington Post* (May 14); Toy, V. 2003. "Wide Island," *New York Times* (November 23).
26. Frank et al. 2004.
27. Although, because these relationships are largely ones of association, one could also read the data to suggest that heavier people watch more television.
28. Hu, F., et al. 2003. "Television Watching and Other Sedentary Behaviors in Relation to Risk of Obesity and Type 2 Diabetes Mellitus in Women," *Journal of the American Medical Association* 289: 1785–1791.
29. Hendry, J. 2001. Reuters health report. www.reutershealth.com/welconnected/dec53.html.
30. Devereux, M. 2004. "Damaged for Life by Too Much TV," *New Zealand Herald* (July 17).
31. French et al. 2001.
32. Ward. 1990.
33. Robinson and Godbey. 1997.
34. Ward. 1990.
35. Saelens, B., et al. 2002. "Home Environmental Influences on Children's Television Watching from Early to Middle Childhood," *Journal of Developmental and Behavioral Pediatrics* 23: 127–132.
36. The amount of calories burned in basal metabolism is primarily a function of weight. A 155-pound man expends about 1,800 calories per day without exercising, a 132-pound woman about 1,400 calories per day.
37. Cutler et al. 2003.
38. "USDA Exercise Guidelines May Be Too Low to Combat Obesity," *Obesity Week* (April 7, 2002). www.obesityweek.com.
39. Mokdad, A. H., J. S. Marks, D. F. Stroup, and J. L. Gerberding. 2004. "Actual Causes of Death in the United States, 2000," *Journal of the American Medical Association* 291: 1238–1245.
40. See, for example, Mokdad et al. 2004.

41. Winslow, R. 2002. "Study Shows Even Moderate Exercise Can Reverse Aging's Effects by Years," *Wall Street Journal* (May 8).
42. Lee, C. D., S. N. Blair, and A. S. Jackson. 1999. "Cardiorespiratory Fitness, Body Composition, and All-Cause and Cardiovascular Disease Mortality in Men," *American Journal of Clinical Nutrition* 69: 3373–3380.
43. Wei, M., et al. 1999. "Relationship between Low Cardio-Respiratory Fitness and Mortality in Normal-Weight, Overweight, and Obese Men," *JAMA* 282: 1547–1553. They did, however, find that among the unfit men, those who were obese had a higher mortality rate than those who were of normal weight, although it is unclear whether this higher mortality rate was due to diet or other factors rather than body weight.
44. McTiernan, A., C. Kooperberg, E. White, S. Wilcox, R. Coates, L. Adams-Campbell, N. Woods, and J. Ockene. 2003. "Recreational Physical Activity and the Risk of Breast Cancer in Postmenopausal Women," *JAMA* 29: 1331–1336.
45. Hu, F., and J. Manson. 2003. "Walking—The Best Medicine for Diabetes?" *Archives of Internal Medicine* 163: 1397–1398.
46. Gregg, E., R. Gerzoff, T. Thompson, and D. Williamson. 2004. "Trying to Lose Weight, Losing Weight, and 9-Year Mortality in Overweight U.S. Adults with Diabetes," *Diabetes Care* 27: 657–662. Although the authors claim that the higher mortality rate associated with weight loss was due to "unintentional" weight loss.
47. Myers, J., M. Prakash, V. Froelicher, D. Do, S. Partington, and J. Atwood. 2002. "Exercise Capacity and Mortality among Men Referred for Exercise Testing," *New England Journal of Medicine* 346: 793–801.
48. Manson, J., et al. 2002. "Walking Compared with Rigorous Exercise for the Prevention of Cardiovascular Events in Women," *New England Journal of Medicine* 347: 716–725.
49. See, for example, Mokdad et al. 2004.
50. De Tocqueville, A. 1835. *Democracy in America*.
51. Freidan, B. 2001 (1961). *The Feminine Mystique*. New York: W. W. Norton.
52. Putnam, R. 2000. *Bowling Alone: The Collapse and Revival of American Community*. New York: Simon and Schuster.

Chapter Eight

1. As quoted in Kiely, K. 2004. "Governor's Healthy State," *USA Today* (July 11).
2. National Public Radio Broadcast. 2004. "A State's Battle against Obesity" (June 15).
3. The low figure is the estimate from the Centers for Disease Control. The high figure comes from a study by pediatrician William Klish at Baylor College of Medicine of children in the Houston school district. Klish, W. 2002. "U.S. Kids Have Shorter Life Expectancy Than Parents Because of Obesity," *Obesity Week* (February 3).
4. Wartik, N. 2003. "Rising Obesity in Children Prompts Call to Action," *New York Times* (August 26).

5. Institute of Medicine. 2004. "Preventing Childhood Obesity: Health in the Balance, 2005," *Report of the Institute of Medicine of the National Academies of Science* (September). For example, my colleague Diane Whitmore found that students who get their foods at school consume about two hundred calories more per day than those who take their lunches from home—a difference that she estimates could contribute to about a 2 percent increase in juvenile obesity. Whitmore, D. 2005. "Do School Lunches Contribute to Childhood Obesity?" working paper.

6. Centers for Disease Control and Prevention. 2000. *School Health Policies and Programs Survey.*

7. Wooton, M. 2004. "Vending Machine Statement," *Nutrition Action Newsletter*, Center for Science in the Public Interest (May 11). This was from a survey of more than 1,400 machines in 251 schools.

8. Data from this survey are listed at www.californiaprojectlean.org.

9. Brownell, K., and K. Horgen. 2003. *Food Fight: The Inside Story of the Food Industry, America's Obesity Crisis, and What We Can Do About It.* Chicago: Contemporary Books. P. 130.

10. Kaufman, M. 1999. "Fighting the Cola Wars in Schools," *Washington Post* (March 23).

11. Oliver, J., and T. Lee. 2005. "Public Opinion and the Politics of Obesity," *Journal of Health Politics, Policy, and Law* (forthcoming).

12. As quoted in Brownell and Horgen. 2003, p. 162.

13. Institute of Medicine. 2004.

14. As quoted in Sweeney, N. 2004. "As Obesity Grows, Schools Cut Physical Education," *Milwaukee Journal Sentinel* (April 24).

15. One of my research assistants, Masataka Harada, derived the findings from a survey of seventeen thousand students between the ages of eleven and seventeen in 386 schools. The data came from the World Health Organization. 2002. *Health Behavior in School-Aged Children, 1997–1998: United States*, ICPSR version. Calverton, MD: Macro International. Using an exploratory statistical procedure (a Chi-squared Automatic Interaction Dectector) from a list of 288 possible explanatory factors (including the hours spent using video games and computers, the frequency of physical activity, and the amount of fast-food consumed) Harada identified the characteristics that had the strongest correlation with juvenile obesity. After tooth brushing the most important factors were ethnicity (Latino and African American kids were more likely to be overweight), parents' education (children whose fathers had no college were more likely to be overweight), and whether the teenager worked (teenagers who work more than fifteen hours a week are more likely to be overweight). Obviously, we did not have a complete list of factors, including genetic sources of weight. Nor are these self-reports 100 percent reliable. Nevertheless, the results raise a striking question of what correlates most strongly with juvenile weight.

16. Ibid.

17. Caballero, B., et al. 2003. "Pathways: A School-Based Randomized Controlled Trial for the Prevention of Obesity in American Indian Schoolchildren," *American Journal of Clinical Nutrition* 78: 1030–1038.

18. Another study in England (James, J., et al. 2004. "Preventing Childhood Obesity by Reducing Consumption of Carbonated Drinks: Cluster Randomized Controlled Trial," *British Medical Journal* 328: 1237) claimed that after only a brief five-session educational program, schoolchildren who were discouraged from drinking soda consumed less soda and did not have a weight gain, compared to a control group that increased soda consumption and had a 7 percent increase in obesity prevalence. This study, however, has a lot of methodological problems and raises some serious questions about its validity (see French, S., et al. 2004. "Too Good to Be True?" *British Medical Journal* 32: E315–316.). Interestingly, this questionable study has been cited much more as evidence about the ability of schools to shape obesity than the Pathways findings, which called this into question.

19. Luepker, R., et al. 1996. "Outcomes of a Field Trial to Improve Children's Dietary and Physical Activity," *Journal of the American Medical Association* 275: 768–776.

20. Brownell and Horgen. 2003, p. 102.

21. Brand, J., and B. Greenberg. 1994. "Commercials in the Classroom: The Impact of Channel One Advertising," *Journal of Advertising Research* 34: 18–23.

22. As quoted in Brownell and Horgen. 2003, p. 102.

23. Ibid.

24. Kluger, R. 1997. *Ashes to Ashes: America's Hundred-Year Cigarette War, the Public Health, and the Unabashed Triumph of Philip Morris.* New York: Vintage.

25. For an excellent account of the politics behind food recommendations, see Nestle, M. 2002. *Food Politics.* Berkeley: University of California Press.

26. Zamiska, N. 2004. "Food Pyramid Frenzy," *Wall Street Journal* (July 29).

27. Ibid., p. 359.

28. Recently, the FDA augmented this list to also include trans fats.

29. USDA. 2000. "Serving Sizes in the Food Guide Pyramid and on the Nutrition Facts Label: What's Different and Why?" *Nutrition Insights* 22 (December).

30. Tarantino, L., Office of Nutritional Products, Labeling, and Dietary Supplements, U.S. Food and Drug Administration. 2004. Letter to food manufacturers about accurate serving size declaration on food products (March 12).

31. Of course, all this discussion about food labeling has left out the content of foods in restaurants. Every day, roughly one in two Americans eats food prepared outside the home, including restaurants, cafeterias, cafes, and take-out. For these venues, there are no government regulations mandating that food makers list the calories or nutritional content of their fare. Although some restaurants claim to post listings of the nutritional and caloric contents of their foods, these are often in remote brochures that are far removed from menus. Many public health experts decry this practice and are calling for more stringent requirements that restaurants list at least the calories next to each serving item. The state legislatures in California and New Hampshire are considering bills that would require restaurants to post the nutritional information of the menus, although how and where this information would be provided is still subject to debate.

32. USDA Nutrition Insights. 2000.
33. Cotterill, R., and A. Franklin. 1995. *The Urban Grocery Store Gap*. Storrs, CT: Food Marketing Policy Center, University of Connecticut.
34. As quoted on www.consumerfreedom.com.
35. Seale, J., A. Regmi, and J. Bernstein. 2003. *International Evidence on Food Consumption Patterns/TB-1904*. Washington, DC: Economic Research Service, USDA.
36. Drewnoski, A., and S. Specter. 2004. "Poverty and Obesity: The Role of Energy Density and Energy Costs," *American Journal of Clinical Nutrition* 79: 6–16.
37. Caravan, S. 2001. "Dietary Intake and Dietary Attitudes among Food Stamp Participants and Other Low-Income Individuals, 2000," USDA Food Service Program Diet Report.
38. Gibson, D. 2003. "Food Stamp Program Participation Is Related to Obesity in Low Income Women," *Journal of Nutrition* 133: 2225–2231.
39. Besharov, D. 2003. "Growing Overweight and Obesity in America: The Potential Role of Federal Nutrition Programs," *Testimony to Congressional Committee on Agriculture, Nutrition, and Forestry* (April 3).
40. Estimate compiled by my research assistant Stephan Whitaker from Economic Research Service, USDA. 2002. *Diet and Health: Food Consumption and Nutrient Intake Tables*. http://ers.usda.gov/Briefing/DietAndHealth/data/food/table6.htm.
41. U.S. Department of Health and Human Services. 2001. *The Surgeon General's Call to Action to Prevent and Decrease Overweight and Obesity*. [Rockville, MD]: U.S. Department of Health and Human Services, Public Health Service, Office of the Surgeon General. Available from: U.S. GPO, Washington, DC.
42. As quoted in Gladwell, M. 1998. "The Pima Paradox," *The New Yorker* (February 18).
43. Agatston, A. 2003. *The South Beach Diet: The Delicious, Doctor-Designed, Foolproof Plan for Fast and Healthy Weight Loss*. New York: Random House. P. 3. (Emphasis added.)
44. Atkins, R. 2002. *Dr. Atkins' New Diet Revolution*. New York: Avon.
45. Of course, this has not prevented Americans from imposing such restrictions. The United States has a long history of moralistic legislation on matters of sex, intoxicants, and political association. For an excellent history of this, I recommend Morone, J. 2002. *Hellfire Nation*. New Haven, CT: Yale University Press.
46. Smith, N. 2004. "Huckabee Unsatisfied with Progress of Health Promotion after Six Months," *Arkansas Democrat-Gazette* (November 8).

Chapter Nine

1. Vardy, J. 2001. "Shopping Is Patriotic, Leaders Say," *National Post of Canada* (September 28).
2. Galbraith, J. 1998 (1958). *The Affluent Society*. New York: Houghton Mifflin.
3. Smith, A. 1976 (1775). *An Inquiry into the Nature and Causes of the Wealth of Nations*. Chicago: University of Chicago Press.

4. Actually, in all fairness, Smith is more sophisticated than this and recognizes many inherent dysfunctions in the market, particularly in the concentration of monopolist power.
5. Easterbrook, G. 2003. *The Progress Paradox: How Life Gets Better While People Feel Worse*. New York: Random House.
6. Lane, R. 2001. *The Loss of Happiness in Market Democracies*. New Haven, CT: Yale University Press.
7. Myers, D. 2001. *The American Paradox: Spiritual Hunger in an Age of Plenty*. New Haven, CT: Yale University Press.
8. Bond, M. 2003. "The Pursuit of Happiness," *New Scientist* 180: 40; Lane. 2001.
9. In fact, by many accounts, we have far more discretionary time than our grandparents did. See Robinson, J., and G. Godbey. 1999. *Time for Life: The Surprising Ways Americans Use Their Time*. State College: Pennsylvania State University Press.
10. For a great examination of this question, see Schwartz, B. 2004. *The Paradox of Choice: Why More Is Less*. New York: Ecco.
11. Several studies find many associations between disease and obesity to be mediated by exercise. See Wessel, T., et al. 2004. "Relationship of Physical Fitness vs. Body Mass Index with Coronary Artery Disease and Cardiovascular Events in Women," *Journal of the American Medical Association* 292: 1179–1187. Carnethon, M., et al. 2003. "Cardiorespiratory Fitness in Young Adulthood and the Development of Cardiovascular Disease Risk Factors," *JAMA* 290: 3092–3100.

Index

Note: Page numbers in *italics* indicate illustrations.